ABOUT THE EDITORS

Jay Mitra is Head of Economic Development and the Innovation Centre at the University of North London, both of which he helped to establish. He is responsible for the university's interface with industry (private, public and voluntary sectors and others involved in economic development), through applied research, vocational training, technology transfer guidance and assessment programmes, and strategic partnerships with key economic stakeholders. He is also a visiting faculty member in the Postgraduate Programme on Corporate Business in the University of Bologna, Project Director of the London Technopole Initiative, and the Director of a small business research forum. He has over 15 years' experience as a consultant, trainer and adviser for SMEs, and has also worked as a consultant for one of the top advertising and marketing companies in Europe.

Piero Formica is Professor of Economics of Innovation and Business Policy at the Postgraduate School of Corporate Business (Technology, Innovation and Entrepreneurship) in the University of Bologna. A graduate of the School of Advanced International Studies at Johns Hopkins University, he is also an expert on various European Union programmes (DG XIII, Science Parks and Regional Innovation and Technology Transfer Infrastructures (RITTS) and DG XVI, Regional Innovation Strategies (RIS)). He is the author of several works in the field of business strategy and innovation, including: *Technopoli: Luoghi e Sentieri dell'innovazione* (1991, Turin); *Mutanti Asiendali: Imprese, Centre di Innovazione e Parchi Scientifici nell'era tecnopolitana*, (1994, Naples); and *The Economics of Science Parks* (edited with Mauricio Guedes, 1996, Rio de Janeiro).

Innovation and Economic Development

University–Enterprise Partnerships in Action

Edited by
Jay Mitra
Piero Formica

Oak Tree Press
Dublin • London

Oak Tree Press
Merrion Building
Lower Merrion Street
Dublin 2, Ireland

A catalogue record of this book is
available from the British Library

ISBN 1-86076-045-7

Printed in Ireland by Colour Books Ltd.

CONTENTS

ABOUT THE CONTRIBUTORS

Emilio Bellini is the Director of the Science and Technology Park in Salerno, Italy.

Y.K. Bhushan is the Director of the Narsee Monjee Institute of Management Studies in Mumbai, India.

Patries Boekholt is a Director of Technopolis, a research and consultancy organisation specialising in innovation policy and based in Brighton (UK) and Amsterdam (NL).

Eugenio Corti is Associate Professor of Management of Technological Innovation at the School of Engineering in the University of Naples "Frederico II", Italy.

Sunanda Easwaran is Professor of Marketing and Entrepreneurship Management at the Narsee Monjee Institute of Management Studies, Mumbai, India.

Mathew J. Manimala is a Senior Member of Faculty in the Human Resource Area at the Administrative Staff College of India in Hyderabad.

Claire Nauwelaers is Senior Research Fellow in the "Regional Innovation Strategies in Europe" research team at MERIT.

F. Marques Reigado is Professor of Regional Economic Planning and Regional Development at the University of Beira Interior in Covilhá, Portugal.

Jan Sadlak is Head of the Higher Education and Research Division of UNESCO in Paris.

Corrado lo Storto is Research Associate in Economic and Management Engineering at the School of Engineering at the University of Naples "Frederico II", Italy.

Mary Lindenstein Walshok is Associate Vice-Chancellor of Extended Studies and Public Service and Adjunct Professor in the Department of Sociology at the University of California, San Diego.

Giuseppe Zollo is Associate Professor of Business Management at the School of Engineering at the University of Naples "Frederico II".

ACKNOWLEDGEMENTS

Many of the ideas and themes in this book have emerged from discussions — formal and informal — and interaction with friends and colleagues across the world. Five years ago we began our "innovation mission" with a brainstorming barney in Brighton, and the two days of intensive exchange and sharing provided the groundwork for this work. Our objectives were to understand the process of innovation and the role of universities as partners of industry in that process. Our thanks are due in large measure to all those who looked at the sea from a Brighton hotel window and lit our creative spark.

Two further conferences have generated more ideas, and this book has been made out of selections from our first "Universities and Industry Working Together" conference held in London in June 1995. We selected particular papers from that conference but we do acknowledge the welter of ideas and thoughts that were generated during the conference sessions. We have learnt a lot from those sessions. Many thanks go out to all colleagues at the Economic Development Unit (EDU) of the University of North London who helped in organising the conference. Three EDU colleagues deserve special mention: Frances Joyce, for remaining calm when the proof-reading and corrections were becoming rather hectic, and when scripts had to be read and re-read from halfway across the world; Agnessi de Amico for her particular expertise with computer graphics; and Monica Lapetra for ensuring that the conference papers were available in the first place.

Our particular appreciation for David Givens and Brian Langan of Oak Tree Press cannot be overstated. They have been very patient, supportive and, most importantly, thorough, in their organisation of the book from a publisher's point of view.

Our colleagues from the University of Bologna have taken much interest and provided considerable support for our work together. Not only have two European universities, one the oldest and the other new, been brought together in a special relationship for university–industry interaction, but personal rapport and friendship have created space for further creative endeavours.

Mario Rinaldi's affection for us, and his belief in our (often messy) pot pourri of ideas, has been a source of much strength.

We have simply edited this book; its strength lies in the contributions made by our colleagues from across the world who share our belief in internationalisation, the need for positive change and innovation. Many thanks to all of them for their early co-operation in revising scripts and for their patience in waiting for the publication.

Universities and industry involve many players who make their own contributions to projects and developments. Their work provides the stimulus for our ideas and actions.

Jay Mitra
Piero Formica

FOREWORD

Policy makers across the world acknowledge that one of the key
development tasks they face is converting their investments in
education into economic returns. Universities contain two of the
keys to economic success — talented people and advanced knowledge or technology. The difficulty lies in converting the opportunities they represent into long-term competitive advantage.

The Economic Development Unit at the University of North
London, under the leadership of Jay Mitra, has achieved an envi-
able international reputation for high quality work exploring the
ways in which universities can contribute to local and national
economic prosperity. In this book, many of the key ideas on this
subject are drawn together through a selection of papers. The papers successfully combine an understanding of the fundamental
questions which underlie any analysis of the university's role in
the community with masses of practical information and guidance.

Jan Sadlak's chapter highlights many of the dilemmas which
face universities and industry in embarking on collaboration.
Many of these issues centre on the different values, expectations
and assumptions of those in higher education and commerce.
These differences are especially apparent in the great research
universities. These are often the most prestigious institutions but,
as Mary Walshok points out, the gap between their worldview and
that of industry is often especially wide. These universities can be
jealous guardians of "the central knowledge resource of their societies". The commercial value of this resource increases as
knowledge becomes the major source of competitive advantage.

Exploiting this source of competitive advantage leads to shifts
in prevailing organisational structures and attitudes. Jay Mitra
and Piero Formica show how many companies are adopting ways
of working and common assumptions that were traditionally associated with education. Learning companies epitomise this shift
while entrepreneurial universities convert an oxymoron into an
axiom. The same theme is extended by Mathew Manimala to
graduates while Y.K. Bhushan and Sunanda Easwaran sharpen
the focus to examine the impact of these shifts on the nature of
innovation. Traditional divides between the scientific investigator,

the innovator and the entrepreneur are increasingly irrelevant in the search for "new solutions and new approaches" to innovation. Effective implementation is the essential counter-point to the traditional emphasis on effective development in the double cycle of innovation.

Patricies Boekholt places these developments in their regional or local context. This analysis of the evidence of innovative clusters in regions challenges the traditional emphasis on institutions and structures. It has particular relevance to local or regional economies striving to maximise their gains from local institutions. Marques Reigado develops this theme in the context of market development and competitive pressures. Eugenio Corti and Corrado lo Storto draw these different strands together. Their approach explores the local structures needed to combine effectively the efforts of the many local actors into a concerted effort to achieve growth through research-based innovation. Emilio Bellini and Giuseppe Zollo continue with this theme, but focus specifically on the dynamics of university–industry relationships, identifying spin-offs as a mechanism for encouraging such relationships and local economic regeneration.

The book sustains high quality analysis throughout while breaking relatively new ground by highlighting the benefits to higher education of innovation, technological development and entrepreneurship. These are especially important in less developed regions where "cultural, organisational and managerial barriers" often undermine efforts to stimulate innovation and economic progress. The scale of investment in this development, allied to the inevitable questions about returns, highlights the importance of effective evaluation. Claire Nauwelaers draws out the importance of establishing methods of linking the evaluation of potential with returns.

This book should be essential reading for all those interested in the increasingly important topic of university–industry interactions for economic development. It has as many lessons and insights for university and industry leaders as it has for policy makers seeking to turn their investment in higher education into jobs and prosperity. All can gain from the overall approach and the specific insights.

Tom Cannon
Chief Executive
Management Charter Initiative

"*I likewise delivered up my watch, which the Emperor was very
curious to see. . . . He asked the opinions of his learned men about
him, which were various and remote, as the reader may well
imagine without my repeating . . .*"
— *Jonathan Swift,* Gulliver's Travels

"Sakuni: *We will play one single throw. Listen carefully: if we lose
we will spend twelve years in the forest clothed in rags, and a
thirteenth year in an unknown place, hidden and disguised. If,
during the course of the thirteenth year, we are discovered, we will
spend a further twelve years in the woods. If you lose, the exile is
yours. At the end of thirteen years, the one or the other will regain
his kingdom*
"Yudhishthira: *Let's play.*" (page 71)

"Krishna: *You must be right. If I can't touch your heart, the ruin of
the earth is near.*
"Karna: *One thing is certain, Krishna. We will make a great
journey together.*" (page 151)

— from *The Mahabharata: A Play based upon the classic Indian
epic*, by Jean-Claude Carrière, translated by Peter Brook,
Methuen, London.

1

INTRODUCTION

Jay Mitra and Piero Formica

The purpose of this book is to examine the nature and scope of the relationship between higher education and economic development, and the strategic implications of such a relationship in the current climate of rapid economic, technological and structural change. Such an examination is not new, the subject matter having already attracted some attention in disparate quarters as the language of our times has tried to explain the meaning of "knowledge" and "information" societies. Much knowledge, particularly "cutting-edge" knowledge, is said to obtain in higher education. Consequently, the extent to which higher education impacts on society and economic development has begun to influence policy agendas of government, the private sector and higher education itself. Our book takes this issue as its central theme but locates the relationship in the context of innovation in terms of assessing whether the higher education – economic development relationship leads to the successful exploitation of new ideas for economic development.

Greater interaction between higher education institutions (HEIs) and economic development players ("industry" for short) can foster the kind of sustainable economic development relevant to today's economies. Such a statement presupposes consideration of many different factors and a wide range of views. Despite recent attention to the subject, how HEIs and industry interact could be considered peripheral to government policy on economic development. Moreover, it is not easy to measure the contribution of such interaction to economic growth and vitality. Much of the importance of the debate is diluted by the often territorial and elitist essays in preserving fundamental, "blue sky" research capability within a limited number of universities at the expense of other considerations of higher education value, such as the "capable" student or the economically active learning organisation.

An important assumption for the book is, therefore, that HEIs and industry together are key players in securing competitive advantage at the micro and macro levels by the way they organise and implement dependent activities and create value for their respective organisations. Another assumption is that such interaction is possible if they see themselves as part of wider and emerging socio-economic clusters where both play strategic roles, defined by themselves and other stakeholders and supported by governments. They are, therefore, seen as integral catalysts for the key determinants of competitive advantage.

THE CONTEXT

The nature, scope and meaning of the interaction between industry and higher education is being examined in the context of cataclysmic change. Europe is said to be lagging behind the United States and Japan in several areas of high technology, and is weak in its production technologies and in exploiting its inventions (Cooley, 1990; European Commission, 1992). Success in business and management is also likely to be heavily dependent on know-how in its widest sense, and the European manufacturing base, which is largely composed of small and medium-sized enterprises (SMEs) and a highly skilled and flexible workforce, can augment this know-how in partnership with HEIs which are intellectual powerhouses, developing know-how through their main functions of education, research, and training. Industry is by no means reliant on academic know-how, and the linearity embedded in the view that academic institutions only generate cutting-edge know-how was never true. This view is particularly unacceptable given the growth of information technologies which enable information and knowledge to be derived from various quarters as part of a constant feedback loop. Recognition of the value of tacit knowledge is another blow for traditional, explicit forms of knowledge generation and dissemination.

What is the role of HEIs in this changing economic and social climate? The stark comment of the *Financial Times* was that:

> British universities are not spawning high-tech companies and transferring technology from lab to market place at the pace required to compete in the twenty-first century. In spite of improved contacts with industry over the past five years, brought

about by government funding cuts, universities are still too divorced from the needs of the business (Tuesday, 2 April 1996).

This comment is corroborated by other evidence from different quarters at both anecdotal and formal levels, all pointing to the significant deficit between education and research provision and industry-based needs in the UK. But such a state of affairs is not restricted to the UK. Hans Gunter Danielmeyer, Director of Corporate Research at Siemens, the electrical and industrial combine, also referred to similar gaps in Germany. Such statements are no consolation to academics, practitioners and policy makers.

Whether new partnerships provide the basis of future economic development is to some extent dependent on the evolution of the relationship between industry and HEIs. This in turn raises two other questions: the background to the relationship; and the development of that relationship.

The particular attention given to the technology transfer process and mechanisms derives from industry's needs to source technology from external sources because of the speed of technological progress, the complexity of the technological base, the growth and sustainability of high technology SMEs, increased global competition, the mismatch between high levels of public spending for research and outcome in terms of enhanced and globally competitive industrial capability, and the increased interest in the sale of technology and related services of universities.

Technology transfer's wide definitional base requires an understanding of the method by which technological know-how is transferred from one point to another, and specifically from ideas to market place. The traditional linear model which considers the sequential progress of ideas from testing to market research, to acceptance by industry, to product development and selling in the market place (the innovation sequence) has long been discredited. Perhaps the most accepted model is the interactive one (or adaptations of Rosenberg's chain-linked model — see Kline and Rosenberg, 1986), because it approximates most closely with reality and practice. The model allows for scientific knowledge to be linked to the innovation process at all stages, thus enabling the mechanisms for HEI–industry links to be available at all stages of the innovation process.

MECHANISMS FOR TECHNOLOGY TRANSFER

Research activities probably constitute the single most important mechanism for technology transfer for universities. Universities carry out most long-term strategic and basic research in science and technology, the social sciences, arts and humanities, and are also involved in a significant proportion of the applied, near-market research collaboratively with industry and other organisations, including government departments. It follows that a major source of HEIs' income is represented by research services which, because of its substantial claims on institutional resources, tend to be institutionalised activities. Only a small part of total research grant income is supported by industry, particularly in the UK. Goddard et al. (1994) estimate that 69 per cent of research income in the UK is derived from the public sector (higher education funding councils, research councils, UK central government, health and hospital authorities). The clamouring for concentration of such public funds among the top-rated, generally older, universities is, therefore, hardly surprising.

Another area of growing research activity is in contract research involving both public and private sector money, with European Commission (EC) contracts being a major area of growth. A combination of both overseas industrial and EC funding rose to over £100 million between 1984/85 and 1990/91 for the "older" universities in the UK. Together with certain other sources (such as charities and overseas research institutes) EC money also represents a significantly growing area of income for the new universities, even though there are considerable variations in the sources of institutional income for different organisations.

Research exploitation may be less common in Europe than in American universities where new or semi-developed technology resulting from research is advanced to the point where patent protection can be acquired and licensing deals with industry negotiated. However, research clubs, affiliation programmes and co-operative research centres, and other examples of multilateral research arrangements, have been operating in Europe for some time now, and this would suggest a closer convergence of interests between industry and HEIs.

Licensing and exploitation of intellectual property are perhaps some of the more specific forms of technology transfer activity arising out of research. Various universities, particularly in the UK, have set up exploitation companies and often spend considerable management time on such negotiations, particularly after the abolition of the automatic granting of negotiating rights to the British Technology Group. For example, according to Department of Trade and Industry (DTI) statistics in the UK, based on findings from 80 universities, 46 of these universities have a wholly or partially owned subsidiary for exploiting research and technology, that gross income for these companies was £172 million for the period from 1 August 1991 to 31 July 1994, and that 757 patents were filed in the same period with the largest number from any one institution being 53 (these patents exclude those arising from industry-funded research which are filed by industry partners).

Another offshoot of research has been the development of spin-off activities. Academic-led innovation partnerships are to be found perhaps most notably in the USA in places such as the Massachusetts Institute of Technology (MIT) and Stanford University. The critical difference between academic spin-offs in places such as MIT and those in many other European institutions is that, in common with many universities in the USA, MIT was created with a view to combining academic studies and applying technology to manufacturing.

There has been a major impact on new business creation in many of these areas. One study found 636 MIT alumni-founded companies in Massachusetts alone with revenues in 1988 of approximately $40 billion. It is believed that these companies account for nearly a third of the Massachusetts economy if secondary job creation is included.

Chalmers University in Gothenburg also boasts of making innovation a particular speciality, generating approximately 40–50 companies per year and several thousand jobs. University start-ups there are said to rival the traditional local shipbuilding industry in levels of employment.

Spin-offs may be divided into two groups — those which have genuinely spun out of research and those in which the HEI retains a majority share. In the UK, spin-off companies have grown rapidly over the years, and of the 80 universities surveyed by the DTI, 277 companies were said to be in existence with a 50/50 split between product- and service-based companies. It is estimated that 163 companies are in incubation and 43 per cent of universities have access to incubation units. It is understood that the average number of spin-offs of 3.3 per cent per university is an underestimate since many academics set up businesses without the support of the university. What is of particular importance here is not so much the extent of wealth creation that is necessarily taking place but the existence of vehicles which should be explored further in terms of regional or national policies for economic development.

Even a cursory reference to research exploitation and diffusion as part of technology transfer cannot be excused without a reference to one of its most glamorous manifestations — the growth of science, technology and research parks with their distinctive local image and proactive involvement of universities. The rise in science parks (an umbrella definition in the current study) has gone hand-in-hand with the rise in entrepreneurship and small firms, and despite some degree of criticism (particularly relating to real academic involvement), it remains a key area of development and policy. In London alone there are at least four new parks under consideration, rather late in the day after the Cambridge phenomenon has already made its legendary mark on the high technology business scene. The main issue about science parks and their role in economic development is that they represent tangible, superior, bricks-and-mortar-based models of technology transfer and economic development activity. There are legitimate questions as to their effectiveness in terms of both these outputs, and most analyses have demonstrated some considerable deficits in employment creation, economic sustainability, wealth creation and distribution. This is a difficult argument, and perhaps one of the stumbling blocks in assessing the effectiveness of science parks has been the tendency to study them as generators of economic development by themselves as opposed to being considered as one of many vehicles which could be used for such purpose.

Consultancy and continuing education (in particular continuing vocational education) are other forms of technology transfer or diffusion which have historically been carried out on an *ad hoc* basis — by individual academics in the case of consultancy, or in a more organised institutional fashion by the vocationally oriented institutions. It is interesting to note that both in terms of measures of growth and actual activity, training and continuing vocational education tend to have a lower profile, even though they may constitute a more pronounced area of activity for the new universities in the UK, for example. This tendency reflects a bias towards a traditional academic approach to the study of any one subject, and towards a context of learning through teaching and research. This has to some extent influenced the design of curricula and research in more vocational subjects such as leisure and tourism, with explicit scholarship and original curiosity-based research dominating over other forms of learning (for example in the workplace or "learning by doing"). The fact that academics do not train as teachers may also have something to do with training's "poor cousin" status, or indeed with the view that training does not really have "higher" value content.

Some change can be witnessed in the European Commission's emphasis on continuing education and training, particularly as part of lifelong learning initiatives which have now entered the agenda of most institutions, and indeed have led various public and private organisations to define themselves as "learning organisations" contributing to the development of "learning societies". The upshot of this process is the realisation of the need to link research and training, and to use the mechanism of continuous training and education to keep pace with technological and other changes.

Typically, training programmes that have brought universities and companies together have made significant contributions to business and economic development. For example, SMEs have benefited from opening up to Europe through student placement programmes such as LEONARDO, dissemination of methods and tools created to monitor the evolution of skills, and the development of training tools and human resource management issues. Trainers learn from new working methods, the development of tools such as multimedia, and transnational educational partnerships through European programmes (DG XIII, European Commission, 1995).

Technology transfer and knowledge exchange are effected in their commonest and perhaps most influential form through personnel exchange, including graduate placement schemes, sandwich courses and staff mobility from both sides (industrial secondments for HEI staff and visiting professorships for industrialists).

There are numerous mechanisms of technology transfer bringing HEIs and industry together, and the above snapshot does not do justice to what is a complex, multinational industry from any country's perspective. However, despite the achievements of the schemes, problems of accountability, perception, and notably measurable success remain. This is particularly the case with SMEs.

Universities are large organisations with decentralised management structures and modes of operation. They are also bureaucratic, which, coupled with traditional barriers, make them unattractive to SMEs. Their focus on academic and technical specialism does not allow for business-type solutions to problems faced by SMEs. Moreover, one of the major problems within HEIs in connection with technology transfer activities is that of an organisation that is able, firstly, to co-ordinate the wide range of existing and potential activities, and secondly, to reflect demand-led interests. Most HEIs will claim to making provision for a larger number of support activities, but by and large these are *ad hoc* in nature and spread across a number of disciplines. A multiplicity of services is accompanied by multiple layers of contact points/service providers, vying with each other for income and as part of an almost inherent academic rivalry. As a consequence, the end-user is often left confused. Additionally, HEI contributions are to a great extent limited by their making available only a particular range of expertise which may not match demand either in terms of specific technologies or in terms of market orientation.

Structural and organisational problems are often compounded by the erroneous assumption that the exploitation of intellectual ability equals the exploitation of intellectual property rights (IPR), a major concern (Elliott, 1995). If innovation is the key, then not only are the concepts of exploitation and protection mutually contradictory, but the whole business of IPR, which aims to package and sell knowledge under licence, can be seen as an impediment to "understanding" which is the real value of research, teaching and training. IPR is a highly contentious issue and is not in itself the subject of this introduction or indeed of other contributions in this book. However, its frequent emergence in university–industry platforms raises questions about purpose, policy, structure and outcome. Should HEIs have increased involvement with contract research; generate income (which by all accounts is an arduous process); deflect academics from pursuing knowledge to the pursuit of research that can be licensed; drive a wedge between industrial liaison officers and academics? Or should HEIs working with industry operate on the premise that academic excellence and industrial use are separate measures of any research project, and that it is possible to select projects which score highly on both (Elliott, 1995)? Equally, if institutions are to be rated highly (and funded accordingly) for their superior academic research (with or without IPR), what of those who transmit knowledge excellently through training, networking and other forms of continuing vocational education?

In addressing issues of linkages with industry, much more is implied in terms of change than organisational strategies which are concerned with centralisation of service provision (a corporate approach) or its opposite. To have a firmer grasp of the innovation process which is embedded in a wider system or network of organisations, policies, information systems and people, requires an outward-looking approach which refers to local, national, and international issues from the point of view of HEIs as centres of learning. Aligning a strategy to a regional economic regeneration strategy allows the institution to harness its particular resources and strengths without compromising the wider spectrum of knowledge and expertise (Mitra, 1996).

The traditional, linear model of the innovation process was based on factors such as: science and technology push/ technology pull/ market pull; information flows; and process adaptation of sequential steps — basic research, applied research, prototype development, market research, product development, marketing and selling. It is interesting to note the extent to which public policy has been influenced by such an approach, intervening at different and specific stages by strengthening public infrastructure, and providing incentives (R&D grants, tax credits, etc.) to the private sector which was then expected to transform the technology, patents and systems into new products and processes (Schuetze, 1996). The innovation would be complete in, for example, the development of a new product with a higher customer satisfaction quotient or a new process which would enable an existing product to be made at lower cost or better quality.

This discredited model has given way to an appreciation of the knowledge embedded in the process, as emerging from a variety of sources, not only at the first point of research, and of different actors (scientists, designers, market analysts, financiers and consumers) all operating on a level, connected field despite their individual agendas. Most importantly, whatever their origins, innovations go through constant change, and different inputs at varying times, with feedback from multiple stages. Kline and Rosenberg (1986) referred to the chain-link model, suggesting multi-directional flows, feedback from different stages, and regular interaction between actors. The continuous process of change implied in the invention, innovation and diffusion processes is echoed by Schuetze (1996) in his "cyclical" model that links the various stages of the innovation process in a way similar to a product life-cycle. In addition to Rosenberg's feedback loops, we have the circular nature of the process, and the strong implication that existing scientific knowledge is used throughout the innovation process and not just at the design phase.

The significance of the non-linear models is denoted by their emphasis on multi-directional linkages, interdependency between "hard" technology and "softer" issues of people management and informational flows, cumulative flows which involve individuals, organisations, regions and government, and the social, cultural, economic and institutional bases of innovative action.

THE SOCIAL CONTEXT OF INNOVATION

Our contention is that innovation takes place only when certain social and economic conditions obtain. Innovation is not the act of individual genius realised in a flash of inspiration, although such a nineteenth-century hangover appears to persist. Some light is thrown on the importance of the social context by briefly looking at the simple example of James Watt's invention of the steam engine. The reality of a social/economic network of people and organisations contributing to the discovery is far removed from the mythical picture of a young Watt dreaming in front of a steaming kettle. Key influences on Watt's invention were: the membership of a closely linked group of scientists from Glasgow and Edinburgh; Watt's friendship with Joseph Black, whose discovery of latent heat was critical to Watt's improvement to the Newcomer engine; and of course, the involvement of the industrialist Roebuck, a personal acquaintance of Watt. Higher education institutions, previous research, social networking, and the direct involvement of industry are the key features of technological innovation. It is this multiple interaction between different players which informs the rationale of an innovative environment.

General agreement on the basic features of an entrepreneur tends to suggest that the entrepreneur is an individual who uses their personal drive, technical and managerial competencies to achieve success for the firm, essentially at the start-up stage. However, the theory of the creative individual as the source of all success is challenged by the practical awareness of the fact that few entrepreneurs are really independent given the existence of a complex network of family and administrative staff support.

Moreover, entrepreneurial acts are frequently those of a small number of individual founder directors working in consort.

Typically, with spin-off firms and technical entrepreneurs emerging from an academic environment, it can be said the founder's characteristics are associated with the technological level of the firm's product (Miller et al., 1988; Lefebvre and Lefebvre, 1992). A schematic model suggests that new companies are dependent at their formation on the technological base learned by the entrepreneur from incubating sources such as former companies, university laboratories, engineering departments. While personal abilities and individual attitudes are critical to the success of the entrepreneur, such abilities are forged in the smithy of collaboration. Even if it is believed that entrepreneurship is a solo act to begin with, it is virtually impossible to achieve any form of growth without cultivating collaborative effort. As Bellini and Zollo point out (see Chapter 10) during the passage from organisational infancy to adulthood the firm undergoes crises of control and direction due to the necessity of reducing the central role of the entrepreneur. Literature surveys show that in order to support its innovative capability, the growing firm must have a minimum size, hold internal skills and maintain a network of stable linkages with external economic agents.

Based on observations made by several writers, two other problems associated with traditional concepts of entrepreneurship can be identified: one is that of the variable impact of entrepreneurship on the growing firm; the other being the wastefulness of individual (entrepreneur) management style. As the firm grows the typical individual entrepreneur often leaves voluntarily (evidence from the UK and USA), implying that the growth of a firm may be attributable to a number of acts of entrepreneurship performed by different individuals or groups of individuals acting in consort. As regards individual acts of management, the key problem lies in balancing responsibilities relating to R&D, marketing, accounting, personnel issues, etc. with an unwillingness to delegate. In many cases the "high-tech" entrepreneur decides to keep the unit of business operation small rather than dilute "control".

The spatial concentration of technology firms indicates that the spirit of entrepreneurship is spawned out of collaboration, focused support from the state and other quarters, and various degrees of networking. Rather than eulogising the wonders of the high-tech entrepreneur and their individual acts of entrepreneurship, it is perhaps worthy of attention to understand the impact of collaboration, interaction between different stakeholders, and networking, on entrepreneurship.

THE ENVIRONMENT OF REFERENCE

The generally accepted idea that innovation is necessary for economic development implies the positive view that better conditions may be created by change. According to this view, the political, cultural, social and technological boundaries move continuously, making available new areas to search for new options that offer greater perceived values at lower perceived costs.

Innovation, then, is related to the creation of value through the exploitation of factors of change. In practical terms this means:

- The development and commercialisation of new products, services, etc., that not only replace the old ones but also satisfy new needs

- The development and implementation of the new processes which produce such products and services, and deliver higher quality with lower consumption of resources

- The creation of new organisational structures which make economic and productive systems more capable of responding to the dynamic evolution of needs.

The factors of change are many and of different nature. Some of them are cultural and are related to what people, as potential users of innovation, value. These factors stem from a consideration of *what is worth doing and why*, and are expressed by changes in market demands, by the evolution of political and socio-economic situations, by the ruling of institutional bodies, etc. Other factors of change explore *what can be done in economic terms and how*. In this case scientific and technological progress has proven to be the most powerful driving force.

It is important to realise that the know-what and the know-hy may be more powerful drives to innovation than the know-w. Innovation requires a vision of the future that is often diffi-t to perceive in underdeveloped environments. This may be the impediment to economic take-off (Nicolò, 1996).

he process of innovation may take advantage of the accumu-stock of scientific and technological knowledge. Neverthe-e exploitation of this stock of knowledge into innovation may mean bearing a cost that is normally far from negligible and accepting a level of risk that is higher than normal. The potential advantages come only after the cost of innovation has been borne and the risk has been accepted. It is important, therefore, that these potential advantages be clearly understood in advance in order to ignite the innovation process.

To make innovation occur there must be organisations and/or entities that are willing to bear the costs and take the risks associated with it, in anticipation of some possible future advantage. These organisations and entities are the actors of innovation. To bear a cost today in order to gain an advantage tomorrow is a typical entrepreneurial attitude; entrepreneurs and enterprises are the main actors of innovation. They are not the only actors and often are not necessarily the critical actors but they are the principal actors. This means that any attempt to establish an innovation model has to take into account the mechanisms and values of entrepreneurial behaviour.

Entrepreneurs interact with their environment, and their choices depend significantly on a number of factors that are not under their direct control. These factors basically concern the nature and structure of the environment within which the entrepreneurs and their enterprises operate. This interaction between the enterprises and their environment of reference is the most intriguing aspect of innovation; understanding the mechanism of such an interaction opens the way to designing possible interventions and development policies for areas that appear to be lagging behind in economic development processes. The modification and improvement of the environment of reference is the area where entities and organisations other than the entrepreneurs — typically educational and social institutions — may qualify as critical actors influencing critical environmental factors of the innovation process.

The concept of environment of reference must be clarified. While it is generally significantly related to the territory by virtue of the geographical location of some determining factors such as people and physical infrastructures for services, research and technology, it is dangerous to identify it strictly with a specific geographical area or territory. The most important characteristic of the environment of reference is its structure, determined by all the possible relations (institutional, social, cultural, financial, commercial, etc.) which link the economic agents (not only enterprises) that operate within it. It is desirable that this network of relationships is widely spread. When it remains contained within an area (especially if it is an underdeveloped area) the visibility of the future and the number of possible options and opportunities rapidly diminish. The environment of reference should not be viewed as a closed spatial niche.

Large enterprises tend to relate more directly to environments with a global geographical extension than small and medium-sized enterprises for which the environment of reference — at first analysis — often appears to be only local and to match the territory within which they operate.

Nevertheless SMEs may indirectly profit from the fact that some of the agents acting in their environment of reference (the institutions, some big enterprises, etc.) also operate in larger and/or more numerous environments, acting as pivots between them. In other words, one can envisage a local environment with a narrow mesh network of relations and a more open environment with a large mesh network. In the interaction between these two environments there is room for innovation in small and medium-sized enterprises. The quality of the environment of reference acts as a multiplier on the value of innovation.

In this sense, investing in the improvement of the environment of reference is an economic activity capable of creating value. Investing in this area is important because many of the environmental factors (such as the demand for innovation, the access to technology or the availability of relevant skills) are generally critical. Nevertheless, it may be unsuitable for single entrepreneurs because they cannot, in general, directly appropriate the value generated by this kind of investment. This is an area where political and social institutions must intervene and invest resources, in an entrepreneurial spirit, for the benefit of the community.

Often the market for small and medium-sized enterprises is formed of larger enterprises. As a consequence, the establishment of some big enterprise in the area may help create the critical mass needed to determine innovation and development. This kind of opportunity should be looked upon favourably.

In order to be able to take advantage of these opportunities, SMEs must be able to access technology and know-how in an efficient way.

It is a widely accepted opinion that most opportunities require the development of science-intensive products and services. Science intensity not only refers to the value of the accumulated stock of research on which the product and/or service is based, but also to the time proximity between the research stage and the commercial exploitation stage. This aspect appears to be very critical in today's world.

The shortening of the product life-cycle can cause significant problems for technological transfer. In fact, these delays have an effect on the length of the time interval necessary for the commercial exploitation of innovative products and cancel the advantage of leadership in the market. If there is a delay in reaching the market, the entire value of the R&D may be lost. The acceleration of technology transfer is one of the most critical variables of the innovation model. To accelerate the transfer, the receivers must be strongly motivated and in touch with their markets. They must also be capable of assimilating the technology they receive. It is here that a good educational and training system in the territory plays a crucial role.

Another very critical variable is the access of SMEs to risk and/or venture capital. In determining this, the vocational character of an area (aerospace, materials, biotechnology, electronics, etc.) appears to be very important. It makes specific skills and technologies available in that area, facilitates contact with the market and also facilitates access to risk or venture capital because it creates communities that can share the culture and understanding of the business. It is in this fertile environment that the provision of all low-cost services gives the highest results.

TERRITORIAL ECOSYSTEMS OF INNOVATION

Typical examples of fertile environments are the Italian "industrial district" of the 1970s and the 1980s, and the "territorial value chain of innovation" (or "territorial ecosystem", TEI) of the 1990s, whose main attributes are shown in Appendix A at the end of this chapter (Formica and Mitra 1996). A TEI is a system whose "ecology" promotes competitive co-operation relationships.

A "territorial value chain" is built up from the primary resources of the indigenous potential represented by knowledge, including organisational knowledge, and information. These resources are renewable, not exhaustible, self-generating, but they also require a highly skilled know-how. They are conveyed towards a set of activities (higher and advanced education, research and technology transfer, university–industry co-operation, innovative and science-based entrepreneurship, seed and venture capital, etc.) whose common denominator is given by the "intellectual technologies" — that is, a set of methodologies (operative research, managerial science, simulation of forecasting models, etc.) trying to replace any intuitive judgement by means of an algorithm. These activities are supported by a broad range of knowledge and "intellectual infrastructures" that take the form of entrepreneurial organisations — e.g., university–industry interfaces and companies, technology transfer centres, business innovation centres, science and technology parks, whose critical mass shapes a "territorial ecosystem of innovation" (TEI) or an "innovative milieu".

TEIs highlight the need for a sound mix of policies that make a clear distinction between "nominal" factors of growth (such as public deficit, public debt/GDP ratio interest rate/inflation differentials and exchange rates) and "real" ones (knowledge and information, education and human capital; science and technology, R&D, technology transfer; entrepreneurship; corporate real investment; social infrastructures such as transport and communications).

TEIs exhibit two basic organisational forms, namely the "holding" and "partnership" forms. According to the type of prevalent design and form, the above-mentioned entrepreneurial organisations play different roles.

In the science-and-technology-park-driven territorial ecosystem of innovation ("science park ecosystem"), the STP plays the role of team leader instead of being a mere property development scheme. In this context the institutional form could be described as a "holding" type (e.g. a company such as "STP Ltd") under which umbrella other organisations (e.g. tenant firms of the STP) operate. The "STP Ltd" company would be the organisational manifestation of the TEI.

The "partnership" form is a bottom-up and incremental model of organisation. In this context the STP organisation is motivated primarily by property development and (on some occasions) regional or territorial marketing and inward investment issues. The organisational manifestation of the TEI might be that of a virtual company or of a federation arising from the co-operation and competition between the STP and other related institutions, such as the business technology centre, the technology transfer centre, the advanced technology centre, the industrial liaison centre, etc.

Compared to TEIs, BEs are emerging as clusters of interlocked activities both from the transformation of the large corporation and the evolution of territorial industrial complexes of small and medium-sized enterprises (SMEs). Examples are represented by the mature Italian industrial districts (e.g. clothing and ceramics in Northern Italy) where some SMEs, driven by product development and customer service, have increased in size and product lines. To be effective, BEs need suitable territorial points of reference, of which TEIs represent the most advanced achievement.

Intellectual Entrepreneurship in the Research Domain

Central to the innovations process in a TEI is the relationship between critical aspects of value — intellectual ("know-how"), economic ("know-what"), and philosophical/social ("know why"). A holistic model of innovation incorporates all three dimensions and provides for the foundation of knowledge-based entrepreneurship.

The existence of TEIs allows for greater value to be attached to "know-what" (what is worth doing and what can be done in economic terms) and "know-why" (rationale for competitiveness) than "know-how", as far as innovation in the local economy is concerned. In this context research provides the ground for intellectual entrepreneurship: that is, the basis for applying the invisible capital of knowledge, which the research itself has generated, to the creation of new industries, the transformation of existing ones, the exploitation of new opportunities, and the constant improvement of current activity. Thus, within a TEI, the knowledge of business development is as relevant as knowledge of developments in science and technology.

The non-linear process of innovation suggests that, at the macro level, innovation in companies is not necessarily the result of university graduates applying their knowledge in business. Previous knowledge is worked upon, transformed and often "unlearnt" to contribute to business development. Moreover, in today's rapidly changing technological climate, relevant cutting-edge knowledge cannot wait for a body of knowledge to be incubated theoretically before it finds application. Intellectual entrepreneurship calls for a closer, continually evolving relationship between what is researched, studied and learnt at higher education institutions and what is researched, produced, marketed and learnt in business.

Much of the development of a holistic model of innovation can be examined in the context of university–industry co-operation.

The two traditionally disparate sectors are now interlocked in the competition for production of knowledge in a learning society. It is, therefore, appropriate to turn at this stage to a short review of the nature of co-operation between industry and higher education, and their combined role in strengthening intellectual entrepreneurship.

Increasing the Value of Intellectual Entrepreneurship

Significant changes are associated with research organisations. Between the last quarter of the nineteenth century and the current decade, university–industry co-operation has influenced the organisational development of science and technology.

The birth of science-based industries, such as the electrical and the chemical industries, emphasised the role of science as a normal means of production. Innovative companies, which generate as well as exploit scientific ideas, built the first industrial research laboratories which opened up the possibilities of university–industry co-operation.

The beginning of the nineteenth century marked the birth of cross-fertilisation between industry and academic work. This cross-fertilisation was best manifested in the laboratories of companies such as General Electric, AT&T and Westinghouse. The process found its most fertile soil in the USA since it was there that in the nineteenth century, European pioneer experiments exploring the marriage between science and technology flourished through the creation of technology universities, modelled on the German experience of technical education and the French École Centrale des Arts et Manufactures. Table 1.1 traces the history of early forms of university–industry co-operation in the USA.

R&D activities are rationalised in laboratories by teams of specialists who come from university and industry. Their task is to ensure that innovation is an organised and routine activity. These laboratories, which are conceived to obtain high productivity in research (an ordinary invention every ten days and a great invention every six months, as Edison said), often come up against the obstacle of bureaucratic procedures which can stifle those individuals who have a propensity for entrepreneurship. Way back in 1935, when the vital industrial laboratories were still on the rise, Schumpeter foresaw the demise of US industrial giants equipped with big research centres. Schumpeter's predictions may be debatable, but the recent examples of IBM and Apple point to the inadequacy of proprietary strategies related to technology, innovation and organisation, as opposed to co-operation with smaller firms and universities.

TABLE 1.1: THE INCUBATION OF UNIVERSITY–INDUSTRY
CO-OPERATION IN THE USA, 1824–1913

1824	Foundation of the Rensselaer School on the French model of the École Centrale des Arts et Manufactures.
1849	Foundation of the Rensselaer Polytechnic Institute.
1865	Foundation of the MIT School of Industrial Science to study science for practical purposes and not only as an elegant form of learning.
Mid-1890s	A series of universities (Johns Hopkins, Harvard, Columbia, Chicago) inaugurate courses oriented towards research on the model of German universities.
1905	Foundation of the MIT Department of Co-operation and Industrial Research.
1913	Foundation of the Mellon Institute of Industrial Research at Pittsburgh University.

Source: Noble, 1977

The era of the industrial research laboratories lasted nearly 70 years (from the 1880s to the 1950s). As the influence of laboratories has declined, university–industry co-operation has increasingly witnessed organisational innovations, of which the university–industry company could be the innovative organisation which will gain momentum over the next few years. Such a company would be the archetypal TEI's "infrastructural innovation", designed as a joint-stock entrepreneurial body whose distinctive stakeholders are university and industry.

With its rationale of commercialising knowledge and generating spin-offs from academe and other (industrial, private and public) research centres, the university–industrial model company creates an atmosphere for the cultivation of intellectual entrepreneurship.

Commercialising Knowledge

The fruits of university research activity have little economic value unless they are systematically harvested in the marketplace. The university–industry company changes the status of services/products based on academic research which would otherwise be generated and sold well below the cost of production. Return from the commercialisation of academic work can be invested in the advancement of knowledge, and new solutions can be transferred internally to the TEI, thereby generating new resources for new investments.

Stimulating the reverse movement of knowledge from industry to university, the university–industry company could take advantage of the potential opening of doors in business corporations to R&D collaboration (as costs of keeping up with a larger number of different technologies continue to rise, more companies are using external sources of R&D). With SMEs, a consortium approach — involving a cluster of firms across or within sectors — could be taken to generate interaction.

Knowledge commercialisation involves issues related to patents and licences springing from intellectual property activity. The university–industry company can promote a patent policy that boosts entrepreneurship. The relaxation of proprietary restrictions on the dissemination of information, patent and royalty rights, with the purpose of granting licences or royalty arrangements, should allow students and research staff to set up their own companies.

Much intellectual property is in the minds of researchers and goes with them if they change jobs. Offering these people the opportunity of directly exploiting their innovative ideas on a commercial basis (or capitalising on business development realised by other potential entrepreneurs) is an effective way of both retaining and commercialising knowledge within the territorial ecosystem of innovation.

Generating Academic Spin-Off

The university is the symbolic milieu of "creators": *intrate spectatores exite creatores* ("those who enter as spectators exit as creators") is the inscription found at the entrance to one of the Italian universities. "Those who enter creators exit entrepreneurs" might be the complementary epigraph for the university–industry company, as such a company surveys the student body and personnel from the university and other research centres to identify potential entrepreneurs.

The university–industry company creates a supportive environment for the three types of spin-offs:

- Enterprises set up by the teaching or research staff of university and other research centres who wish to exploit commercially the results of research conducted in academic environments.

- Enterprises founded by graduates to exploit commercially the results of research in which they have been involved at their institution (see Appendix B at the end of this chapter for the example of the "TOP" programme devised by the University of Twente in the Netherlands).

- Enterprises run by people from outside the university (for example, employed professional managers in the private sector moving from their job to business ownership), who decide to exploit commercially results of the university's or their own research. The objective of the University of Twente's TOP programme is to match spin-offs ideas and entrepreneurs. Once realistic spin-off ideas have been detected within an academic environment, an advertising campaign is launched in appropriate newspapers and magazines, asking for experienced entrepreneurs with a technical and commercial background to back the product and/or create new ventures based on the research ideas.

Some of these examples of spin-offs could be established by the university–industry company on a joint-venture basis. Application and development of such work as "ideas generation" (the creative process) for business development delineates a new path of knowledge transfer (Figure 1.1, Scenarios B and C), which itself is an important element of spin-off activity.

The scenarios depicted in Figure 1.1 show the way in which university–industry relationships, through technology transfer, can evolve from a traditional model (Scenario A) to that of market-oriented ones (Scenarios A and B), with the last model offering the prospect of the creation of a discrete, spin-off company, that rises above the separate domain of either the university or industry. The evolution of this model shifts attention from individual vested interests to issues concerned with benefits to the wider community and economic development of a region.

FIGURE 1.1: THE PROCESS OF TECHNOLOGY TRANSFER

SCENARIO A

University supply-led technology transfer

("academic lubricant to get the wheels going")

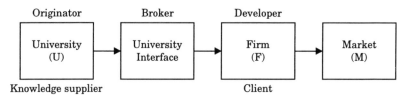

SCENARIO B

Market-led technology transfer

("creating conections with markets that generate demands for new products/services")

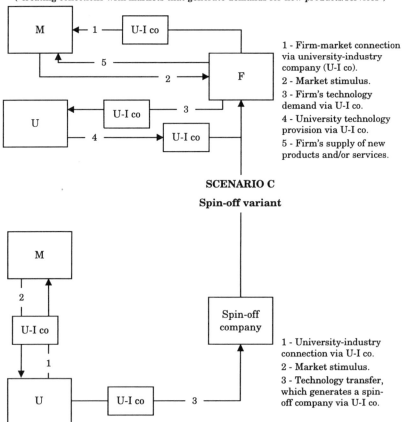

1 - Firm-market connection via university-industry company (U-I co).

2 - Market stimulus.

3 - Firm's technology demand via U-I co.

4 - University technology provision via U-I co.

5 - Firm's supply of new products and/or services.

SCENARIO C

Spin-off variant

1 - University-industry connection via U-I co.

2 - Market stimulus.

3 - Technology transfer, which generates a spin-off company via U-I co.

Source: Formica and Mitra, 1996

The Regional Development Dimension

In our consideration of the evolution and characteristics of university–industry relationships, and of the process of innovation, we have referred often to the involvement of multiple players and of their influence on both the relationships and the innovation process. Innovation as a social process means that universities and industry engage in relationships for generating, applying, transforming and distributing knowledge. It means that there are technological, organisational, social and cultural factors involved at all levels, and that innovation and change occur when individuals and institutions are mutually dependent on each other for accumulating and diffusing knowledge through learning, direct experience and interaction. This is a more comprehensive approach to the role of universities and industry, acknowledging that, in the development of that relationship, many other institutions, processes and factors are involved as a part of a wider knowledge network.

Inherent in the consideration of a "knowledge network" is the importance of the spatial concept of innovation. Such a concept builds on the idea of innovation being demand-driven and a product of policies, institutional strategies and economic conditions. As Annalee Saxenian (1994) has pointed out, various factors, such as the cultural and social factors of a region, the networks and structure of the industrial sector (labour market, competitive factors, etc.) and the structure of the organisation, all taken together, have had a direct influence on the development of an "innovative milieu" such as Silicon Valley. The visionary role of Stanford University in spawning high technology and innovative companies close to its campus emphasises the role of the university in exploiting spatial, knowledge-based resources.

The emergence of the region, and in particular the knowledge-based region, as the centre for economic activity, underscores the growing importance of the regional environment in helping firms to innovate, operate globally, and invest in the locational advantages of regional innovation systems, which include well-developed technology transfer systems, a good skill base, dynamic education/R&D facilities, and well-equipped suppliers as part of a strong network or an industrial district. In this scenario, the innovation process is not simply afforded by the university–industry technology transfer mechanisms, but by the interaction

between producers and users, between consumers and distributors, and by the mutual proximity of all these players.

The complex environment of reference calls for the university–
industry company to:

- Identify the needs of the community as the fundamental process in promoting innovation.

- Encourage the creation of demand for innovative products and
  services by giving priority to financial support for the development of new technology

- Encourage greater co-operation between individual departments within universities and companies (with perhaps a
  lesser degree of centralisation of activities) at the operational
  level

- Facilitate the operational level by providing information services on the market, commercialising know-how, generating new
  activities, co-ordinating multi-disciplinary effort and funding
  opportunities, finding suitable partners, and participating directly at policy forums at the local, national and international
  levels

- Establish knowledge networks with other institutions and with
  companies at the hub of such networks

- Attract firms to participate on network forums and in specific
  programmes from their inception

- Generate greater awareness within universities and within
  education systems (particularly funding bodies) of the need for
  recognition of incentives for direct work with industry

- Making strategic, programme-based and synergetic links between research, continuing vocational education, outreach and
  other development activities

- The greater encouragement of action research activities on
  economic, social and technological threats and opportunities in
  the region, supported by specific action programmes

- The encouragement of spin-offs.

The type of university–industry interface company envisaged
above requires a form of stakeholding which reflects the interest
and participation of additional stakeholders, outside higher education and industry. The idea of a "network" organisation is predi-

cated upon two factors: the involvement of all institutions which provide or imbibe from education (including research, teaching and training) as part of a hub-and-spoke system; and the drawing-up of a regional agenda within higher education institutions. This approach recognises the salient fact of learning occurring in different environments (within universities and outside in companies), and the importance of collaboration at different levels within a region to create a learning culture. Linking inward investment strategies with, for example, skills training, technology transfer, international strategic alliances, and property development in a region would require co-ordinated activity of key stakeholders. The shift is from adversarial strategies based on institutional hegemony to information sharing and collaborative activity based on regional, market-oriented advantage.

Such networking is further enhanced with the advent of telematics and the ability to generate and transfer knowledge across distances. Apart from the benefit to immediate business transactions, the acquisition, processing and reorganisation of different sources of information speedily allows for co-operation and co-ordination of different types of expertise both within and outside organisations.

We are deliberately stressing the university–industry dimension to regional networks. Most universities are, however, characterised by the absence of any regional policy, and this position is unlikely to be corrected if the role of universities is not given sufficient prominence within regional and economic development agendas, along with appropriate recognition and reward for participation by universities at the regional level. In order for such recognition and reward to be incorporated into policy agendas, it would be necessary to appreciate some of the specific advantages derived from the university–industry dimension of regional networking. Reference has already been made to the sourcing of data and information for the production, easily and speedily, of new knowledge both within and outside the institution. There is greater value to be obtained when we consider who can benefit most from such developments. SMEs are more likely to favour multi-disciplinary packages for research, training and information services, but they also lack capabilities. They are also very vulnerable to the rapid changes that now affect most businesses. Subject to proper packaging of appropriate services, universities could be major players in the development of relevant services for SMEs and regional competitive advantage capability. This resource needs to be harnessed, as much through the reorganisation of university strategies and structures as with the clear understanding of its benefit by local policy makers.

The development of a regional innovation strategy by the Economic Development Unit of the University of North London is an example of university-led action based on valorising academic expertise and mixing it with know-how derived from other organisations. The strategy is to promote new business creation (the spin-off of new firms and the development of young and innovative firms). The objective is to look for organic development with a particular focus on generating, coding and disseminating appropriate information, which was identified in a major survey as the main impediment to innovation for local SMEs. The implementation plan includes the creation of a forum for SMEs to meet and discuss issues of relevance through workshops, seminars, local and overseas company visits and one-to-one meetings. Information generated, informally and formally, is collated, analysed and then disseminated for a variety of purposes. The demand-side forum is matched by a "Service Suppliers' Network" which consists of local policy makers and actors. The objective here is to coordinate strategies for innovation and technology transfer by feeding back information from each other and from the demandside forum. The essential information is put together and used through an Information Brokerage Service which is used by both SMEs and supply-side stakeholders. During the nine months of its operation, 70 firms have become members, along with local authorities, training and enterprise councils, and business support services.

There are many good examples of networking models emerging across the world. The Scottish Enterprise model of entrepreneurship, Sheffield 2000, the creation of the new Foundation by the University of Bologna, the CONNECT programme at the University of California, San Diego, and the proposed development of the Enterprise Innovation Centre in India, are examples of existing or emerging networks involving a variety of institutions with different agendas to work together. The issue is that of developing such networks, not which organisation leads them. Vision, openness, informal architecture, are more important than proprietary control by any one organisation. Such networks do not solve economic development problems by themselves; they act as harbingers and catalysts for change through new ways of working.

CONCLUSION

Greater university–industry collaboration is likely to emerge in the future in the fuzzy domain of networking. It will be based on interconnectedness, interdependency, recognition of values that lie in learning by using, doing, and interacting. It is already apparent that such collaboration will not only be brought about by combining the interests of the two parties but also by the involvement of other institutions acting in a regional capacity. There is an interesting parallel between the emergence of convergent technologies as seen in the interdependencies between microprocessing and ergonomics in miniaturisation, or between internet and e-mail, and the links between pure and applied research, explicit and tacit forms of learning and between disparate organisations in a network as they approach the millennium. Industry, higher education, government and the wider community are raw characters in the hypertext of information flows today.

APPENDIX A

THE EVOLUTIONARY TREND OF THE INDUSTRIAL DISTRICT

Definition

An industrial district can be defined as a geographical proximity of many independent firms where:

- The firms are interlocked in a set of operations for manufacturing a specific product (e.g. tiles, knitwear, leather, packaging machines).

- Often each firm specialises in the production of a single component of the final product.

- There is a co-evolution of firms specialised in the production of customised machine tools and equipment related to that final product.

Key Features

Co-ordination

Co-ordination between firms in an industrial district usually takes either of two forms:

- The *original form*, based on voluntary (i.e. moral and social) reciprocal commitment and trust, which leads to a swarm of small firms of equal status (like a "Roman phalanx" — a body of soldiers in close formation acting individually but presenting a united front in battle). This lead to *productive decentralisation* ("separate but together"), where there is a chain of small and micro firms, each participant being specialised in only one phase of the cycle.

- The *evolutionary form*, a mixture of commitment and hierarchy, the latter stemming from the intervention of a decision-maker (for example, a leading company as a local pivot/champion). The "Roman phalanx" configuration is transformed into a set of "wedges", each of which has the leading company at its "sharp end" — that is, at the point of contact with the market. This leads to the formation of *Business Ecosystems* ("All in the family").

A Business Ecosystem (BE) is a supply chain made up of several companies interacting rapidly with each other and with the outside world. A BE embraces:

- A leader, which holds the intellectual leadership and is the node of human networks supported by information technology interconnections.

- A few direct primary suppliers (co-makers), involved in the early phase of the leader's development process.

- A platform of secondary and tertiary subcontractors surrounding the new business configuration.

Relationships

There are three major types of relationship scenarios within industrial districts:

1. Deep-rooted informal and implicit relationships based on unwritten rules and unwritten codes of behaviour. They are the cornerstone of more advanced and structured forms of collaboration. In this scenario, *trust is a social dividend* which springs from the individual's need to preserve their own reputation within a small local community. The behavioural rules are mainly related to professional correctitude and honesty.

2. Uncertainty and instability fostered by the non-observance of the local codes, e.g.: not imitating/counterfeiting the competitors' model; not exacerbating price competition. This avoidance

of local codes corresponds to what could be characterised as *"hit-and-run" behaviour*, where short-termist firms are always willing to sacrifice future markets gains to short-term profits, disregarding the district's general interest. Therefore, the architecture of trust relationships shows a large grey area between a propensity to binding commitments and a propensity to opportunistic actions.

3. Building trust for competition: the new formula of relational contracts within business ecosystems is based on the *establishment of long-term relationships* which imply continuity and stability. In this scenario, the BE's leading company is keen to cultivate a long-term supplier strategy. Whenever there is a trade-off between short-term profits and investments for breeding the BE competitiveness, the latter prevails.

Information

An individualistic ethos will always affect the process of sharing the information. This can be illustrated using a number of analogies:

- *"Between a shooting and a passing game"*: Using an analogy from soccer, this type of ethos implies an attitude where *"my scores really count; the club's scores might count"*. Small entrepreneurs must still overcome the reluctance of opening the business to outsiders and accept the idea of sharing experiences with competitors, for example:

  ◊ giving competitors information about the solvency of the potential clients

  ◊ if the company is unable to solve a client's problem, they should be open to giving them the name of a competitor who may be able to help them.

- *The "well" architecture:* The supplier who needs water (i.e. information) goes to the assembler's well. The well owner wants to supply the best available water, in terms of quality and quantity. The owner sets a limit to the water's distribution. Partial and opportunistic disclosure of information generates a climate of uncertainty within the supplier's environment.

- *The "plumbing network" architecture:* A more open, co-operative environment leads to what could be described as a "plumbing network". This type of architecture allows the establishment of a consummate co-operative relationship between the parties. Competition arises from each network-partner's capability to use the flow of information. The flow of information is rich, continuous, rapid, free, and reciprocal. All the parties operate in the context of competitive co-operation: they work co-operatively and competitively to support new products, satisfy customer needs, and eventually incorporate the next round of innovations. Competitive co-operation is practised through the Business Service Centre located in the district.

Business Service Centre

The Business Service Centre (BSC) is a provider of specialist added-value "structural services" (*servizi reali*, or real services, as opposed to monetary incentives), which encourage structural changes (e.g. product diversification, process restructuring, market penetration), within the SMEs located in the district. The BSC promotes the SMEs' collective upgrading of autonomy, innovation and competitiveness.

Generally, a BSC is a limited liability consortium company, publicly and privately financed, which links hundreds of firms of various sizes (within the SMEs) with productive topology. These firms are subscribers of the Centre's services. The BSC usually evolves in three distinct phases:

- *Inception phase* (0–4 years): the Centre's start-up mission is the creation of a social consensus around the idea of setting up a common language and culture, and a shared view of the future strategy for the development of the district.

- *First phase* (5–10 years): delivering information services via meetings, training courses, publications.

- *Second phase* (after 10 years): providing advanced methods and tools for technological innovation, quality and internationalisation.

Implicit, Trust-Based or Relational Contracts

The long term is assumed as the time horizon of relational contracts. The type of relational contract affects the long-term relationship. There are two main types of contract:

- The most frequent form is the spot contract, which may be renewed by the parties. According to this contract, the long-term relationship is continuously jeopardised by the parties' opportunistic behaviour. The implicit commitment of long-term links induces the parties to invest in the relationship. Yet, once the investment has made, the party in the strongest bargaining position (usually, the assembler) attempts to exploit the relationship, even if that behaviour leads to its cessation. The weaker parties take the risks ("zero assurance" from the stronger party) and receive incentives (they share the gains with the stronger party, even though these may be unequally distributed).

- The new, experimental type of relational contract based on the principle of competitive co-operation. Here, risks (assurance) and gains (incentives) rest on an even division between the parties involved. The new contract calls for a network structure whose main features are (Miles and Snow, 1992):

  ◊ *Voluntarism*: Partners are free to withdraw from relationships they believe are unfairly structures

  ◊ *Openness*: Network relationships are highly visible to all parties

  ◊ *Explicitness*: External, visible relationships specify the performance that is expected from each partner, and how the performance will be measure and compensated

  ◊ *Simplicity*: "The less you sign, the more you achieve"

  ◊ *Performance*: Network relationships are guided by performance rather than by procedures. Partners are pushed towards performance-based equity.

  ◊ *Information accessibility*: full disclosure information systems ensure that all decisions are made objectively and fairly

  ◊ *Capacity for self-renewal*: the operating logic of the network is the ability to adapt (i.e. change configuration) without losing effectiveness.

The Evolutionary Trend

The evolutionary trend of the industrial district indicates an innovative, outward-looking local milieu (the "territorial ecosystem of innovation"). The competitive challenges of the 1990s in areas such as business leadership within the district and technology, finance, and market access are far more complex in terms of scope and degree. From a self-contained territorial community the district evolves as an innovative local milieu with the capacity to establish international relations.

There are a number of forces spanning the boundaries of the industrial district's economy:

- Business diversification around the firm's core competence.

- International delocalisation of manufacturing and services for better performance both in terms of cost-effectiveness and market competitiveness.

- New forms of organisation of economic activities (e.g. firms' networks and network-firms), which, in turn, create links beyond the local area.

- New district-actors other than small entrepreneurs, such as universities, research institutions, knowledge centres, which encourage an international vision of the local development.

APPENDIX B

THE TOP PROGRAMME AT THE UNIVERSITY OF TWENTE (UT), THE NETHERLANDS.

The University of Twente runs a Temporal Entrepreneurial Placements (TOP) programme. The pivot of the Programme is the University's Industrial Liaison Centre, Transfer, Research and Development (TRD).

University and entrepreneur: sharing opportunities

A UT research group offers a part-time position for one year to a graduate who must develop a business plan in order to be accepted for a place on a TOP Programme. The new entrepreneur works half-time for the research group on contracted research projects and for the remainder they are free to develop their product or service, or to work on first orders from clients.

A supportive business school

UT's graduate students in Business Management help the potential entrepreneurs to develop the business plan.

The evaluation phase

The TOP Steering Committee (consisting of the TRD product manager, the Director of the Business Technology Centre and the Director of Innovation Consultants — itself one of the first UT spin-off companies) assesses the business plan of the entrepreneur before a decision is made whether or not to award a TOP place. The Committee also evaluates the TOP entrepreneurs after they have been in business for six months.

The training phase

At the UT's Centre of Innovative Entrepreneurship, TOP graduates are trained on "How to Become an Entrepreneur."

The "mentor"

An experienced entrepreneur is asked to provide support in management issues to the new entrepreneur during the first year. This service is provided free of charge. After the first year the "mentor" tends to stay with the entrepreneur on a consultancy basis.

TOP entrepreneurs, vehicle of technology transfer

TOP entrepreneurs become important partners in further developing results of scientific research into applicable technologies. They have also turned out to be excellent agents for transferring the technologies to industry and into marketable products.

Financing: revolving fund mechanism

For the first five years (1984–89) the Programme was financed (DFL 5,525,000 — approx. £1.85 million) by the Dutch Ministry of Economic Affairs on the basis of starting 15 companies per years. Today the programme is financed through a revolving fund supported by the European Social Fund and by TOP entrepreneurs' profits.

Results (1984–1986)

Since the scheme began, 220 places have been awarded, 170 new firms have been established, of which only 35 have ceased their activities and 1100 new jobs have been generated over ten years (not counting additional jobs with supplier companies).

Source: Kobus and van Barneveld, 1994.

References

Cooley, M. (on behalf of the European Expert Group) (1990), "European Competitiveness in the Twenty-first Century — Integration of Work, Culture and Technology", a Contribution to the FAST Proposal for an R&D Programme on Human Work in Advanced Technological Environments, Commission of the European Communities, DGXII, Brussels

Elliott, C. (1995), "Exploitation or Partnership? An Alternative Approach to University–Industry Collaboration", *Industry and Higher Education Journal*, February.

European Commission (1992), "Advanced Training for Competitive Advantage", Communication from the Commission to the Council and the European Parliament concerning European Higher Education–Industry Co-operation, Brussels, 9 December.

Formica, P. and Mitra, J. (1996), "Co-operation and Competition: the Creation of Ecosystems of Innovation", *Industry and Higher Education Journal*, June.

Goddard, J., Charles, D., Pike, A., Potts, G. and Bradley, D. (1994), "Universities and Communities: A Report by the Centre for Urban and Regional Development Studies", University of Newcastle, for the Committee of Vice Chancellors and Principals, London.

Hull, C.J. (1990), "Technology Transfer Between Higher Education and Industry in Europe: Obstacles to its Development and Proposals for Helping to Overcome Them", *Technology, Innovation, Information*, Luxembourg.

Kline, S.J. and Rosenberg, N. (1986), "An Overview of Innovation", in National Academy of Engineering, *The Positive Sum Strategy*, Washington, DC: National Academy Press.

Kobus, J.A. and van Barneveld D. (1994), "Spin-off Projects in Twente", in *Technology Transfer Practice in Europe*, Conference Papers, Hanover, 28–29 April.

Lefebvre, E. and Lefebvre, L.A. (1992), "Firm Innovativeness and CEO Characteristics in Small Manufacturing Firms", *Journal of Engineering and Technology Management*, No. 9.

Miles, R.E. and Snow, C.C. (1992), "Causes of Failures in Networking Organizations", *California Management Review*, Summer.

Miller, D., Droge, C. and Toulouse, J.M. (1988), "Strategic Process & Content as Mediators between Organisational Context and Structure", *Academy of Management Journal*, Vol. 31, No. 3.

Mitra, J. (1996), "Managing Change: a Holistic Approach to Higher Education–Industry Interaction in the United Kingdom", Paper presented at the UNESCO World Conference on Engineering Education, Paris, May.

Monck, C.P.S., Porter, R.B., Quintas, A., Storey, D.J. and Wynarczyk, P. (1988), *Science Parks and the Growth of High Technology Firms*, London: Croom Helm.

Nicolò, V. (1996), "Technology Transfer through Connection with Stimulating Markets" in Guedes, M. and Formica, P. (eds.), *The Economics of Science Parks*, ANPROTEC, The International Association of Science Parks/Association of University Related Research Parks, Rio de Janeiro.

Noble, D.T. (1977), *America by Design: Science, Technology and the Rise of Corporate Capitalism*, New York: Alfred A. Knopf.

Saxenian, A. (1994), *Regional Advantage: Culture and Competition in Silicon Valley and Route 128*, Cambridge, MA: Harvard University Press.

Schuetze, H.G. (1996), "Innovation Systems, Regional Development and the Role of Universities in Industrial Innovation", *Industry and Higher Education Journal*, April.

Williams, B.R. (1985), *The Direct and Indirect Role of Higher Education in Industrial Innovation: What Should we Expect?* London: Technical Change Centre.

2

HIGHER EDUCATION–INDUSTRY CO-OPERATION: BETWEEN HESITANT PARTNERSHIP AND STRATEGIC ALLIANCE

Jan Sadlak[*]

INTRODUCTION

A broad paradigm by which higher education–industry co-operation is currently debated is based on two assumptions. First, the cumulative impact of scientific and technological progress — particularly with regard to communications and information technology and the internationalisation/globalisation of markets and manufacturing processes — implies appropriate adjustments which can be formulated as a need for economic restructuring and social regeneration, particularly at the local and regional levels. Second, that co-operation between higher education and industry is important and can make a significant contribution to these dynamic processes of adjustment. These two assumptions must be kept in mind while analysing recent developments in higher education.

To begin with, one does not have to be very observant to note that the economic and political environment has been altered quite abruptly in the course of the last decade or so, changing the global situation beyond recognition. An important factor in this development is associated with the demise of ideologically motivated bipolar confrontations. In hindsight, however, it was a collective illusion that a relatively peaceful implosion of the communist system and its national varieties in Central and Eastern Europe would bring about an immediate, massive and equitable reallocation of resources to economic and social development.

---

[*] The views expressed in this chapter are those of the author.

The list of achievements and failures caused by these developments depends on the specific issue, regional context, political persuasion or even personal opinion. But we are only now beginning to realise how profound these changes are and how many aspects of our economic and social life and their respective institutions need to be rethought and modified. In many regards, we have to operate in the context of a multiplicity of powers and trends, which raises the level of complexity of policy development and its implementation.

Consider the situation in higher education, where ongoing debate is a much more arduous task than simply a healthy critical examination of the intellectual objectives of higher education and the functioning of its institutions, or the search for corrective measures for its cyclical problems. It is also more profound than making end-of-the-century speculations and formulating prospects for the new millennium. It is not the first time in the history of universities that their missions and functioning are being fundamentally questioned. What is novel in the current debate is that calls for comprehensive reappraisal and decisive changes are not limited to one region or country. Even if the economic and social conditions behind the functioning of higher education institutions are sometimes very different, even within a given country, there are a number of problems shared by the whole of higher education enterprise.

The list of challenges facing higher education depends very much on the local and national context but, if higher education is to have a meaningful role in economic and social regeneration, we need to keep the following five issues and trends in mind when searching for solutions:

1. The size and rapid diversification of student populations

2. The limits of public funding for higher education

3. Absolute and relative advancement of science

4. The paradigm shift between information and communication technologies and higher education

5. Higher education and the "world of work".

These five issues are discussed below in detail.

THE SIZE AND RAPID DIVERSIFICATION OF STUDENT POPULATIONS

In many countries a policy of mass access to higher education is nowadays more a rule than an exception. Consequently, the number of students in higher education in some countries now exceeds the number of such traditionally important socio-professional groups as farmers.

The level of student enrolment for a traditionally predominant college-age group of 18–22/24 year-olds has reached 50 per cent, which is considered, even if rather arbitrarily, to be the threshold level for a "mass" system of higher education.[1] Quite a number of countries, and not only the rich and highly developed ones, are determined to reach the North American level of sending up to 60 per cent of school-leavers to colleges and universities in order to ensure that at least some 30 per cent of the workforce have academic and higher level vocational qualifications. It is worth noting that in Japan in 1995, 64.7 per cent of 18–22 year-olds were enrolled in various types of higher education institution such as universities, junior colleges, colleges of technology and special training colleges.

The argument for such expansion of higher education provisions is based on various estimations concerning the evolution of labour markets which show, for example, that in the course of the next decade, 40 per cent of all jobs in the industrialised countries will require 16 years of schooling and training and 60 per cent of all jobs will require a high school diploma.

Another major factor in a growing student enrolment is related to increased demand for higher education from people other than those in the "traditional age-group" and "full-time" students. This non-traditional clientele is diverse not only from the point of view of age but also from the point of view of educational and professional development needs, formal academic status, financial means, etc. This is also the category of student population where the most rapid growth can be observed.

The policy of mass access is to be continued for economic as well as social reasons, but it is not a risk-free policy for higher education or for other interested constituencies. The problems of quality of students, organisation and curriculum, employability of graduates, formation of professional and civil service "elites", all add up to a major, even if greatly simplified, question: are we

opening higher education to the masses or are we creating a sec-
ond-rate system?

THE LIMITS OF PUBLIC FUNDING FOR HIGHER EDUCATION

It is no longer a viable strategy for higher education, including
public institutions, to rely solely on seeking bigger and bigger al-
locations from public budgets. Even very optimistic assumptions
do not permit us to see "new public money" for higher education
on the horizon. The public budget strain is felt almost everywhere
and at every level of government. Many projections show that
current policies and cost-sharing patterns are just unsustainable.
Generally speaking and despite various innovative formulae for
the allocation of public and institutional budgets, in real terms
public spending per student is declining, which, sooner or later,
will also mean an overall decline in the quality of higher education enterprise.

The pattern of monetary flows in higher education systems is
also changing — more and more public money is being diverted
from "education" to "student support" and other types of social
assistance programmes which are rapidly growing. In many
cases, this is not evidence of the emancipation of students but the
symptoms of encroaching decline of the income of young people,
their families or even whole segments of society.

Another burning issue, even if its heat is not yet radiating
much outside academia, is the level of academic and support-staff
salaries in higher education. Some would argue that "professors
are not meant to be rich" but it is also true that the economic
status of the academic profession, measured by the level of academic salaries, particularly for the lower ranks and part-time
staff, should be an issue of serious concern. The satisfaction of
"doing interesting things" and relative job security, as is the case
for those university teachers who have tenure or status of "public
service" functionaries, are still strong reasons for choosing an
academic career. But there is a real risk, particularly if this tendency is to continue, that such a career might not be sufficiently
attractive, particularly for the most able academics and those
with an established record in industry and business, who could
contribute to enriching university teaching and research.

From the point of view of particular higher education institutions, a policy of greater efficiency in running their operations by
charging overseas students the full cost of studies, generating in-

come from "selling research capacity", renting office space etc., can be important sources of additional revenue. Some of them report, with justified satisfaction, that their corporate partners shoulder quite a substantial proportion of their research budget. If university–industry partnerships in research (with their "tax credits") are the most promising area, it is doubtful that these can bring about a system-wide solution to the funding crisis in higher education — not to mention that, if the search for external income is pursued with excessive zeal, it might raise reservations with regard to the overall mission of the university and its intellectual independence. Striking the right balance is therefore a growing part of the art of governance of academic institutions.

There is a great need for a comprehensive policy review of the system-wide funding of higher education. Taxpayers, corporations, philanthropists, parents and students are, and will remain, the principal actors in sharing the costs of higher education; but the ways, means and proportions of financial responsibility will have to be re-examined. In most cases this will have to be carried out in conjunction with a broadly understood social welfare reform, redistribution of social benefits, corporate and individual tax responsibilities, etc. Higher education needs to be more effective in persuading legislators, governments and corporate partners, as well as the general public, that when funding policies are decided, they should be considered more from the point of view of long-term commitment than of short-term budgetary allocation.

ABSOLUTE AND RELATIVE ADVANCEMENT OF SCIENCE

Mastery of science has become one of the indicators of the indigenous mastery of developmental processes. Access to scientific knowledge is becoming equally as important as access to higher education. Unlike other levels of education, higher education as a whole can only thrive in the symbiotic presence of scientific endeavour. The institutional culture of the university, and of other academic institutions similar in mission, thrives on research. For, good or bad, university teachers/professors will more likely identify themselves with "researchers" in academies, medical centres, space and telecommunications organisations and industrial research laboratories than with "teachers" in primary or secondary schools.

The advancement of science has also been marked by the development of a number of academic disciplines. But at the same time there is a growing awareness of the need to promote inter-disciplinary and multidisciplinary approaches and methods in teaching, training and research. In this context, pressure is also being exerted to dissociate teaching and research functions at the system and institutional levels for intellectual as well as cost reasons.

It is also clear that science has become very expensive. The sheer dimension of the cost of research activities and laboratories has rendered it imperative to make the process of allocation of scarce resources not only very competitive, but also a highly politicised process, affecting a whole range of interest groups, of which "university scientists" are only one. At the same time, there is more and more pressure on higher education institutions to recover "full economic costs" from externally sponsored contract research, or else risk being accused of "subsidising commercial work from the public purse".

To some extent, the discussion on public funding of research is difficult because, for a variety of reasons, a society, even in countries whose economies depend on research-generated knowledge and technology, is not particularly comfortable with the work of academic or industrial scientists and not particularly appreciative of the direct and indirect economic and social contribution of their work. As they say in the public relations business, there is a "problem of image". The following biting remark made by a contemporary Polish writer, Tadeusz Konwicki (1982), illustrates this argument well:

> In the days of my childhood, a university professor meant the highest incarnation of humanism. I was not marching after the army, I was running after the academics. While the nineteenth century lovingly embraced science, the late twentieth century started to attack its holy shrines. Yesterday we were putting our future into its hands, today we suggest that it should take a little rest and stop bugging us so much.[2]

This kind of reservation should draw our attention and mobilise all concerned parties to common action, showing the catalytic role of academic research as well as the need for a reinforcement of the humanistic and ethical perspectives of research; it is from this perspective that technological development should then be derived.

THE PARADIGM SHIFT BETWEEN INFORMATION AND COMMUNICATION TECHNOLOGIES AND HIGHER EDUCATION

We are witnessing a rapid change in the way students acquire knowledge, scientists carry out their work and communicate among themselves, and institutions of higher education function. The information super-highway is changing the pattern of international, national and local academic communication. Daily academic discourse, which occupies various networks, especially the Internet, has become so routine as to be indispensable.

The next area in which we can expect significant impact within higher education is the application of educational software, especially where this allows interactive learning and experiments. There are even more radical designs in circulation. It has been suggested that universities should provide all lecture and tutorial material on a computer database, accessible to students and staff on and off campus, to the general public who may wish to follow these courses and to graduates and professionals in industry who need to update their skills and knowledge. It will still be some time before such "database universities", in which classrooms are made of "bytes not bricks", become a reality for students and graduates, but the potential educational, financial and economic benefits of this technology, particularly for continuing education programmes, should be granted greater attention and recognition within the academic community. Also, this is an area in which higher education–industry co-operation is both needed and promising. This can be attained only if the issue of intellectual property is resolved in a way which will accommodate both the needs of the academic community for the circulation of knowledge on a non-profit basis, and the legitimate interests of the "for-profit" companies for which patents and other forms of intellectual property can be a most important asset.

HIGHER EDUCATION AND THE "WORLD OF WORK"

We seem to be approaching a point which will require a redefinition of our relations with the "world of work" and related notions of employment and unemployment, jobs and job-sharing, qualifications, social and professional mobility, productive activity, etc. The link between economic cycles and labour market has become even more confused as it is not impossible to observe increases in productivity while restricting employment. We can even foresee questions arising concerning the very purpose of employment; traditionally, employment has been seen as a mechanism for a meritocratic redistribution of purchasing power amongst the individual members of society. But for the time being, our main concern, at least in industrialised countries, lies in finding new areas in which graduates of schools and universities will be able to find jobs.

This problem conspicuously leads us to a "last frontier" on the sectoral ladder of the economy — services. The traditional services, as well as various forms of entertainment, sport and leisure industries, are still prime areas where opportunities for new "jobs" can be created and sought. But, for this author, the most promising area is going to be the *education sector*. Education is already a "big business". It is not only a broadly understood "key to prosperity" but also as good a vehicle for creating jobs and fostering local and regional development as any other economic activity. The tasks in this sector are labour-intensive and usually have positive results with regard to aspects such as professional satisfaction and self-fulfilment. The starting capital and operational budget per workplace is usually lower if compared with manufacturing or such public service institutions as prisons.

SUMMARY

The above list of developments and challenges for higher education is not a comprehensive one, and different analyses are possible. They have already been discussed, among other topics, during the debates and studies carried out by such international organisations as UNESCO and OECD. The essential message from those discussions and the trends and developments outlined above is that any serious debate about economic and social development, which is also a paramount framework of relations between higher education and industry, must take account of their growing interdependence and complexity of functioning. It is clear that higher education needs to be more effective in building alliances. Generally speaking, the relationship between university and industry is as old as the history of many higher education institutions. The nature, character and motivations for enhancing or restraining such relationships have been the subject of continuous change. But, in many respects, the further development of higher education, as with industry, is going to be marked by the growing role played by knowledge creation and use. We are in a period of searching for more adequate concepts, policies and institutional forms, both within higher education and industry. It is neither too early nor too late for this debate. Because, as Nobel laureate in literature Isaac Bashevis Singer wisely observed in his 1984 lecture at the New York Public Library: "We are living in the epoch where the real struggle for existence takes place in universities, laboratories, libraries".[3]

Notes

[1] For example, Martin Trow suggests that when the participation rate in full-time higher education is greater than 50 percent, this figure indicates the breakthrough point between "elite" and "mass" higher education, because the distinguishing characteristics of elite higher education could not by fully sustained across a whole system. See, Oliver Fulton (1988), "Elite Survivals? Entry 'Standards' and Procedures for Higher Education Admission", *Studies in Higher Education*, Vol. 13, No. 1, p. 15.

[2] Tadeusz Konwicki (1982), *Kalendarz–klepsydra*, Warsaw: Czytelnik, p. 318.

[3] Isaac Bashevis Singer (1984), "Of Providence, Free Will and the Future of Learning", *The New York Times Book Review*, 17 January.

3

EXPANDING ROLES FOR RESEARCH UNIVERSITIES IN ECONOMIC DEVELOPMENT

Mary Lindenstein Walshok

INTRODUCTION

The late 1960s were a heady time of civil rights and antiwar activism in the United States of America, even in the conservative midwest. In that context, Serbo-Croat Studies at Indiana University would appear to be totally irrelevant to the needs of a society being torn asunder by civil unrest. A narrow, blinkered approach would have phased out esoteric fields such as Serbo-Croat Studies and increased support for applied social studies relevant to the more immediate needs of the day: poverty, civil rights, the war in Vietnam and larger questions of the emerging third world.

In the 1990s, however, with the end of the Cold War and the unravelling of the fragile USSR, those concerned with the language, culture and history of Eastern European peoples, and the knowledge they have been developing about this region of the world, have moved centre-stage.

Similarly, in the 1960s, those interested in aggregate data analysis of major social trends worked tirelessly on Monroe calculators, keypunch machines and card sorters, all brought together in the auditorium-sized computer centres needed to run their cross-tabulations and statistical tests of validity. Today, a simple powerbook personal computer is linked to worldwide data banks, colleagues and programmeming capabilities, all of which would have been unimaginable 25 years ago.

These examples represent the extraordinary social benefit of ongoing research and scholarship that the USA as a nation supports through its major research universities. In contrast to the European model, the USA has allocated growing amounts of public finds, and has vested in universities, rather than freestanding institutes, the primary responsibility for the development of new knowledge and the provision of advanced education and knowledge.

As a consequence, America's major universities have made unique contributions to society well beyond the education of young people through degree programmes. Research universities have developed into major centres of expertise for business, government and industry; many are centres of new ideas and intellectual movements in the arts, humanities and the social sciences. Their research in the sciences has been a primary resource in the development of the post-World War II economy and in the development of the new technology products and enterprises shaping the global economy of the next century. Even though the professors of Eastern European studies, whose work gave rise to the benefits people have received as citizens, did not begin their research with an "application" or a use in mind, the nature of the knowledge discovery and development process is such that ideas and innovations eventually connect to needs and markets, at least in a rapidly changing market economy.

As we emerge from the twentieth into the twenty-first century, knowledge is clearly *the* critical resource in the growth and development of individuals, organisations, and the economy. Virtually every action and decision in which we engage — at home, at work, in communities, and in the economy — contains a significant component of advanced knowledge with which we must deal. Telephones, microwaves, and medications at home; computers, complex manuals, and analytical reports at work; toxic waste, transportation and bi-lingual education in our communities; industrial decline, modernising enterprises and corporate downsizing in the economy — these are all knowledge-based forces with which we deal daily.

Research universities, particularly in the United States, have become more central in their societies in the latter part of this century, primarily because they represent the central knowledge resources in those societies. As new knowledge and its applications and absorption increases in significance at all levels of society — economy, organisation and individual — institutions whose "primary business" is knowledge increase in significance. Over the last one hundred years, the United States has focused the discovery, development, application, and preservation of all forms of knowledge — scientific, humanistic, and social scientific — in a network of privately and publicly funded research universities.

These institutions are therefore being called upon to participate more actively in knowledge-linking activities which have more tangible influences over regional economics, support organisational and community change, and increase the competencies of workers and professionals. However, precisely what we must do is unclear because of the lack of a well-developed "economy theory" for the role of knowledge (Drucker, 1993); few sophisticated analytical tools and human strategies to adequately capture the expanding role of "knowledge workers" in the economy (Marshall, 1987; Reich, 1992); and a surfeit of civic institutions through which advanced knowledge can be shared and evaluated in order to develop informed "public judgements" (Corson, 1988; Bender, 1993).

Knowledge Without Boundaries (Walshok, 1995) provides a detailed discussion of the characteristics of knowledge transformations and constituency needs giving rise to these increased public demands on research universities. It also provides case studies of universities which are providing important "knowledge linkages" in their communities in support of economic development, workforce competencies, and civic education. The purpose of this chapter is to zero in on the first of these issues with a more detailed presentation of the varied ways in which universities can contribute to regional economic development.

This discussion proceeds from a set of assumptions which need to be explicit at the outset. These are that economic development (be it growth, expansion, or structural transformations) depends on a variety of regional (or natural) capacities, only one of which is scientific and technological developments. As Harold Shapiro (1991), President of Princeton University, so aptly states it:

> The truth — however obvious — is that technological progress, productivity, and economic leadership result from the capacity to sustain the vitality of a large number of mutually interdependent elements of our national life. Even technological progress itself depends critically on such cultural and environmental factors as public policy, political stability, life expectancy, nutrition, attitude towards risk, geography, natural resources, and religion.

Thus, any thoughtful discussion of the role of research universities in regional economic development should capture the full range of knowledge development and support activities essential to the process.

THE MULTIPLE INFLUENCES ON REGIONAL ECONOMIC DEVELOPMENT

Studies of regional economic development over the past two decades have focused on the extraordinary interdependencies between research, capital, business services and public policy in the formation and growth of regions which are coming to be known as "technolopolises" — Silicon Valley in California, Route 128 in Massachusetts, Cambridge and Silicon Glen in the United Kingdom. In addition, sociological analyses, such as that by Rogers and Larsen (1984) on Silicon Valley, suggest the extraordinary significance of leadership and social networks — the human infrastructure, as it were — to the development of the shared values and mutual trust so critical to communities dealing with continuous change and innovation. This complex array of essential factors suggests the need for a variety of activities and resources uniquely suited to the capabilities of research universities. At the most general level they include:

- Understanding the global context and local issues affecting regional economic development

- Managing the technical and social "drivers" of development

- Assuring "linking mechanisms" and support systems which give rise to the "culture" essential to knowledge-based economic development.

Table 3.1 provides a summary of the key knowledge-based activities critical to regional economic development to which research universities can make a unique contribution. These activities include:

- Assuring a supportive public policy environment among citizens *and* officials

- Assessing market needs and opportunities

- Expanding regional capabilities, *vis-à-vis* access to advanced professional and management services, sources of capital, marketing and distribution links, quality of life, etc.

- New product development and industry formation

TABLE 3.1: REGIONAL KNOWLEDGE-BASED ECONOMIC DEVELOPMENT ACTIVITIES

Value Added Research University Activities	Supportive Public Opinion & Policy Environment	Assessing Market Needs	Expanding Regional Capabilities	Technology Product Development	Organisational Change and Development	Human Capital Development	Nourishing the "Culture"
Regional Economical/Social Research	X	X	X			X	
Basic & Applied Research	X	X	X	X	X	X	
Technology Commercialisation			X	X	X	X	X
Workforce Development and Education					X	X	X
Organisational Assessments and Management Development		X	X	X	X	X	X
Organisation of New & Interdisciplinary Knowledge	X	X	X	X	X	X	
Community Forums and Leadership Briefings		X	X				X
Regional Convenor of Groups Concerned About the Role of Knowledge	X	X	X		X	X	X

- Developing flexible organisations/industries capable of continuous change

- Building and continuously developing human capital resources

- Nourishing a "culture" of change, innovation, and "trust".

Table 3.1 also spells out the specific capabilities research universities can call upon to assist in addressing these seven challenges. It summarises eight critical relationships in this process. These capabilities are laid out below in more detail. Research universities possess much of the "raw material" essential to putting knowledge to work. They can utilise a wide range of resources, including: a broad range of competencies in the faculty; the availability of libraries, computer centres and databases; and the large numbers of undergraduate, and particularly, graduate students. The aim of the remainder of this chapter is to elucidate the institutional mechanisms which need to be put in place to mobilise these university assets to serve economic development goals.

THE UNIQUE CONTRIBUTION OF RESEARCH UNIVERSITIES

Research universities are uniquely qualified to discover and develop new knowledge, to acknowledge gaps in their communities, to provide economic, social, cultural and organisational trend analyses, to educate and train individuals and to convene groups concerned about informed, rational discourse on issues of common concern. These capabilities of universities reside in many places within the academy — not just schools of business, engineering, and public policy. However, these capabilities are rarely called upon by the larger society, much less offered by the typically "sheltered" academic faculty because, to date, universities have not been sufficiently organised and staffed to mobilise their diverse knowledge resources to serve public needs, particularly across the range of issues and at the pace of change characterising the world today. Table 3.1 suggests universities can contribute to economic development in a variety of important ways, some obvious and others not so obvious. These include:

- Regional economic and social research, i.e. industry, cluster studies, asset mapping *vis-à-vis* infrastructure and quality of life, assessing support service capabilities

- Basic and applied research activities

- Technology transfer and commercialisation initiatives

- Workforce needs assessment, development and education

- Organisational assessments and management development

- Organisation of new and interdisciplinary knowledge for problem solving and capacity building

- Serving as a regional convenor of groups concerned about the role of knowledge and technology in regional development

- Organising community forums and leadership briefings on issues of regional significance.

These eight activities are all essential to a comprehensive economic development strategy. Economic and social research enables a region to identify strategic assets and important gaps in its industrial base, infrastructure, geographic and service capabilities. Basic and applied research activities drive new product development, which in turn gives rise to new companies and new jobs. Technology transfer and commercialisation initiatives are the means by which basic research and the marketplace encounter one another and ideas are transformed into products favourable to new business formation. Workforce assessments need to go on continuously so that universities can partner with employers in the development of basic and continuing education programmes supportive of the skills needed to be economically competitive. Organisational assessments and management development programmes focus on the fact that *all* organisations must change and adapt to changing economic, demographic, and market conditions. They need assistance in making these transitions and developing the necessary management skills. The organisation of new and interdisciplinary knowledge for problem solving and capacity building is essential to providing skill development programmes for new and emerging fields of practice.

Competency areas as varied as toxic and hazardous waste management and desk-top publishing are needed by industry and require training programmes which do not intrinsically come from any single department within the university. Universities can also serve as convenors of leadership groups from government, industry, and non-profit organisations who are critical to building local support for specific development strategies. In addition, they can organise community forums and leadership briefings to introduce new ideas and opportunities for economic development. Without broad public and leadership understanding and support of the complex issues affecting regional development, it is very difficult to make change. In sum, each of these activities has a unique contribution to make and, in each case, the university has a role to play.

Many of these activities are becoming a more essential part of university programmes because of growing public demand, government incentives, private sector support and key faculty leaders. This is especially true with regard to regional capabilities assessments, applied research, technology commercialisation, and workforce education, particularly continuing education and advanced retraining. However, in the United States, even these activities are for the most part *ad hoc* and occurring at the margins, particularly, within the top research universities throughout the country. As Gary Anders (1992) notes:

> The list of public service-sounding programmes with economic development overtones at some campuses is impressive, and some universities are doing a credible job of integrating campus resources with off-campus needs. However, in the main, public service programmes are not well integrated with the mainstream of campus activities, and only occasionally do faculty participate freely in both activities.

Technology transfer programmes, industrial liaison activities, business incubators, and small business development centres are proliferating throughout the United States. What little evaluation of their effectiveness exists is inconclusive with regard to their true value to business expansion, business formation, and new job creation, the ultimate goals of regional economic development. In fact, Meyer and Fasenfest, summarising a broad range of papers at a symposium on local economic development reports in *Policy Studies Review* (Meyer and Fasenfest, 1991: 177), suggest that local communities for the most part have adopted the wrong tactics if a) they rely heavily on external, time-bound sources of funds for programmes and b) they rely on public administrators for leadership, rather than business or community leaders with specialised expertise. Such approaches have had uncertain effects according to the symposium participants. The range of initiatives discussed at the symposium included papers from both the US and the UK and are summarised in Figure 3.1.

FIGURE 3.1: LOCAL ECONOMIC DEVELOPMENT INTERVENTION

1. **Efforts directed primarily at new business attraction**

   - Relocation subsidies (capital assistance, tax rebates, personnel training)
   - Infrastructure construction (to serve potential in-migrants, rather than local demand)
   - Business facilities construction by the public sector (or private sector use)

2. **Efforts directed primarily at stimulating local business**

   - Small business assistance programmes
   - New product development programmes (grants and public under-writing of inventions)
   - Creation of new for-profit organisations by the public sector or local non-profit groups

3. **Geographically-based interventions**

   - Enterprise Zones (providing tax and other subsidies to firms in a particular area)
   - Target revitalisation zones (special tax districts, urban renewal projects)
   - Neighbourhood or area business groups (Community Development Corporations)

4. **Human capital strategies**

   - Improved basic and broad-based vocational education
   - New and innovative worker training/retraining programmes
   - Provision of day-care, health care and other human services.

5. **Research and analytical efforts**

   - State, Region or Local Economic Planning Organisations (public, private or non-profit)
   - Enterprise Boards (which conduct extensive research on their local economies)
   - Urban Development Corporations (which accomplish a similar analytical role)

Source: Meyer and Fasenfest (1991)

The more complex presentation of the dimensions of the knowledge-driven economic development process is captured by the "paradigm" offered by Smilor, Dietrich, and Gibson in a 1993 UNESCO report on entrepreneurial universities reproduced in Figure 3.2. It touches on the significance *and* interdependence of a multiplicity of capabilities within research universities, all of which must be tapped if the economic impacts achieved around places such as Stanford, the Universities of Texas and North Carolina, or MIT are to be replicated in communities such as Denver, San Diego, or Kansas City.

What is critical in the foregoing paradigm is the emphasis on the simultaneous development of parallel and frequently intersecting factors supportive of new knowledge development, technology commercialisation, education and training and a hospitable regional "climate". This means that economic development draws on knowledge resources institution-wide, not just from a single department, division or school. The economy, the values and capabilities of the community, and the competencies and orientations of individual workers and citizens must all be developing and transforming continuously and simultaneously across a wide range of knowledge issues.

Of course, basic and applied research being conducted in science and engineering is critical and must, when appropriate, be "linked" to industries and organisations seeking new and better products and processes. Of course, schools of business management have critical research, teaching and consulting roles to play, *vis-à-vis* organisations in change and entrepreneurial business development. Of course, labour studies and public policy centres have much to contribute to understanding economic forces, workforce needs, regional capabilities, infrastructure needs, and government. Less obviously, departments of sociology and political science, literature and history have much to contribute in elucidating and addressing the demographic, cultural, linguistic and humanistic issues which provide the larger context in which specific regional economic development strategies will be more or less successful, depending on their attentiveness to such concerns.

The deep, small-town, Midwestern roots of most migrants to Southern California, for example, bring an anti-urbanism and a longing for order and homogeneity which contrasts vividly with the Northeastern urban roots of migrants to Northern California, where being part of a "world class" community is highly valued.

FIGURE 3.2: THE KNOWLEDGE-DRIVEN ECONOMIC DEVELOPMENT PROCESS

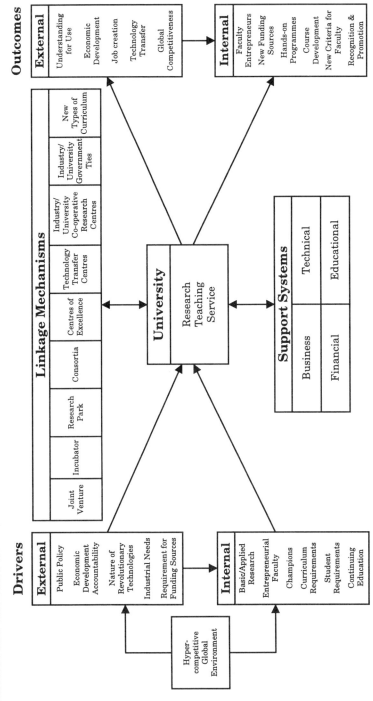

Source: Smilor et al., 1993

Such historical and sociological facts frame how people respond to contemporary crises and new opportunities and can help elucidate how a region can best pursue its economic future. The dance, poetry and music of diverse peoples and classes, their ethical priorities and family values can be elucidated by the work of humanities scholars and incorporated into discussions and decisions about regional alternatives.

The fundamental problem for research universities which have such a rich reservoir of information of value to integrated regional development can be summed up simply. The organisational forms and institutional support and reward systems which have served the expansion of knowledge so well have resulted in (a) fragmented academic disciplines, each with (b) distinct vocabularies and methodologies for developing and communicating about knowledge which are (c) neither easily accessed nor understood by the other smart and dedicated contributors to the knowledge-driven economic development process.

This lack of fit and difficulty in communicating and collaborating across knowledge boundaries which separate spheres of expertise and authority is what needs to be addressed by universities if they are to be truly valuable contributors to regional economic development.

LINKING KNOWLEDGE CAPABILITIES TO REGIONAL ECONOMIC DEVELOPMENT

It has become very fashionable to celebrate uncritically the need for applied over basic research, the value of research parks and incubators and the importance of problem-focused practice-oriented certificate and degree programmes. In fact, many suggest we will see the end of the research university as we know it in Great Britain, Europe, and the USA. They celebrate the emergence of the "relevant" and adaptable "modern" service-driven university. In discussing the role of public universities in local economic development, Gary Anders (1992) sums up this view as follows:

> Unlike the traditional university where classical education and basic research are the principal forms of academic endeavour, the modern university trains specialists, encourages applied research and is involved in the development of new technologies and theoretical analysis for commercial application. This technical orientation necessitates greater involvement in the day-to-day concerns of

practitioners in both business and political circles. A major result of this involvement is the growing integration of the teaching content with the subjects of outside collaboration. Kuhlman (1986: 18) sees these changes as engendering substantial tensions between those faculties in the "quality-oriented" classical disciplines, and those in the "utility-oriented" fields of science, engineering and business. In short, the modern approach stresses applied research and additional collaborations with outside agents such as the federal government and private companies.

The problem with this view as suggested earlier is that evaluation research and critical analyses of the effectiveness of incubators and research parks (Smilor and Gill, 1986) on the relative merits of applied versus basic research (Lederberg, 1987; Kenney, 1988; Shapiro, 1991; Dertouzos et al., 1989) and the workforce benefits of special training programmes (Magaziner, 1989) are uneven at best. On the other hand, what is clear is that those communities with diverse regional capabilities and aspirations which are linked in varied and ongoing ways to a rich array of academic programmes and knowledge resource campuses, tend to be those communities in which significant economic development is taking place. It is the synergies between a multiplicity of specific programmes, services and people which make regional economic development happen. Incubators, entrepreneurial centres, applied research programmes, continuing education, leadership consensus, public support, etc., are all necessary but not sufficient to make development happen.

Rather than reducing the universities' challenge to the need for more "applied" and "relevant" research and teaching, we instead need to better develop the institutional mechanisms through which we broker, exchange, develop, organise, and disseminate knowledge to the growing sectors of the public for whom it is an increasingly essential resource. History suggests that a knowledge economy with continuous innovations depends on the unencumbered pursuit of basic research and independent scholarly pursuits. Experience suggests that the most effective worker or professional is the person who is broadly educated with the intellectual flexibility and solid skill base required to continuously adapt to change and learn new things. History and experience tell us time and time again that what is "esoteric" at one time — whether it be Eastern European Studies or the sex lives of insects — may be central at another when ethnic wars or DNA affect our daily lives.

For these reasons, research universities do not need to abandon what they do well. Rather, they need to expand programmes and develop staff whose primary function is leading or facilitating knowledge linkages across the boundaries now separating knowledge discovery from application, reflection from action, informed discourse from special interest advocacy. Shapiro (1991) of Princeton remarks that:

> As an economist, I have often speculated that what may be required — in certain selected circumstances — is not a new market orientation of university-based research, but a structured set of relationships between a sub-set of university-based researchers, industry-based researchers and government. I have often considered whether or not a variant of the academic health centre model — a partnership that protects the independence of each partner — might make certain types of mutually supportive joint ventures both more natural and more useful.

Protecting the "independence" of each partner while facilitating the sharing of knowledge and the development potential of collaborative efforts may require a variety of new institutional approaches. In my review of research universities "making a difference" for specific communities through innovative approaches to knowledge linkages, what emerged was a variety of characteristics common to all the programmes, whether focused on economic development, civic discourse or workforce training.

Some of these characteristics were:

- Persons and/or academic departments within the university who have a flexible view of knowledge and acknowledge the variable sources of relevant expertise inside and outside the academy

- A desire to learn from these non-university sources as well as to teach them

- A genuine commitment to collaboration expressed through broadly representative funding boards and governing committees who set programme priorities and formats, and identify appropriate sources of expertise

- A commitment to a social dynamic characterised by exchanges, interaction, and networking, and thus an acknowledgement that programmes must support informal as well as formal activities, and a belief that a "community" needs to be developed

- A commitment to flexible and varied formats for information dissemination and knowledge exchange

- An ongoing process of self-evaluation and tracking of programme effects, which often means research and evaluation functions

- Multiple sources of funding — private, university, corporate, membership fees for services — in all the programmes

- Components in all of the programmes that directly or indirectly enhance the central intellectual preoccupations and resource needs of the university

- Programmes are staffed and facilitated by highly educated full-time professionals, who are as at home with academic as with off-campus constituencies and who possess credibility among all the partners in the knowledge exchange

- A significant component of campus leadership support, typically in the person of the provost or the president, associated with every programme.

The characteristics of the people who lead these various initiatives also reflect a kind of knowledge professional within the university that will become increasingly important. These professionals can be described as follows:

- They possess advanced academic credentials in the content areas for which they are responsible

- They have some "hands-on" experience on which to draw in interactions with off-campus constituencies

- They are professionally committed to "knowledge-linking" roles (not unlike clinical faculty documentary film makers/serious journalists)

- They know how to facilitate problem solving, articulate issues, and identify expertise

- They are skilled at providing "linking leadership," serving as convenor in knowledge-related activities

- They are skilled at written and oral communication as well as management of projects (Rosener, 1994).

Research universities need more programmes with these characteristics and more professionals whose primary function is spanning knowledge boundaries between universities and the public in order to be more effective partners in economic development.

CONCLUSIONS

Research universities have an increasingly significant role to play in regional economic development if they do three things:

1. Embrace a wider and deeper understanding of the unique character and multiplicity of factors affecting economic development in a knowledge society

2. See their role in society as mobilising and making accessible campus-wide academic resources — from the sciences to the humanities — relevant to the knowledge problems confronting advanced economies.

3. Invest (politically and financially) in the development of institutional mechanisms whose central role is to facilitate, broker and develop knowledge across the internal boundaries of academic disciplines and across the external boundaries currently separating the highly valuable "traditional" research and teaching programmes from the concerns and challenges confronting society at large.

This means going beyond the development of technology transfer programmes, science parks and special applied degrees, few of which are needed. It means reaffirming what we do — basic research and liberal arts degree programmes. It also means recognising that new linkages need to be developed campus-wide. Such linkages must create bridges between a variety of academic programmes and a variety of constituencies in the community. Otherwise, we cannot be sure that the scientific, management, workforce, and cultural climate issues productive of meaningful economic development will be addressed.

References

Anders, Gary C. (1992), "The Changing Role of the Public University in Local Economic Development" *Economic Development Review* Vol. 10, No. 4, pp. 76–79.

Bender, T. (1993), *Intellect and Public Life: Essays on the Social History of Academic Intellectuals in the United States*, Baltimore, MD: Johns Hopkins University Press.

Corson, R. (1988), "Democracy in Action", Conference Report on Lifelong Learning and Citizenship in Sweden and the United States, National Issues Forum, St. Paul, MN, October.

Dertouzos, M.L., Lester, R.K., Solow, R.M. and the MIT Commission on Industrial Productivity (1989), *Made in America: Regaining the Productive Edge*, Cambridge, MA: MIT Press.

Drucker, P.F. (1993), *Post-Capitalist Society*, New York: Harper Collins.

Kenney, M. (1988), *Biotechnology: The University–Industrial Complex*, New Haven, CT: Yale University Press.

Kuhlman, James A. (1986), "Industry, Universities, and the Technological Imperative", *Business and Economic Review* No. 32, pp. 415–19.

Larson, Thomas D. (1989), "New Uses for the University", *Educational Record,* Summer/Fall: pp. 61–65.

Lederberg, J. (1987), "Does Scientific Progress Come for Projects or People?", Address at the Centenary Meeting of the National Association of State Universities and Land Grant Colleges, 7 November.

Magaziner, I.C. and Patinkin, M. (1989), *The Silent War: Inside the Global Business Battles Shaping America's Future*, New York: Random House.

Marshall, F.R. (1987), *Unheard Voices: Labor and Economic Policy in a Competitive World*, New York: Basic Books.

Meyer, Peter B. and Fasenfest, David (1991), "The Comparative Politics of Local Economic Development: Introduction to the Symposium", *Policy Studies Review*, Spring/Summer, Vol. 10, No. 2/3, pp. 89–179.

Reich, R.B. (1992), *The Work of Nations: Preparing Ourselves for the 21st Century Capitalism*, New York: Vintage Books.

Rogers, E.M., and Larsen, J.K. (1984), *Silicon Valley Fever: Growth of High Technology Culture*, New York: Basic Books.

Rosener, J. (1994), "Watch for a New Style in the Workplace — 'Linking Leadership'" *Los Angeles Times*, 11 September, Business Section, p. D2.

Shapiro, Harold T. (1991), "The Research University and the Economy", *Queen's Quarterly*, Vol. 98, No. 3, p. 577.

Smilor, Raymond W., Dietrich Glenn B., and Gibson, David V. (1993), "The Entrepreneurial University: The Role of Higher Education in the United States in Technology, Commercialisation and Economic Development", UNESCO, pp. 1–11.

Smilor, R.W. and Gill, Michael Doud, Jr. (1986), *The New Business Incubator: Linking Talent, Technology, Capital and Know-How*, Lexington, MA: Lexington Books.

Smilor, R.W., Kozmetsky,, G., and Gibson, D.V. (eds.), (1988), *Creating the Technopolis: Linking Technology Commercialisation and Economic Development,* New York: Harper Collins.

Walshok, Mary L. (1995), *Knowledge Without Boundaries: What America's Research Universities Can Do for the Economy, the Workplace and the Community,* San Francisco, CA: Jossey-Bass.

4

INNOVATIVE PLAYERS IN ECONOMIC DEVELOPMENT IN EUROPE: "LEARNING COMPANIES" AND "ENTREPRENEURIAL UNIVERSITIES" IN ACTION

Jay Mitra and Piero Formica[*]

Summary

This chapter analyses the behaviour of "learning companies" and "entrepreneurial universities" in the context of the territorial and business ecosystems of innovation in which they are involved. Against a background of fundamental differences between the higher education and commercial sectors, and the history of university–industry co-operation in Europe, the characteristics of territorial ecosystems of innovation (TEIs) are set out and the holistic, networking and interactive models of knowledge and technology transfer are discussed. This analysis provides a conceptual framework for the successful development of territorial ecosystems of innovation which are identified as crucial for future successful European socio-economic development. As concrete examples of activities which contribute towards this end, the authors offer brief case studies of the Economic Development Unit and Innovation Centre at the University of North London and the London Technopole Initiative.

INTRODUCTION

On 1 May 1995 the *Financial Times* published two articles on how companies are reshaping their research policy. Referring to Xerox, it said that the company, after having failed in the 1970s to

---

[*] The views and opinions expressed in this chapter are those of the authors and do not necessarily represent those of their respective organisations.

exploit the pioneering work done in personal computing at its Palo Alto Research Centre (PARC), had

> changed the process by which creativity is harnessed within the organisation. In the 1970s PARC viewed itself as an academic community. We have changed that orientation to one where the researchers view their success as to whether it is commercially successful to Xerox.

Mitsubishi Heavy Industries, the Japanese industrial group, "seeking a fresh approach to its European marketing strategy, decided to tap the originality of Pembroke College in Cambridge". These two cases are good examples of "learning companies" striving to foster marketable innovation.

On the academic front, the process of universities designing and managing activities necessary to the commercialisation of knowledge and the production of spin-off companies by graduates, professors, researchers and external people, is becoming increasingly visible. Such institutions are "entrepreneurial universities" and are the academic counterpart of learning companies.

Learning companies and entrepreneurial universities contribute to a quick and self-reinforcing pace of long-term economic development. This chapter provides an insight into the behaviour of both players through the lenses of the territorial and business ecosystems of innovation in which they are embedded.

THE DIVIDE BETWEEN UNIVERSITIES AND ENTREPRENEURIAL COMPANIES

Entrepreneurs are clearly and, often, solely concerned with problems which they can observe directly and solve empirically. They are concerned with sales rather than marketing, with cash rather than profit, and with output rather than productivity. Their skills and knowledge are directed toward the primary task of the organisation which they have created and are directing.

Universities are concerned with abstracting and generalising knowledge. Their priorities and interests lie in the "second order", with entrepreneurs being "first order" managers (Jones and Lakin, 1977; for a fuller account, see also Jones and Lakin, 1978). They are concerned with marketing rather than sales, profit rather than cash, and productivity rather than output. Where they offer their services to entrepreneurial companies, they frequently talk with a vocabulary that does not have a resonance with the entrepreneurs.

Entrepreneurs, worried about the level of sales of their products, will not be looking for lectures, or advice on abstract matters such as segmentation of the market — they simply want to sell more. Similarly, if output is down they want assistance, not with work study or productivity bargaining schemes — they simply want to make more.

The divide between universities and entrepreneurial companies (mainly small and medium-sized enterprises — SMEs) is visible on the other side as well. There have been attempts to impose the language and motivation of entrepreneurs on university departments. Cooley (1987) has described methods of organising universities as *factories* within which the students are referred to as *commodities*, the examinations as *quality control procedures*, graduation as *delivery* and the professors as *operators*. Cooley uses a Frank Wolf algorithm (computer-based) to work out the rate at which the professors are *producing*.

However, as well as being rooted in the abstract, universities are large, highly structured organisations that display precious little flexibility. In contrast, entrepreneurial companies are small, unstructured and highly flexible. The staff of the universities are generally motivated by the prospect of preferment in the promotion race, and status on the academic circuit. The company staff are perhaps more driven by the need for their businesses to survive and to produce cash.

Universities are good at "generalised" solutions and the application of abstract principles, arriving at accurate analysis and prescription after a suitable period of study. Companies want specific answers to specific questions — and they want them now.

In short, companies and universities are widely different institutions with little in common. Interaction between them is made more difficult by differences in culture, style, timescales and aspirations. They do not have shared interests, philosophies or even a shared *lingua franca* in which to communicate.

Such perceptions and views about the divide between learning organisations and entrepreneurial institutions has to be studied against the context of higher education–industry co-operation in Europe.

HIGHER EDUCATION–INDUSTRY CO-OPERATION: THE EUROPEAN BACKGROUND

Higher education and industry have co-operated with essentially three objectives in mind (European Commission, 1992):

- Faster industrial applications of the results of fundamental research

- Improved output of technical skills

- More effective transfer of technology between sectors and regions.

Numerous examples of HE–industry partnerships, policies for interaction, networks and institutions are to be found all over Europe, with particular European Commission (EC) programmes, such as COMETT, playing an important role in their development. HEIs have included traditional universities, polytechnics, technical colleges, *grands écoles*, *Fachhochschulen*, and other post-secondary research and teaching institutions. Proper historical documentation and analysis are likely to reveal both depth and breadth in the historical relationship, but increasing demands on higher education to play a fuller role in the innovation process have been a feature of the last decade. In the UK, universities have been under pressure since the 1950s to make their curricula and activities more relevant to the needs of the workplace, and, therefore, to contribute to economic development.

The "academic" bias and lack of practical training in engineering courses, for example, was the underlying reason for what the Finniston Committee of 1980 described as their inferiority and for the lack of partnership between UK universities and industry (Monck et al., 1988). Economic and financial constraints have also added to this pressure, as government funding for research has declined over the years.

Technology transfer has been the usual term used to describe the interaction between HEIs and industry, and has been understood as the supply of technical knowledge or know-how by HEIs to industrial firms.

Technology transfer activities can be grouped under four main headings (Hull, 1990):

- Research services

- Consultancy services

- Training and continuing education services

- Research exploitation.

It is unlikely that any one institution practises all forms of technology transfer, and the emphasis in any one institution in any one country is, to a great extent, determined by cultural traditions, institutional structures, public policies and its ratings on the scale of innovation and technology development.

The transfer activity itself can take various forms, including (Williams, 1985):

- The provision of opportunities for students to acquire knowledge, skills and attitudes which could be used to create and promote the success of SMEs

- The promotion of research into high technology which may create opportunities for innovation by small firms

- Encouragement of staff to provide consultancy and training services

- Allowing staff to create or take part in the creation of small, especially high-technology firms

- Setting up companies to exploit research, design and development activities of staff.

Against the backdrop painted above, it is possible to envisage a situation or a future scenario in which innovative forms of co-operation between higher education and industry can generate economic development for a "learning" society. It is, therefore, appropriate to appreciate the scope of future "learning companies" and "entrepreneurial universities", before presenting a hypothesis for the future.

LEARNING COMPANIES AND ENTREPRENEURIAL UNIVERSITIES

Learning is a process of growth of resources which provide new prospects of a company's success, a process which, without a doubt, initially concerns the human resource, whose task it is to work on ideas and modify knowledge, drawing from the reservoir of accumulated know-how and experiences matured within the organisation.

A "learning" organisation is an organisation able to support internal, consistent innovation, having as immediate objectives the improvement of quality, the strengthening of relations with clients and suppliers, and the achievement of a more effective corporate strategy (Mills and Friesen, 1992).

Companies are becoming places of culture, creativity and innovation by moving their central focus from material to information flows. The advanced company of the 1990s can be seen as a network having its centre in a "training and research institute" transmitting signals to the different points of the network: technology, management, organisation, marketing, finance, etc. The essential components of the new competitive formula are the absorption of intellectual capital through strong immaterial investments (in R&D, training, information and information systems, marketing and communication) together with internationally oriented location strategies and an increasing propensity to operate abroad.

While industries are assuming more and more culturally distinguishing features, universities and other HEIs are being led to identify commercial aspects of their activities. These typically non-profit organisations have flourished in protected environmental conditions until recently against an increasingly turbulent economic climate that has shaken the entrepreneurial world. However, educational institutions are now exposed to the winds of competition. In fact, universities are confronted by the enlarged competition coming from other species — companies which generate, through their "training and research institutes", the new markets of advanced education and attack the traditional education milieu whose life-cycle is declining — and also by competition among themselves, some being successful in the new arena of global competition with respect to training and promotion of human resources.

Such a change takes place in a period marked, at international level, by organisational gaps and budget deficits in universities, in addition to sharp reductions in public expenditures which put the traditional mechanism of financial regulation based on endowment funds in a critical position.

Universities are thus compelled to adopt an entrepreneurial policy stance, having to operate in an open environment where the number and species of competitors are growing in the domain of production, acquisition and transfer of knowledge through the development of training and research activities. Co-operation with industry offers precisely this opportunity. This does not mean simply a passive transfer of financial resources from industry to university; rather, it involves the innovation of systems dating back to the eighteenth century. It also means the evolution of the company as a "learning" organisation and of the non-profit educational institution as an "entrepreneurial system".

The convergence of interests between the two partners and the foundation of a common vision are achieved through hybrid bodies of entrepreneurial style and co-operative mission. The effectiveness of such convergence is best understood through a consideration of the economics of territorial ecosystems of innovation. The purpose of this exercise is to locate the prospective future forms of relationship between higher education and industry in the context of changing economic and social realities.

THE ECONOMICS OF TERRITORIAL ECOSYSTEMS OF INNOVATION

In the 1990s a new type of industry — the industry of "innovative milieux" or "territorial ecosystems of innovation" (TEIs) — is emerging under the stimulus of the plummeting costs of information and communication technologies and the new infrastructure of the information superhighway, in addition to a market- and society-led trend in science and technology advancement.

TABLE 4.1. "PRODUCT OUT" AND "MARKET AND SERVICE-IN" AGES

"Product-out" age *(1955-74)*	*"Market and service-in" age* *(since 1974)*
Selling what is produced	Producing what can be sold
Mass production	Mass personalisation
Long product life-cycle	Short product life-cycle
Volume/scale-driven costs	Variety-driven costs
Volume-driven competitors	Variety-driven competitors
Cost-oriented strategies (internal efficiency)	Time-oriented strategies (time-based external results)

TEIs appear as the counterpart of "business ecosystems" (BEs), the new champions of continental/global competition, which encircle a variety of firms sharing the same views of the new "market and service-in age" (Table 4.1). BEs are springing from the learning processes, contributing to the transformation of the large corporations as well as to the evolution of territorial industrial complexes of SMEs as clusters of interrelated activities (Porter, 1990). Examples may be found in the mature Italian industrial fields (such as apparel, sweaters, ceramics) where some SMEs, driven by product development and customer service, have increased in size and product lines.

Building trust for competition is the *modus operandi* of BEs. To be effective, BEs need suitable territorial environments, of which TEIs represent the most advanced achievement. A TEI is informed by a set of institutions that co-evolve capabilities around a broad range of infrastructural innovations, strengthening the capacity for local development and providing the breeding ground for BEs. These institutions include:

- Universities, other HEIs and research institutions

- Public/private, local/regional development agencies

- Local/regional public authorities

- The business community; the local chamber of commerce; industrial associations; financial institutions; companies; networks of companies (business ecosystems).

TEI organisations work co-operatively and competitively to organise, initiate, provide information and support service to the market; they also initiate ecosystem-driven development projects that bring together a number of real factors of growth, such as:

- Knowledge and information, education and human capital

- Science and technology, R&D, technology transfer

- Entrepreneurship

- Corporate real investments

- Social infrastructures (transport, information communication technologies).

Infrastructural innovations take the form of entrepreneurial organisations for innovation, well known examples of which are science and technology parks (STPs); business innovation centres (BICs) and business technology centres (BTCs); technology transfer centres (TTCs); advanced technology centres (ATCs); university–industry interfaces (industrial liaison centres (ILCs), focused on university–industry co-operation); and other organisations, such as those for territorial marketing, site development and financing of innovation (Gueder and Formica, 1996). All these organisations appear as transactional leaders (mediators, facilitators, etc.) that run and process the gamut of the market- and innovation-driven projects. Altogether, they define an innovative milieu that is, at local level, the architectural aspect of BEs.

Outputs of the TEI industry are both material (sites/location opportunities) and immaterial (services) activities that provide customers with effective means of securing competitive advantage, such as:

- Facilitating technological development and technology transfer

- Developing the commercial potential of R&D, education and training (e.g. academic–industry spin-offs for new companies)

- Creating connections with markets that generate demand for innovative products and services (e.g. non-linear process of idea–research–prototype–product–market)

- Improving supply chains (a facet of BEs) in terms of applying technology (e.g. a network of new technology-based suppliers in the local economy could attract/help retain large industrial clients and also generate the emergence of new activities).

The TEI industry is not yet informed by a standard or dominant design. In the current decade, the early 1950s "campus model" (university-based real-estate development as the ancestor of TEI) still survives, together with its 1970s version (the "territorial model" of national/regional/local authorities-based property development enriched by some experimental services), beside the fresh "network model" which enhances the value of the intangible activities for economic development.

In the network model, a variety of interdependent organisations pursue hybrid tasks. Thus industrial companies are loci of the generation, not only the application, of knowledge (for example, company-owned schools of advanced technical and management training). By contrast, HEIs, besides the generation of knowledge, carry out its dissemination as well as the generation and management of business (for example, university-owned firms and "teaching companies", where an HEI participates through its students and staff in a company project to achieve substantial and comprehensive changes, raising both industrial and academic performance by the effective use of reciprocal expertise).

THE WAY FORWARD

HEIs and industry have not acquired collaborative sophistication by following a linear route which is either technology-driven or market-driven. Old notions of basic research chasing companies with an understanding of the market, who are in turn chasing HEIs for applied research, have become outmoded.

Holistic, Networking Model of Knowledge and Technology Transfer

Conventional wisdom has it that technology or a particular kind of knowledge, precursor to technology, once disseminated, will somehow find its application. The technology push will bring about the possible innovations. Technology transfer is therefore viewed as a unidirectional process, from the knowledge supplier — the scientific and academic community which is the originator of knowledge — to the industrial client, the developer.

The holistic model moves away from the notion of technology transfer as once-off hand-out from the university and research institutions to the firm, replacing it with a broader vision, which encompasses an ongoing two-way exchange between the partners. This model makes available to companies a "fast-food" menu of new applications of existing technologies. Its transfer mechanism does not contemplate the replacement of an old technology with a new one, but, rather, works like a drill to dig out new possible uses of an existing technology, or like a mirror which duplicates the images combining technologies of different fields in an innovative way. This last operation, the so-called "technological fusion", creates a climate of collaboration among companies in order to produce the fusion. Companies, separated from each other in terms of culture and sector of activity, can find some points of linkage which act as a prelude to the formation and development of industrial clusters, reaching critical mass when they achieve complete success (Mitra, 1993).

Functional forms of technology transfer (such as the exchange of research samples, articles in publications, patents and licensing agreements, participation in co-operative research projects, and personnel transfers) would be empowered by innovative organisational forms of university–industry interaction addressed to creating links with markets that give rise to demand for innovative products/services (market-led instead of supply-led technology transfer).

Interactive Models for Co-operation

Collaboration, like technology transfer itself, relies on interactive models for a better understanding of the interface between different institutions. Institutions pursuing different activities are increasingly reliant on each other.

Interaction not only takes place between academic disciplines but also between organisations, between HEIs and businesses, between research groups and industry, and between individuals within organisations. The new forms of organisational interaction are characterised by interdependencies which suggest that no one organisation can meet the challenge of change alone. Traditional assumptions of, for example, universities and industry in relation to research and training have changed. HEIs can no longer pride themselves as the loci for the creation and dissemination of knowledge, as industries themselves carry out even more fundamental research within their own laboratories. Indeed, much R&D is carried out within industry, and some companies (mainly large ones) have set up their own schools of advanced technical and management training.

THE THEORY IN PRACTICE

The following brief case studies are offered as two examples of activities contributing to the networking, holistic and interactive models of innovation and economic development.

The University of North London

The development of the Economic Development Unit (EDU) at the University of North London has helped to establish a platform for stakeholder networking between a disparate group of players (local authorities, training and enterprise councils, enterprise agencies, higher and further education institutions, and, more recently, Business Links, a government-supplied intermediary acting as a one-stop shop for business support service activities) to be engaged in a proactive partnership for economic development. This results from an understanding of the fact that there is no longer one, single patron for economic development (traditionally the local authority) and a wider range of reactive economic development supplier agencies (such as educational and training institutions). There is now a greater requirement for all parties to play an active part through forums such as European Regional Development Funds and the EU's LEONARDO programme, to address issues as diverse as unemployment, continuing vocational education, innovation and technology, business competitiveness and skills shortages.

The EDU has taken a proactive stand towards economic regeneration on three fronts:

- The co-ordination of institutional business development, vocational training, specific industry-related R&D, technology transfer and related activities

- A strategic involvement with different stakeholders through participation at various forums to influence policy and decision-making, particularly on education and training for economic development

- Operational involvement with stakeholders through training, consultancy and R&D programmes.

Operating on a self-financing basis, its portfolio includes programmes as varied as Refugee Assessment and Guidance, Women Returners to Work, and Regional Innovation and Technology Transfer Strategies. The objective is to try to draw from this diverse range a pattern of economic activity which can meet the needs of different individuals and organisations, and offer opportunities for both work and higher education. By developing initiatives in both local and international markets, and in conjunction with some of the stakeholders mentioned above, it is able to contribute widely to economic development and regeneration.

One of the main project-based developments for the EDU is the new Innovation Centre, which is located alongside and within a major new University development (the Learning Centre) concentrating on computer, language, library and media services. The objective of the Innovation Centre is to contribute to economic development through the promotion of technological, organisational, and social forms of innovation in SMEs and supply-side organisation. This it has started to do by:

- Identifying innovations in all EDU programmes and promoting them

- Acting as a "virtual" innovation centre by being a catalyst for the promotion of innovation as opposed to a traditional centre which accommodates small, generally high-technology start-ups (the University of North London's centre is more concerned with the involvement of people in innovation, whether that be technological innovation or managerial innovation, through specific programmes)

- Serving as a state-of-the-art resource base for all sectors of industry (resources include databases, seminar training and brainstorming facilities, teleworking facilities;

- Acting as a central point for University-wide industry-oriented activities and a forum for wider stakeholder partnerships.

The London Technopole Initiative

Alongside the development of a "virtual" infrastructure for innovation and economic development stands the EDU's spearheading of an action research and networking programme on regional innovation and technology transfer infrastructures and strategies. Commissioned by the SPRINT programme of the European Commission (Strategic Programme for Innovation and Technology Transfer), the main objectives of the initiative are to:

- Carry out demand and supply-side analyses of the technology transfer capabilities and the capacity for innovation of organisations

- Identify the gaps, deficiencies, and strengths for creating a networking strategy for technology transfer and innovation infrastructures

- Draw up implementation plans for the establishment of appropriate infrastructures.

The initiative involves the partnership of several local authorities, Training and Enterprise Councils (TECs) and small firms with the EDU to realise the objectives of the project. Perhaps the most important aspect of the initiative is the work on the creation of a practical plan for the promotion of innovation for economic development, and the interaction between different stakeholders as part of a holistic, networking model. What follows is the drive towards the establishment of a territorial ecosystem of innovation by organisations that wish to "learn" and be "entrepreneurial".

THE FUTURE AGENDA

The strategic implications for the future centre around the role of both HEIs and companies as economic entities and as learning organisations in economic development. In strategic terms, universities can play a specialised role in attracting, retaining and generating SMEs in their innovative economic environment. The mix of attraction, retention, and generation, create a "territorial value chain" (Formica, 1992) which is built up from those particular basic resources of an area's endogenous potential represented by knowledge and information.

Knowledge and information resources are conveyed towards a set of activities by a set of methodologies, such as research (operational, scientific, skills analysis, labour market), management development seminars, etc. Such activities range from advanced education through to industrial liaison, entrepreneurship, venture capital provision, and local authority infrastructure support, to name but a few. Specific structures are set up to support these activities and they include science/technology parks, innovation centres, business centres, one-stop shops and, by extension, enterprise agencies and other linked support services.

Universities play direct and indirect roles in developing firm structures through action research, management development programmes, and other means. They are involved in both supply and demand creation through education and training provision leading to enhanced skills of employees in small firms, and, again, through research and development can contribute to the development of related industries. Such involvement is of particular value to small firms, which, because of resource constraints, find it difficult to negotiate the paths to business and economic development. The strategic, macro-level link-up can only help to support operational interaction for the purpose of collaborative work. Hull (1990) and the Centre for the Exploitation of Science and Technology (1992) have propagated the interactive model for collaboration which allows for different technological, market and business insights to create the initial business concept. This is then followed by the development of the concept through, for example, prototyping market research for product and process technologies. Commercial development is effected through the manufacturing and marketing processes. It should be noted that at all stages both HEIs and industry add value to the product and the process of commercialisation.

What emerges from committed collaboration and the pooling of activities, is a "quality dividend" which best describes the benefits to both HEIs and companies, in particular SMEs. Such a dividend is derived from high-quality training materials, the quality of graduates, obtaining greater pay-off from R&D investment by linked training effort, cost savings in training, the training dimension in technology transfer, and the ability of HEIs to adapt to changing needs (European Commission, 1992). As stated earlier, such effort is demonstrated not merely through the adoption of innovative programmes but also through organisational change, particularly for universities. The European agenda for HEI–industry collaboration for the future is based on the central theme of socio-economic development. This paper is a simple, conceptual contribution towards attainment of that objective.

References

Centre for Exploitation of Science and Technology (1992), *The Faraday Programme: Final Report to the Working Group on Innovation*, London: CEST.

Commission of the European Communities (1992), *Communication from the Commission to the Council and the European Parliament Concerning European Higher Education–Industry Cooperation: Advanced Training for Competitive Advantage*, European Commission, Brussels, 9 December, p. 3.

Cooley, M. (1987), *Architect or Bee? The Human Price of Technology*, London: The Hogarth Press/Chatto and Windus.

Formica, P. (1992), "Science Parks and Companies: Strategic Implications", Paper presented to the conference on Science Parks — Strategies for Success, Commission for the European Communities, DG XIII, Luxembourg.

Gueder, M. and Formica, P. (eds.) (1996), *The Economics of Science Parks*, ANPROTEC, IASP, AURRP, Rio de Janeiro.

Hull, C.J. (1990), *Technology Transfer between Higher Education and Industry in Europe — Obstacles to its Development and Proposal for Helping to Overcome them*, Luxembourg: Technology Innovation Information (TII).

Jones, R. and Lakin, C. (1977), "The Four Orders of Administration", *Management Decision*, Vol. 15, No. 4.

Jones, R. and Lakin, C. (1978), *The Carpetmakers,* New York: McGraw-Hill.

Mills, D.Q. and Friesen, B. (1992), "The learning organisation", *European Management Journal*, Vol. 1, No. 2.

Mitra, J. (1993), "Universities and SMEs — from Technology Transfer to Economic Development: Strategic Considerations and Implications Relating to the Institutional Interface", Paper presented at the First Venezuelan SME Management Seminar.

Monck, C.S.P., Quintas, P., Porter, R.B., Storey, D.J. and Wyranczyk, P. (1988), *Science Parks and the Growth of High Technology Firms*, London: Croom Helm.

Porter, M.E. (1990), *The Competitive Advantage of Nations*, London: Macmillan.

Williams, B.R. (1985), *The Direct and Indirect Role of Higher Education in Industrial Innovation — What Should we Expect?*, London: Technical Change Centre.

5

INNOVATION: THE CONCEPT, THE PROCESS, THE PEOPLE

Y.K. Bhushan and Sunanda Easwaran

Summary

Economic and political changes during the last decade or so have given rise to a totally new structure of socio-economic relationships between and within nations round the world. Yet, the contradictions of extreme poverty and wealth not only co-exist, but have become more marked. The direction the economies of the world will take in the coming years is by no means clear. What is clear, however, is that a new framework will have to be identified and new solutions found within it, to problems that exist today and even those that might arise in future.

Defining "innovation" in terms of these new solutions and new approaches to problems, this chapter discusses the concept and the history of innovation, and its applications in the field of entrepreneurship and small business. It talks of social and economic innovation as two strands of the concept of social growth and attempts to identify who contributes to innovation and how. Characteristics of the innovator-entrepreneur are identified, and the role of socio-cultural and economic environment in "fashioning innovative entrepreneurship", so to speak, is discussed.

The chapter discusses the process of innovation and makes the point that innovation springs from contextual need. The innovator-entrepreneur, contrary to popular belief, is a visionary leader, integrated with the realities of their own environment and not a loner concerned with ideas alone. On the contrary, the true innovator-entrepreneur performs the roles of innovator and co-ordinator, and is concerned with ensuring implementation of their innovations as an agent of change. Innovation therefore has to be contextual and continuous in order to be meaningful.

INTRODUCTION: THE ENIGMATIC FUTURE
AND ITS CHALLENGES

It is not just a platitude to observe that the world has undergone a bout of unprecedented and mind-boggling change over the last five years. The icons of yesterday lie in dust and the solutions of yesteryear appear to be fit only for safe storage in archives. A truly brave new world is emerging on the horizon, what with information and communication technology coalescing the vast spread of physical distances into a borderless global village. So sudden and discontinuous have been the changes in the political and economic life of the people across the world that they are in many ways moving through that transitory phase of disorientation which was succinctly described by Alvin Toffler (1983) as "The Future Shock".

The new emerging world is characterised by an abrupt end to the balance of power, the sudden demise of socialism, a loud assertion of human rights and individual freedom, and a free flow of resources across the world, depending upon where they would net the best return. The bipolarity that marked the world almost throughout the current century has been replaced by a unipolarity of ideology and economic doctrine even before the end of the present millennium. As a result, "the human society", in the words of Jacques Marcovitch of the University of Sao Paulo in Brazil, "lives in a global, competitive, heterogeneous, interdependent and shrinking world".

While the euphoria about the emergence of a new world continues to regale and excite people, one cannot turn away from the contradictions that are still inherent in the socio-economic scenario in a substantial part of the world. The spectre of poverty, deprivation, unemployment, stark inequity among and within countries, a fast degenerating environment under serious attack from non-degradable waste accumulation, and the uncontrolled and puzzling incidence of new communicable diseases, haunts the future generations as much as the present one. The sixty-four-million-dollar question that confronts us menacingly is: what is the next millennium going to be like? A period of want-free enjoyment of life at its fullest for all down to the lowest stratum of society, or an age of conflict, misery and destruction never experienced hitherto in the history of mankind? The future seems to be pregnant with dilemmas which make it so very enigmatic.

NEED FOR PARADIGM SHIFT

How is the challenge of change and the new future going to be met? How are the new and unfamiliar problems of health and human behaviour going to be resolved? Will the sturdy, old time-tested keys of economics, sociology and health-care help to unlock the new set of problems? If the current confusion of the world is any guide, the new challenges can be met essentially through new modes and directions of thinking and action. As Albert Einstein aptly put it, "the world we have created today as a result of our thinking thus far has problems which cannot be solved by thinking the way we thought when we created them". There is a need today, more than ever before in the history of mankind, for a shifting of old paradigms through fresh, unfettered thinking and bold new modes of action. Creative thinking about the world and its problems is the urgent demand of the present times. Quick collective action through creative applications of the new thinking is an equally urgent requirement of the society. Innovation truly holds the key to a future that will see the human race and its physical and social ecology in "dynamic harmony".

THE ESSENCE OF INNOVATION

The concept of "innovation" has been looked at differently in various contexts. The common thread running through them all is that innovation is the expression of creativity in a practical context, involving applications of new thinking to problem-solving. It is necessary, however, to view it in context, since by its very nature it is needs-based and thus related to the context in which its need arises. Scientists have often derided the importance of context, claiming that "true" innovation does not seek to "solve" problems in the environment but like beauty, is its own justification. Faraday was one such, concerned with the search for "supreme truth". However, for the present purpose, without engaging in the controversy of positivism vs. normativism, it suffices to reiterate that innovation is not only an essential but also a natural means of solving problems that prove too intractable to be solved by conventional, known means. In this sense, it would also be useful to draw a distinction between "invention" and "innovation". Invention is the production of new ideas, solutions and applications in the format of thought structures, models or scheme. Innovation consists in making new things happen in terms of new results. The successful innovator, is "therefore, a doer — someone with imagination who can visualise the possibilities of an idea and who has a strong desire and resource management skills to see it realised in a concrete form" (adapted from Davis, 1987).

STAGES IN INNOVATION

Everett Rogers, the consumer behaviour guru, delineated three types or stages of innovation:

1. The discontinuous innovation or "new to the world" idea, which has elsewhere been referred to as the universal innovation and which according to Rogers requires complete change in lifestyle;

2. The dynamically continuous innovation, which builds on a discontinuous innovation already in place and requires moderate change in behaviour; and

3. The continuous innovation, which is primarily an extension or adaptation of an "existing" innovation, requiring little or no behavioural modification (Rogers, 1987).

The second and third have been referred to as relative innovations of varying degrees by other authors. Again, an "innovation" in a particular context may have been in place elsewhere for a long period and would therefore not qualify for the hallowed title of "universal innovation". The concept of "contextual innovation" find its validity in this sense.

INNOVATION AND ENTREPRENEURSHIP

Schumpeter first defined entrepreneurship, as distinct from small business, in the context of innovation. His theory of economic change defines the entrepreneur as a change-agent, taking the economic system into a new direction (Schumpter, 1954; quoted in Cuevas). Since then, a number of authors have extended the notion of entrepreneurship beyond economic processes. The economist Baumol refers to entrepreneurs as creative people not necessarily engaged in business, but allocating their talents on the basis of the reward-structure prevailing in a society (Baumol, 1990; quoted in Gopakumar, 1995). Peter Drucker considers innovation as the specific instrument of entrepreneurship and as the act that endows resources with a new capacity to create wealth. Significantly, he also refers to "social innovation" as an essential aspect of entrepreneurship (Drucker, 1991). It is thus possible and even necessary to think of innovation in economic and non-economic contexts, embracing both technological and social areas and not just new economic uses of newly identified resources. It is important to treat them not as separate entities, but as different starting points towards the ultimate objective of social growth, all finding expression in the development of entrepreneurship for meeting the challenges posed by new problems and contradictions in the world.

If innovation is needs-based, it is also linked inextricably to the specific strengths that the innovator/entrepreneur brings to bear on the problem to be solved. The kind of solution that will ultimately provide the most effective answer stems not only from "a newly identified need", but depends in equal measure on the manner in which the need is perceived and interpreted by the entrepreneur, and the specific match arrived at between the need-dimensions and entrepreneurial capabilities.

INNOVATIONS IN ENTREPRENEURSHIP

This variation in the need/strength permutations results in a variety of forms that entrepreneurship can take. In the context of business alone, for example, it is possible to think of three structural variants. These variants are discussed briefly in the context of India, a fast developing country.

1. **Group enterprises** like SEWA (Self-Employed Women's Association): the overriding need for economic self-sufficiency, coupled with the paucity of self-confidence and financial resources that women, the exclusive members of this group, displayed as a result of generations of economic and social repression, almost dictated that strength for achievement of their objectives would have to be found in this structure of a group enterprise. As a model, group enterprise has found many adherents, especially in developing economies, where the disadvantaged individual's paucity of resources finds solutions for growth through the collective strengths of the group. SEWA, which began in 1972 with 400 members, today claims a membership of more than 100,000 women.

2. **Co-operatives** like LIJJAT (Shri Mahila Grih Udyog Lijjat Papad) present the other side of the coin, harnessing strengths

like traditional domestic skills for achievement of common economic objectives. The overall goal of such enterprises is the greatest good of the greatest number, and the functioning is based on the ideology of SARVODAYA (development of all). LI-JJAT, which was founded on 15 March 1959 and officially registered as a society on 25 July 1966, started with 4 members and registered sales of less than RS10,000 (£175) in the first year. Today the organisation has 44 units (branches) all over the country and registered sales of RS632 million in 1993/94. It has diversified into a number of household products like spices, pickles and detergents.

3. **Individual enterprises** based, in India as in other countries, on a plethora of motivations, and drawing upon a variety of sources of strength and expertise. Technology-based enterprises are typical examples, with entrepreneurs deciding to "go into business for themselves" on the strength of experience and technical knowledge acquired while working in the industry. Innovation in such enterprises often takes the form of process innovation, though product innovation of the "dynamically continuous" type is not unheard of. In a study of 46 high-tech SMEs, Ramachandran and Nair (1996) cite cases of entrepreneurs "who started in their known territory but quickly switched over to products new to the Indian market. For instance, one firm which started with process control equipment soon switched over to computer visual display units and keyboards which were not being manufactured in India in any significant way."

The choice of the most appropriate form of enterprise has often been an extremely difficult decision and examples abound of firms which have registered trend-setting successes in one area failing miserably in another field. In India, the co-operative model, for example, which was almost exclusively responsible for lifting the dairy industry out of its morass, has been an utter failure in the edible oils industry by the admission of Dr Kurien himself, whose brainchild it was.

FORMS OF INNOVATION

Two conclusions can be drawn from this discussion:

1. Process innovation can be an effective catalyst for growth

2. Models of innovation have to be rooted in the social and economic realities of the situation.

This, in turn, implies that innovations, economic as well as non-economic, could take a variety of forms:

- **Innovation in Target Group Definition:** A holistic approach to the twin objectives of quicker employment generation and self-development through enterprise training led the Narsee Monjee Institute of Management Studies (NMIMS) to concentrate on the urban middle-income group rather than the traditional emphasis on the rural and the urban poor for women's enterprise training.

- **Innovation in Opportunity Identification:** This refers to the identification of an opportunity before it has been identified by anyone else, or in a field where no opportunity was seen to exist. This is the most popular interpretation of the term "enterprise", and examples are numerous. Manimala (1992) cites the example of Ambani of Reliance Industries, who spotted an opportunity in a particularly unfavourable environment. He noted that powerlooms, which had governmental patronage in terms of tax structure, produced high quality goods but could not market them. He got the powerlooms to produce high quality textiles to his specifications and marketed them under his brand name. Today Reliance is the largest private sector company in India, with net sales of about L1,000 million (£17.8 million) in 1994/95.

- **Innovation in Delivery Mechanism:** Any element of the marketing mix could be the result of the innovation process: the "product", the promotion strategy, or the distribution channel. A case in point is Mr Panse of Mintage Electro Equipments, a Bombay-based SME with a turnover of L 2.2 million (£39,000) in the first year of operation, who has hit upon the innovative scheme of marketing their portable emergency lights through exclusive commission agents rather than a full-time field force to be employed by his firm. The commission agents are entrepreneurs in their own right, trained by Mintage but operating as independent entities, and maintaining fully fledged organisations if they so wish. Selection of these MBAs (Mintage Business Associates) is through a rigorous procedure and the opportunity is not made available to traditional, established dealers in electrical goods. The scheme, while on the one hand creating a large number of entrepreneurs through the multiplier effect, has at the same time helped Mintage gain access to a vast distribution network with the minimum of expense and made available to them the benefits of the various incentive schemes offered by the government for employment generation.

Another company that made marketing history in India a few years ago is Eureka-Forbes, the L 30 million (£530,000) Indian affiliate of the Swedish giant Electrolux, which introduced the concept of domestic vacuum cleaners to India in the late 1980s. Recognising that the market for this product was nascent and small and also that as a new concept, the product required personal demonstration, Eureka-Forbes decided to market their vacuum cleaners through door-to-door selling, instead of following the conventional channel of:

Manufacturer → Wholesaler → Retailer

Their success has since then motivated a number of other manufactures of consumer durables to follow the same direct sales route.

Yet another example of innovative delivery mechanisms comes from the field of social innovation. With the objective of delivering quality education to minority schools, NMIMS has been running a programme in Bombay and another city in western India, aimed at professionalising the management of selected minority schools. The programme is aimed at head teachers, administrators and teachers who are being trained in the process of managing change on their own. An innovative off-shoot of the programme is the entrepreneurship development programmes proposed for the parents of school-going children, aimed at improving their economic status in order to bring down the children's drop-out rates.

- **Innovation in Organisation Structure:** In most of the instances listed above, innovations elsewhere have been accompanied by changes in the organisation structure. The case of

Mintage was referred to in this context earlier. Both LIJJAT and SEWA are characterised by very flat organisations, and at LIJJAT in particular, even the top functionaries are elected through open ballot for a fixed period of time. The result therefore, is greater parity in relationships and linkages between the various stakeholders, and the ensuing sense of enhanced involvement with the organisation.

*   **Strategic Innovations:** Mintage, of course, is a classical instance of strategic innovation. Not only have they ensured product superiority over competition, they have also adopted the strategy of wearing many hats successfully: that of the technology-oriented entrepreneur, that of the savvy marketer, and that of the socially conscious employer, generating not just employment but enterprise. They have gained from all of these strategies.

    Another classically successful case of strategic innovation, now cited in every Indian textbook of marketing, has been that of NIRMA, the low-quality, low-price detergent that gave the detergent giant Levers a run for its money by expanding the market for detergents downwards. And the most savvy strategic innovator of them all was Mahatma Gandhi, who realised long ago that industrialisation of rural India was essential for balanced growth, and the quickest route to rural industrialisation was through traditional skill-based industries.

It is a fact of elementary economics that, unlike land and capital, the other three factors of production, namely, labour, management and entrepreneurship are essentially linked to the persona of the entrepreneur, and are therefore related to their attitudinal approach. Entrepreneurial processes in the society can therefore be brought about only through attitude change, by making people more entrepreneurial. These entrepreneurial processes, in turn, have to be rooted in the local, situational and cultural context. Universal models of entrepreneurship and enterprise training will usually not work. That is the only constant to be expected with models of entrepreneurship and innovation; that is, they have to be based on the "here and now" of cultures.

THE PROCESS OF INNOVATION

What sparks off the process of innovation? Drucker (1991), talking in the context of business, lists a number of forces, some in the environment and others integral to the organisation. The environmental forces he lists are: demographics, changes in perceptions, meaning and moods, and increased knowledge. Forces integral to the firm that contribute to innovative changes are: unexpected outside events, dissonance between reality and the desired states and finally, opportunity based on identification of process needs. A few years ago, Eureka-Forbes introduced yet another innovative concept in the after-sales service of their durables. Introducing the idea of franchising in after-sales-service for the first time, they offered to recruit and train anyone who could provide premises for stocking spare parts, had some understanding of engineering or could hire such a person and had access to a telephone. Spare parts would be the property of Eureka-Forbes and therefore did not involve any payment apart from a deposit. This scheme has found many enthusiastic followers and helped create a number of entrepreneurs, including women.

Even more pervasive is the innovation that arises as a new solution to existing needs or problems, in answer to requirements of increased efficiency or when old, tried and trusted methods are no longer adequate. This is as much a result of changing demographics as what Drucker refers to as changes in perceptions, meaning and moods. Newly developing suburbs in metropolitan areas like Bombay, primarily populated by first generation immigrants of the middle and upper middle class and with a large number of young working couples, are today seeing a spurt in eateries that specialise in take-away and home delivery services: "an idea whose time has come".

Writing in the World Executive Digest, David Perry, Director of Client Services, The Technology Group, traces the change over the decades in the way marketers have changed their perceptions of their customers, from mass-audience with similar requirements in the 1950s to the matrixed or niche perceptions today, when customer groups are divided by prices, features and applications, so that "the market is not a mass segmented or sub-segmented group, but rather a conglomeration of niches, each with a specific price/feature/need profile" (Perry, 1990). The innovator/ entrepreneur spots these niches before others, and moves into the one where their match with the niche-profile is optimised. Long before formal courier services were introduced on a large scale in India, an innovative group in Western India identified the need for safe, speedy mail delivery and introduced the "Angadia" service. Today it is perceived as being the quickest and most reliable of courier services.

INNOVATION: THE PEOPLE

Quinn (1985) talks of the innovative entrepreneur's impatience with long-drawn out procedures and fanatic conviction about the success-potential of his idea, born in the main of his expertise. This is often interpreted to mean that an innovator is a maverick and a loner. Organisations are usually advised to treat these birds of paradise with kid gloves. While it may be true that innovators can spot both the problem and the solution much ahead of everyone else and, being "doers", are more concerned with implementing change than with structure and formality, by their very nature they are visionary leaders of people, and therefore usually not confined to ivory towers. All the examples discussed earlier point to one reality: the innovator-entrepreneurs, because they are innovators and entrepreneurs, do not always wait and follow the prescribed path or look for traditional inputs in order to fill gaps in the process of output achievement. In their hurry to achieve their goal, they innovate the means, forever "making do" with whatever alternative comes to hand, rather than waiting for the "correct one" to become available. They trust their expertise and intuition to assess the suitability of the new alternative. Culture plays a major role, too, in the integration of the innovator-entrepreneur with the environment: in cultures like India, for example, where the individual is so strongly integrated in the family, the western concept of the innovator loner finds no relevance.

While the twin concepts of entrepreneur and innovator transcend the boundaries of economic enterprise, they have been developed primarily by the economic and human resources schools of thought, beginning with the former. The economist Leibenstein pointed out that in the context of a firm, there is no one-to-one relationship between inputs and output, and gaps often exist between the two. Accordingly, the primary role that the entrepreneur plays is that of a "gap-filler" and "input-completer" (Leibenstein, 1968; quoted in Gopakumar, 1995). Extending this concept beyond the firm loses none of its applicability, but does project the entrepreneur-innovator in the role of a resource mobiliser. This in turn presupposes that the entrepreneur-innovator has to be a networker. At this stage, it may be useful to extend the classical definition of Schumpeter that postulates an entrepreneur as a change agent disturbing an economic system in equilibrium and taking it into a new direction. It would seem logical to assume that while the entrepreneur in their role as an innovator may do just that, in their role as co-ordinator they would assume responsibility for institutionalising the change, so that it could have a permanent, or at least a long-term impact. This defines for the entrepreneur the role of a normative innovator, steeped in social reality. This also implies that the entrepreneur has a two-way relationship with the environment, simultaneously being influenced by it in the process of opportunity identification and influencing it through the changes they introduce.

As these changes are essential if cultures and societies are not to stagnate and die, it becomes imperative for us to not only create a climate where the entrepreneurial spirit can grow, but we need to go a step further and actively plan for nurturing it. This would require that societies:

1. Foster creativity and innovation through the education system from early stages, to train the individual to think creatively. The role of universities and other educational institutions has to be expanded so that they not only act as change-agents themselves, but they also mould individual thinking towards seeking, accepting, preparing for and actively assisting change. Mere competency training, while essential for the successful handling of today's situation, will prove inadequate in proactive training for tomorrow.

2. Reward technical/technological relevance to everyday life, in addition to rewarding technological innovation. A western example that can easily and fruitfully be adapted the world over is to be found in the John Logie Baird awards for innovation in Scotland. Aimed at encouraging innovative business projects from companies and individuals, these awards are presented each year to companies and entrepreneurs with innovative business ideas which can be commercially exploited with success.

3. Plan and provide for innovative/entrepreneurial networking

4. Ensure that innovation is rooted in contextual/cultural realities, for greater and speedier diffusion.

CONCLUSION

The final word on innovation can never be said, if it is to be true to its spirit. However, entrepreneurial characteristics can certainly be identified:

- Creativity of thought, coupled with a certain degree of restlessness

- The desire to excel and the belief that things ought to be and can be made better

- The ability to identify an opportunity before anyone else

- A certain pragmatism that helps in the translation of an innovative idea into practical reality

- Ability to network and mobilise resources

- Visionary leadership and the ability to take people along with oneself, coupled with some degree of charisma

- Activism — the innovator is a doer

- Social awareness and sensitivity combined with business skills — superordination

- Organising ability

- Developing leaders among co-workers and subordinates

- Self-confidence in the face of scepticism and criticism.

The entrepreneurial process is dynamic and needs constant redefinition. In developing societies, the context has to be primarily one of social innovation, with economic innovation being used as a means for achieving it. The problems of deprivation cannot be solved in the same manner as the problems of plenty, and innovation therefore needs to be constantly "innovated", if it is to be relevant.

References

Baumol, W.J. (1990), "Entrepreneurship: Productive, Unproductive and Destructive", *Journal of Political Economy,* XCVIII-5; quoted in K. Gopakumar (1995), "The Entrepreneur in Economic Thought: A Thematic Overview", *The Journal of Entrepreneurship,* Vol. 4, No. 1, p. 14.

Davis, William (1987), *The Innovators*, London: Ebony Press (adapted).

Drucker, P.F. (1991), *Innovation and Entrepreneurship*, New Delhi: East West Press, pp. 31–34.

Leibenstein, H. (1968), "Entrepreneurship and Development", *American Economic Review* (Papers & Proceedings), LVIII-2; as quoted in K. Gopakumar (1995), "The Entrepreneur in Economic Thought: A Thematic Overview", *The Journal of Entrepreneurship,* Vol. 4, No. 1, p. 12.

Manimala, M.J. (1992), "Innovative Entrepreneurship: Testing the Theory of Environmental Determinism" in *Innovations in Management for Development*, Maheshwari, B.L. (ed.), New Delhi: Tata McGraw-Hill, pp. 100–119.

Perry, David (1990), "Marketing Distribution in the 1990s" in *World Executive Digest,* January, pp. 50–52.

Quinn, J.B. (1985), "Managing Innovation: Controlled Chaos" in *Innovation,* Harvard Business Review paperbacks, pp. 17–28.

Ramachandran, K. and Nair, E. (1996), "Strategies of Technology Intensive Firms", Working Paper 1296, Ahmedabad: Indian Institute of Management: p. 2.

Rogers, Everett (1987), *Diffusion of Innovation,* New York: Free Press.

Schumpter, J.A. (1954), *History of Economic Analysis*, Oxford: Oxford University Press.

Toffler, Alvin (1983), *The Future Shock*, London: Pan Books.

6

HIGHER EDUCATION–ENTERPRISE CO-OPERATION AND THE ENTREPRENEURIAL GRADUATE: THE NEED FOR A NEW PARADIGM

Mathew J. Manimala

Summary

Deviating from their traditional focus on the abstract and the theoretical, universities and higher education institutions (HEIs) have, of late, been paying a lot of attention to the practical applications of the knowledge generated in the HEI system. Developing new products and services from research output and commercialising them through entrepreneurial ventures have been taken up by many HEIs with a view to making useful contributions to the economy and thereby improving the quality of life in the community. Prominent among the schemes undertaken by HEIs in this regard are:

1. Science and technology parks

2. University companies

3. Promotion of academic entrepreneurs.

A review of these schemes using the findings of various evaluation studies and case studies has shown that they had very limited success not only in developing countries, but even in developed countries. In fact, the celebration of isolated successes of these schemes in some developed countries has been shielding the lacklustre performance of the majority. It appears that the paradigm of direct involvement and action by HEIs in the development of new products and services and their commercialisation through entrepreneurial activities has not been appropriate. An alternative paradigm for the HEIs would be to contribute to the

development of entrepreneurial individuals rather than of entrepreneurial ventures.

INTRODUCTION

Universities and higher education institutions (HEIs) have traditionally been more concerned with the abstract and the theoretical than with practical applications. Efforts have been made from
time to time to make university programmes practical and useful
to society by placing progressively greater emphasis on applied
sciences. In spite of such efforts, the fact still remains that very
few HEIs have been able to keep pace with the times and match
their services with the emerging needs of society. In 1980, for example, the Finniston Committee in the UK observed that engineering courses in the UK were inferior because of weak links between universities and industry (Monck et al., 1988). If this is the
case in an industrially advanced country, it can only be (indeed it
is) far worse in developing countries.

Universities and HEIs are urged to contribute to improving the
quality of life of the society in which they operate. Quality of life
in a society would, to a large extent, depend on the availability of
innovative products and services and a level of purchasing power
high enough for people to afford them. It is against this context
that creation of innovative, high technology enterprises is considered to be a double-edged weapon capable of achieving the twin
objectives of generating wealth as well as products and services.
Research studies have shown that employment growth in smaller
firms is higher than in larger firms. Besides, it was also observed
that high technology firms show faster employment growth than
conventional firms (Morse, 1976; Rothwell and Zegveld, 1982;
Breheny and McQuaid, 1987; Cambridge City Council, 1986; Storey, 1985), although a few later studies have produced evidence to
the contrary (Keeble and Kelly, 1986; Oakey, 1991; 1995). On the
issue of innovativeness also, the evidence is mixed. It was observed by Pavitt et al. (1987) that innovations take place both in
smaller as well as larger firms, but not so much in medium-sized
firms. This may be because, as Rothwell (1986; 1994) points out,
innovations are helped by certain features of small firms such as
ability to react quickly, willingness to take risks, and better internal communication as well as by certain other features of large
firms such as the ability to raise resources, to market the new
products through their existing dealer networks and to liaise with

external agencies especially the government. Thus it is only for certain types of innovation that the smaller firm may be better suited than the larger firm. All the same, it is the belief that small enterprises are the primary instruments of innovation, wealth creation and employment generation that universities and HEIs are urged to take an active part in creating such ventures.

THE TRADITIONAL MODEL

The existing model of university–enterprise collaboration is based on a few quasi-empirical assumptions. As mentioned above, many of these assumptions are supported by empirical evidence. Or, wherever the evidence is contrary to the assumptions, it is conveniently ignored. Though researchers generally claim that they believe what they see, there are many cases where they try to see what they believe in. These issues will be discussed in subsequent sections. In this section, we shall try to explicitly state the assumptions underlying the existing model of HEI–enterprise collaboration and briefly outline the expectations under this model.

Assumptions

The existing HEI–enterprise co-operation model operates on the following assumptions:

- The ultimate objective of HEIs should be to contribute to material welfare (creating wealth and employment and improving the quality of physical life), which would be best achieved by stimulating enterprise creation based on new ideas generated in the HEI system.

- Most inventions can be converted into commercial products without much additional investment in time or money.

- Commercial innovations, especially the introduction of new products, is primarily the function of "technology push" rather than "market pull". Hence a new product/service based on an invention is bound to be a success in the market.

- Entrepreneurial individuals look at universities and research institutions as a major source of new ideas.

- If appropriate encouragement is given, researchers and academics could turn out to be successful entrepreneurs.

- Continuous interaction with research institutions is important for the sustained growth of high-tech enterprises and therefore such enterprises would like to locate themselves near research institutions.

Expectations

Under these assumptions, it is but natural that society expects HEIs to contribute to general economic development. Williams (1985) summarises these expectations by enumerating five ways in which universities/HEIs can contribute to the creation of new technology-based firms (NTBFs):

1. By providing opportunities for students to acquire skills and attitudes which could be used to create or promote the successful NTBFs

2. By promoting research in high technology which may create opportunities for innovation by small firms

3. By encouraging staff to provide advice and consultancy services in the field of high technology

4. By allowing staff to create or take part in the creation of firms to exploit high technology

5. By creating companies to exploit the research or design and development activities of staff in the fields of high technology.

Similar is the view held by the report of the Economist Intelligence Unit (1985) which identified four major kinds of tasks for universities, namely:

1. Facilitating communications

2. Providing professional and financial support

3. Establishing enterprises and research centres

4. Collaborating with outside bodies.

Recognising these expectations, HEIs, especially in the industrialised western countries, have initiated several schemes to actively promote the commercialisation of their research output.

THE MODEL IN ACTION

Among the many schemes, policies and activities launched by universities and HEIs following the assumptions and prescriptions of the model, the prominent ones are:

- University-owned companies

- Liberal and facilitating changes in intellectual property right (IPR) rules

- Encouragement to academic staff to start their own enterprises

- Science and technology parks, and so on.

The most celebrated scheme among these is, of course, the science parks, which are often cited as illustrious examples of university–enterprise co-operation. Evaluations of the science park experiment along with the other schemes of the universities is one of the ways in which the validity of the model as well as the tenability of the assumptions could be tested.

Science Parks

The concept of science parks originated in the work of Terman and others at Stanford University in the United States. The idea was to help industries to enhance their competitiveness using the research output from the universities. During the 1960s the movement spread to Europe. In the UK, the first science park was developed by Cambridge University followed by Heriot-Watt. But the real boom of science parks in the UK occurred in the early 1980s.

Developing countries are also taking the initiative for creating similar facilities near HEIs. India, for example, has launched a project called Science and Technology Entrepreneurs Park (STEP). There are at present 12 such parks in India. The initiative, however, comes primarily from the Department of Science and Technology (DST), and not from the universities or research institutions.

There are several studies on the UK science parks; some of them are conceptual and others empirical (Currie, 1985; Dalton, 1985; Eul, 1985; Lowe, 1985; Segal, 1985; Cambridge City Council, 1986; Southern, 1986; Monck, 1986, 1987; McDonald, 1987; Monck et al., 1988; Storey and Strange, 1992; Mitra et al, 1993; Hauschildt and Steinkuhler, 1994; Westhead and Storey, 1994; Mitra and Jinkinson, 1995). While the evaluation studies generally confirm the beneficial impact of high-tech firms on the economy, they have shown hardly any difference between high-tech firms on science parks and those located elsewhere. Apparently, the "HEI connection" does not give any special advantages to the science park firms. Monck et al. (1988) provide interesting comparisons between on-park and off-park high-tech firms on the various aspects of their performance. A few of their findings are given below, most of which are confirmed by other studies as well.

- Out of the 42 science parks surveyed, only nine (21 per cent) received some kind of funding support from universities, whose share in the expenditure was 19 per cent, the balance being from the government, local authorities, tenant companies and private sector institutions.

- As for the number of founders with university degrees, the proportions were similar on science parks (75 per cent) and outside (79 per cent). But there were more founders with higher degrees on science parks (52 per cent versus 16 per cent).

- Unemployment prior to start-up was similar on science parks (18 per cent) and outside (20 per cent).

- Knowledge of the specific market (not of process and technology) was the single most important motivator for start-up in both cases.

- Prior managerial experience of founders was the same for both the groups (74 per cent versus 75 per cent). Similarly, prior ownership experience was also comparable (29 per cent versus 22 per cent).

- Among the reasons for being near an HEI, the most important one was the general prestige/image of the site and, significantly, not the prestige of the university, nor the facilities and ideas offered by the HEI.

- R&D intensity in terms of the number of qualified scientists and engineers was higher in science park firms. Similarly, patenting activity was also higher in science parks.

- While informal contacts with the local HEI were higher for the science park firms, project-based contacts were higher for firms outside the parks.

- Academic-owned firms were proportionately higher in science parks, but their performance was poorer.

- In terms of the overall performance of the firms there was hardly any difference between science park firms and others. However, there was a difference between high-tech and low-tech firms, the former performing better than the latter.

It is clear that UK science park firms are not significantly different from other high-tech firms located outside the science parks. The experience on the continent is also broadly similar. In a study of German TS-parks, Hauschildt and Steinkuhler (1994) concludes that the size and growth of TS-park companies do not differ from companies that develop outside the parks. More importantly, they question the assumption that TS-parks contribute to the development of the region. In fact, the traffic usually flows the other way. Prior development of a region is one of the preconditions of attracting TS-parks to that region. So the fortunes of the TS-park firms depend on the fortunes of the region, not vice versa. Besides, the parks can also be a source of costs for the region as many of these firms are subsidised by the local authorities because of the social prestige associated with maintaining TS-parks.

University Companies[*]

The more enterprising of the universities in the West have taken the initiative of founding their own companies with the objective of commercialising the new ideas generated in their research departments. Typically the objectives of such a company are as follows:

- Identify commercially feasible projects from among the new ideas generated by university's/HEI's researchers

- Invest (subject to certain limits) in the further development of research ideas, either alone or in joint ventures

- Apply for and secure patent protection for the university's/HEI's ideas

- Identify buyers for the patented ideas or partners for developing them further

---

[*] This section is based on a study of a university company carried out by the author in 1991. The company wishes to remain anonymous.

- Negotiate collaboration/licence agreements on behalf of the university and its staff

- Provide technical, commercial, legal and marketing advice to partners/licensees

- Create subsidiary companies around new ideas and sell them off with a view to making profits or at least recovering the cost of patenting, developing, etc.

Thus the university companies generally do not engage in the manufacturing or marketing of products and services, which are the main functions of a normal enterprise. In other words, the products they sell are new product ideas and/or semi-developed technologies. These are obviously irregular in production, uncertain in development and difficult to sell. This may be why during the ten years of existence of the university company under study, there were less than five fully developed commercial products, even though there were more than 970 new ideas offered for sale. It was pointed out that these technology-transfer companies operate under serious constraints:

- Shortage of investment funds is a major problem for the university companies. Universities themselves are on budget support, and therefore are unable to invest the funds required for the further development of new ideas. It is also difficult to raise funds from capital markets and financial institutions because of the uncertainty and long gestation period associated with the development of ideas generated in the laboratory.

- Government funding for the universities is generally based on the number of students, and not on the number of research projects. Research therefore gets a low priority in the universities, which would, in turn, reduce the generation of new ideas.

- There is no regular supply of the "raw material" for the university companies, which are the new ideas from the laboratories. Such irregular and unpredictable supplies make it difficult for the company to ensure continuity in its business. Obviously, it is almost impossible for the company to do any strategic planning or even to deliberate on the broad directions of its future business. The university companies therefore are often forced to adopt a "reactive" rather than "proactive" business strategy.

- Getting researchers (and industry) interested in the commercial development of new ideas is another major problem. According to one estimate, only 5–6 per cent of the inventors are interested in leaving their research jobs for the commercial development of their inventions and eventual setting up of an enterprise.

- Added to the natural lack of interest on the part of the inventor, there are disincentives emerging from the Intellectual Property Rights (IPR) policies of universities. In the case of the university whose company was studied, the individual inventor has no rights over their invention. All the rights are held by the university. So the first hurdle for an inventor wishing to commercialise their new idea is to get the university bureaucracy interested in it.

- Even in universities which claim to have an IPR policy favouring the individual inventor, there are several operational difficulties. In a study of the IPR policy of nine universities in the UK, Harvey (1994) pointed out many such operational problems. Out of the nine universities, only one was helpful to the start-up of new-technology-based firms, even though there were five others who had favourable policies. Three of the latter did very little to implement their policies. Two others failed to communicate their policies to the implementing officers, who then became hindrances rather than facilitators.

- There are also disincentives arising from the formula for sharing the gains. In the university studied above, only one-third of the surplus goes to the inventor. The remaining portion is equally divided between the concerned department and the university. Also, there are built-in disincentives in the calculation of the surplus. All the direct and indirect expenses of product development are deducted from the initial sales figures itself, so that the surplus would often be quite meagre and belated. It was pointed out that in the case of one invention, the inventor had to wait ten years for some share in the surplus after commercial sales of the product started. The period for product development was extra.

- Just as investors are shy about new products and technologies because of the inherent uncertainties of the commercial outcome and the long gestation periods involved, there are also difficulties in marketing such a new product whose credentials

are yet to be established. This is especially the case if the
product is the result of "technology push" rather than "market
pull". The problem is further compounded if the new product is
designed for a global niche rather than a local market. It may
be noted that the universities and their small partners have
limited marketing capabilities even in a local market.

* Finally, university companies experience competition from two
  other large systems. One source of competition is the large
  companies whose R&D departments are better equipped for
  the development of application-oriented new products and
  their marketing. Secondly, there are technology transfer organisations such as the British Technology Group (BTG) and
  the Investors in Industry (3i), whose sources are wider than
  the research departments of one university. As the sources of
  their new ideas are larger, they can specialise in relevant areas, plan for growth and diversification, and have better capabilities for commercial development and technology transfer.

The Academic Entrepreneur

It was observed above that very often the IPR policies of universities stand in the way of stimulating entrepreneurship among
academic professionals. Additionally, it was observed that among
the inventors, only about 5–6 per cent are interested in undertak-
ing the commercialisation of their inventions. Thus, even with the
most favourable IPR and other policies of universities, it is unlikely that many academic researchers would venture into the
start-up of new enterprises based on their own inventions. In a
few case studies of academics becoming entrepreneurs it was
found that the factors influencing the plunge were not necessarily
the positive ones such as a perceived commercial use of the invention or the encouragement from colleagues or mentors, but in
many cases the stimulus came from negative factors such as the
denial of promotion, lack of recognition for one's work, the need of
the family to be in a certain locality, and so on (Manimala, 1988,
1992c; Piramal and Herdeck, 1985). Interestingly, in most cases,
the initial products were also not directly related to the field of
their research.

It appears that academic research and entrepreneurship have
nothing much in common and that the emergence of the academic
entrepreneur is more a function of the extraneous circumstances
than the recognition of the intrinsic commercial value of the in-

ventions. In a study of academic entrepreneurs among life scientists, Louis et al. (1989) eloquently brought out these points. Their conclusions are apt to throw some light on the issue of promoting the academic entrepreneur:

- There is a general belief among academics that profit making is inconsistent with the pursuit of truth

- There is no evidence of the emergence of a new kind of entrepreneurial scholar in universities

- Scholarly productivity is not an important predictor of commercial entrepreneurship

- The most common form of academic entrepreneurship is in getting large research grants (and not in commercial manufacture and marketing of invention-based new products)

- R&D entrepreneurship apparently requires a different set of competencies than those required for bringing new products to market or organising new firms

- University policies and structures have little impact on faculty entrepreneurship. In other words, institutions cannot easily engineer entrepreneurship. This is because academic entrepreneurship is determined more by group characteristics than by individual characteristics, which would imply that the universities should create strong cultures (Ouchi, 1980) which are supportive of entrepreneurship. However, as universities are loosely coupled systems (Weick, 1976), they are often unable to inculcate a strong culture. Needless to say the academic's strong need for individualism may have prompted them to make self-selection into a university system which is loosely coupled and therefore would allow divergence of views and thought patterns.

EXPERIENCES FROM A DEVELOPING COUNTRY

Developing countries generally have a tendency to copy the "successful" schemes of the developed countries. Following the Western models of promoting university enterprise collaboration, the Department of Science and Technology (DST) of the Government of India created the National Science and Technology Entrepreneurship Development Board (NSTEDB) with the objective of developing science and technology entrepreneurs, especially through collaboration between universities and entrepreneurial individuals. NSTEDB has promoted several schemes such as entrepreneurship awareness camps, science and technology entrepreneurship development programmes (ST-EDPs), entrepreneurship development cells in educational institutions, training for trainers programmes, awards and incentives, science and technology entrepreneurs park (STEP) and so on. Among these, STEP, like the science park scheme in the UK, is the most important initiative for promoting HEI–enterprise collaboration. A major difference here is that the initiative has come from the government, not from the HEIs or the enterprises who are supposed to collaborate.

There are about a dozen STEPs in India now. Though their performance has not been formally evaluated, there are reports of their lacklustre performance. In fact, there has not been a single STEP entrepreneur selected for the "Science and Technology Entrepreneur of the Year" Award instituted by NSTEDB. Brief profiles of four entrepreneurs who were selected for the above award (in recent years) are given below. The "caselets" show that even those entrepreneurs who were adjudged to be the best among Science and Technology Entrepreneurs have not been associated with STEP or HEIs.

- A science graduate works with a private sector company for a few years then decides to start on her own. She attends an STEDP and starts exporting carved articles and furniture. Later she diversifies into health foods where the modern co-extrusion technology is used. Significantly, the relatively "high-tech" food processing unit was located in a backward area, not in a university town!

- An electrical engineer quits a promising career in a large public sector organisation after nine years of distinguished service with them. He was bitten by the urge to be his own boss, and the major source of his inspiration was his family. He too attends an STEDP, and later starts a unit for the manufacture of transformers and chokes for electronic applications. These were the products of his previous employer, but the smaller scale operation carefully monitored by an individual entrepreneur has improved the quality and dramatically brought down the rejection rate from 50 per cent in his parent company to just 1 per cent.

- A graduate in polymer sciences, who wanted to manufacture injection moulded plastic goods, refuses job offers and tries unsuccessfully for three months to start his venture. He then joins and STEDP, who provide him with training as well as contacts for raw material and power connection. The unit gets started and the entrepreneur makes a few innovative designs.

- A postgraduate in chemistry works as a teacher and a tourism guide for some years. Later, having decided to start her own enterprise, she attends an STEDP and starts manufacturing ready-made garments. Subsequently, she diversifies into bicycle parts, for which the manufacturing unit was set up in a backward rural area.

Such examples could be picked up from among other "high-tech" entrepreneurs also. The choice here is limited to S&T Entrepreneurship Award winners because they are more likely to have been influenced by HEIs. This is expected to be the case especially because the awards were instituted by an agency which is committed to promoting HEI–enterprise interaction. Conversely, if these awardees have not been influenced by the HEIs, it is unlikely that HEIs are actively collaborating with enterprises in India. It may also be noted that none of the above awardees came from Science and Technology Entrepreneurs Parks which is a specific scheme of NSTEDB for promoting HEI–enterprise collaboration.

An analysis of the four "caselets" shows that, except probably for the third one, where the entrepreneur moves directly from his college to the start-up, there is no perceptible influence of HEIs on entrepreneurs. The products of these "S&T enterprises" are not the typical "high-tech" ones. Similarly, they do not seem to be selected on the basis of the entrepreneurs' previous training and specialisation. The most important consideration, especially in the case of the initial product, seems to be what one can sell rather than what one knows how to make. Thus technology is of secondary importance even to the S&T entrepreneur. As for the agencies/organisations influencing the potential entrepreneur, the more powerful influences seem to come from one's family, previous employer, and the government sponsored promotional agencies. There is hardly any direct involvement from HEIs. Backward area concessions which offer certain financial advantages seem to be given greater weight than proximity to HEIs. In fact, when one moves to rural and backward areas, the possibilities for interaction with HEIs are further reduced.

It may perhaps be argued that research in Indian universities is still at a primitive stage with hardly any commercially usable output. Though this is largely true, it may not be the only reason for the passive relationship and lack of interaction between HEIs and enterprises. As we have seen above, the experience of the developed countries in the West is also not very different. Making an overall assessment of the scenario, Oakey (1994) states that the Silicon Valley and Cambridge Science Parks are exceptions rather than the rule. Similarly in one of the celebrated examples of university–enterprise collaboration in the UK, namely that of T-Disc Oil Skimmer, the development of the commercial product involved much more collaboration between the enterprise and other agencies than between the enterprise and the university. The gestation period was more than 10 years, and after the product was successfully developed and commercialised, the "entrepreneur" wanted to sell off the business because he wanted to be more involved in designing than manufacturing and selling (Manimala and Pearson, 1991; Manimala, 1992a). Apparently, the entrepreneur who came forward to collaborate with the university was not really an entrepreneur but a researcher or rather a designer. This is probably another confirmation of the limited nature of university–enterprise collaboration.

THE AGGREGATE EVIDENCE

The aggregate evidence emerging from this discussion does not offer much justification for HEIs getting directly and actively involved in enterprise promotion. The observations made above in this regard and a few other relevant research findings are briefly summarised below.

- Science park firms hardly differed from off-park firms except in the number of R&D personnel and patenting activity. It is significant to note that the park firms did not have any higher degree of interaction with the universities. In fact, the off-park firms had larger number of project-based contacts with universities. Locational choices on the parks were influenced more by the general prestige associated with the place than by the nearness to universities. The Indian efforts at replicating the science parks did not originate from the HEIs but from a gov-

ernmental agency. There was no substantial increase in HEI–
enterprise interaction because of these efforts. In fact, among
the enterprises promoted under the science and technology entrepreneurship scheme, only 30 per cent of the entrepreneurs
had specialised qualifications. Similarly, a large number of
them were in low-tech areas often unrelated to their speciali-
sations (Mohan, 1992). Even the best among them — that is,
the award winners — never thought of locating their enterprises near a university or HEI. Finance and market considerations were naturally more important for them than process
and R&D.

* University companies for technology transfer are beset with
  several problems, which are unfamiliar to a normal manufac-
  turing/service company. These problems include the need for
  heavy development funds, long gestation periods with uncertain results, shortage of investment funds, irregular supply of
  raw materials (that is, new ideas) and the consequent inability
  to do strategic planning, lack of interest among academic staff
  for applied research and commercialisation of new ideas, unfavourable IPR and gainsharing policies, delays due to bureaucratic procedures and individualistic attitudes, callous indif-
  ference to market needs because of an unstated but strongly
  rooted belief in the superiority of technology over market, and
  so on. Also, these thorny problems are to be managed by a
  group of people who are not even equipped to manage a routine
  manufacturing/service company!

* Serious doubts have been expressed about the compatibility
  between academic/research competence and entrepreneurial
  competence. The study of academic entrepreneurs by Louis et
  al. (1989), whose conclusions are outlined above, is thought-
  provoking. Basic or theoretical research would call for independent, individualistic and divergent thinking capabilities.
  Application or implementation, on the other hand, would need
  more of convergent thinking and group efforts. Moreover, the
  academic can look at a process, material, phenomenon, etc., independent of what market needs it might serve, whereas for an
  entrepreneur, no technology, process, or product would be interesting unless a market need already existed or could be created. Thus, the orientation for academic research is unlikely to
  be compatible with the orientation for entrepreneurial activity.
  This may be why even the limited number of academic entre-

preneurs who were based on the UK science parks were less successful than their non-academic counterparts (Monck et al., 1988). An analysis of some recent commercial breakthroughs described in Nayak and Ketteringham (1986) has shown that hardly any of the breakthroughs originated with an academic researcher. It appears that although academic research may provide the basic idea for many a commercial product or service, the academic researcher may not be the best person for commercialising these ideas.

- The incompatibilities involved in academic institutions directly getting into entrepreneurial activities have been highlighted by McDonald (1987) also. It was pointed out that even in science parks there is hardly any interaction with universities, which is because the kind of information usually available in science and engineering departments are not much use to the firms. Besides, as no new technology is acceptable for commercial production until after substantial development, most technology transfers take place between firms who are constantly in touch with the market. Hence the role of universities in this is minimal. Finally, it was argued that there are high social costs in converting a first-rate academic into a third-rate entrepreneur!

- It is an observed fact that as far as educational qualifications are concerned, the entrepreneur is substantially less qualified than the academic. Though Monck et al. (1988) found that more than 50 per cent of the high-tech entrepreneurs were graduates, Storey (1982) cites other studies to show that among entrepreneurs in general, the proportion of graduates is as low as 5 per cent. Further, in a recent study of British entrepreneurs by the author (Manimala, 1993; Manimala and Pearson, 1995), it was found that entrepreneurs had relatively low levels of education, most of them being non-graduates. In this matter there was no difference between founders of high-growth ventures and low-growth ventures. It appears that there is an inverse correlation between university education and entrepreneurship! Conversely, there may be a self-selection process whereby the individuals who are interested in employment or professions seek to acquire better qualifications, whereas those who have entrepreneurial inclinations would perhaps refuse to proceed further with academic and theoretical studies.

CONCLUSION: THE NEED FOR A NEW PARADIGM

It is not the intention in this chapter to argue that scientific research and training at HEIs have nothing to do with the development and commercialisation of new products and technologies. There is no denying the fact that more and more commercial products and technologies are based on scientific research and inventions. What is questioned here is the existing model of HEI–enterprise interaction which assigns a direct and active role for the HEIs in the commercialisation of their research output or in the promotion of enterprises.

We have seen above that HEIs have difficulties with enterprise promotion both on account of the type of individuals they have as constituents and the kind of organisations they are. Studies on academic professionals have shown that they are the embodiment of attitudes, orientations and thought patterns which are far from appropriate for an entrepreneurial career (Louis et al., 1989; McDonald, 1987). As an organisation, an HEI is a loosely coupled system (Weick, 1976), which is required for generating independent thought and divergent ideas. Such a system, however, is not appropriate for enterprise creation or promotion. For the latter kind of activity, there is a need for a clan culture (Ouchi, 1980) which enables members of the group to share strong common beliefs and embark on joint action. Even in the cases of collaborative projects, entrepreneurs are not very interested in working with HEIs because the primary interest of the academic is in publishing the output, whereas the entrepreneur wants his projects to be closely guarded so as to ward off competition. During my interviews with a few Indian entrepreneurs on the subject of university–enterprise collaboration, it was pointed out that the most common service availed of from the universities is the testing service. This is because in India university services are still substantially low-priced. Joint research projects between universities and enterprises are very rare in India.

As it is obvious from the evidence represented in this chapter that the existing model of active involvement by HEIs is inadequate both on account of conceptual as well as practical reasons, it is necessary to look for alternative models or paradigms. In this connection, it is relevant to look at the findings of a recent study by the author (Manimala, 1992b) on the impact of environmental factors on the emergence of innovative entrepreneurs. It was found that the task environment did not have much influence on the formation of the innovative entrepreneur whereas the general environment did. The task environment consists of factors that have a specific impact on business activities such as:

- Customers including both distributors and users

- Suppliers and materials, labour, capital, technology and work space

- Competitors for markets and resources

- Regulatory groups including governmental agencies, unions and interfirm associations (Thompson, 1967).

The general environment consists of the economic, legal-political, socio-cultural and educational systems (Khandwalla, 1977). Universities and HEIs forming part of the educational system are important factors influencing this general environment and therefore have a vital role to play in the making of innovative entrepreneurs. However, if universities/HEIs are viewed primarily as a source of technology, they would be a part of the task environment whose influence on the making of innovative entrepreneurs is observed to be minimal. In other words, while a favourable task environment would definitely channel the energies of a large number of entrepreneurial individuals into the concerned field, the converse is unlikely to be true. That is, a favourable task environment is not a sufficient condition for creating the entrepreneurial motive and competencies in individuals. The latter is mainly a function of the general environment. In fact, the entrepreneurial individual can, to some extent, compensate for the inadequacies of the task environment through their innovative actions. Viewed against this and the reported unsuccessful attempts of HEIs to create a favourable task environment for entrepreneurship, it appears that it is more appropriate for the HEIs to focus on the general environment.

The new paradigm is necessitated because the assumptions on which the old one was based have not found much empirical support. Hence the old set of assumptions will have to be replaced by a new set, which could be formulated as follows:

1. The primary objective of HEIs is to create and disseminate knowledge. Though the applications of such knowledge can generate commercial activities and wealth, HEIs would be better off leaving this part to other agencies rather than getting directly involved.

2. Converting inventions into commercial products requires heavy investment in terms of time as well as money which is often beyond the capacity of an HEI or a small enterprise. Moreover, small enterprises and academic institutions are often unable to absorb the high degree of uncertainty associated with the commercial development of an invention.

3. It is a myth that smaller organisations are better suited for all kinds of innovations. Similarly, their ability to generate sustained growth in employment and wealth is also questionable. Hence the HEI–enterprise collaboration may not produce the material benefits to society as is often claimed.

4. Even though innovative products are sometimes brought into the market as a result of "technology push", the more common route is likely to be that of "market pull". In fact, for the entrepreneur, the most important consideration is the market, not technology or process.

5. There is a mistaken notion that entrepreneurs look towards HEIs as an important source of new commercial ideas. Similarly, they have no special preference to be located near an HEI. Nor do they think that interaction with HEIs could be an important stimulus for the growth of their enterprises.

6. Academics and researchers are generally not interested in entrepreneurial pursuits even if the latter are based on their own inventions. And, in the rare cases where academics become entrepreneurs, their performance is poorer than their non-academic counterparts.

These new set of "assumptions" which enjoy a fair degree of empirical support call for a new paradigm of HEI–enterprise collaboration, wherein HEIs are to be treated not primarily as a source of new commercial ideas but as a source of skilled and entrepreneurial individuals. In other words, HEIs can contribute a great deal towards the development of technical skills and entrepreneurial orientation in their graduates. However, if HEIs get directly and actively involved in the commercialisation of inventions and the creation or stimulation of enterprises, they would be dissipating their focus and thereby engaging in a less productive use of their resources.

References

Breheny, M.J. and McQuaid, R. (1987), "The Development of the United Kingdom's Major Centre of High Technology Industry", in M.J. Breheny and R. McQuaid (eds.), *The Development of High Technology Industries*, London: Croom Helm.

Cambridge City Council (1986), *Employment Development Strategy: High-Tech and Conventional Manufacturing Industry*, Cambridge: Cambridge City Council.

Currie, J. (1985), *Science Parks in Britain: Their Role for the Late 1980s*, Cardiff: CSP Economic Publications.

Dalton, I. (1985), "The Objectives and Development of the Heriot-Watt University Research Park", in J.M. Gibb (ed.), *Science Parks and Innovation Centres: Their Economic and Social Impact*, Amsterdam: Elsevier.

Economist Intelligence Unit (1985), *Universities and Industry*, Special Report No. 213, London: EIU.

Eul, F.M. (1985), "Science Parks and Innovation Centres: Property, the Unconsidered Element", in J.M. Gibb (ed.), *Science Parks and Innovation Centres: Their Economic and Social Impact*, Amsterdam: Elsevier.

Harvey, K.A. (1994), "The Impact of Institutional Intellectual Property Policy on the Propensity of Individual UK Universities to Incubate NTBFs", in R.P. Oakey (ed.), *New Technology-Based Firms in the 1990s*, London: Paul Chapman, pp. 136–148.

Hauschildt, J. and Steinkuhler, R.H. (1994), "The Role for Science and Technology Parks in NTBF Development", in R.P. Oakey (ed.), *New Technology-Based Firms in the 1990s*, London: Paul Chapman, pp. 181–191.

Keeble, D. and Kelly, T. (1986), "New Firms and High Technology Industry in the United Kingdom: The Case of Computer Electronics" in D. Keeble and E. Wever (eds.), *New Firms and Regional Development in Europe*, London: Croom Helm.

Khandwalla, P.N. (1977), *Design of Organisations*, New York: Harcourt Brace Jovanovich.

Louis, K.S., Blumenthal, D., Gluck, M.E. and Stoto, M.A. (1989), "Entrepreneurs in Academe: An Exploration of Behaviours Among Life Scientists", *Administrative Science Quarterly*, 34, March, pp. 110–131.

Lowe, J. (1985), "Science Parks in the UK", *Lloyds Bank Review*, No. 156, April, pp. 31–42.

Manimala, M.J. (1988), "Managerial Heuristics of Pioneering-Innovative Entrepreneurs: An Exploratory Study", Unpublished Doctoral Dissertation, Indian Institute of Management, Ahmedabad.

Manimala, M.J. (1992a), "Interorganisational Collaboration for Technology Development: A Comparative Analysis of a British Case and an Indian Case", Paper presented at the International Seminar on Innovation and Technology Transfer: European and Indian Perspectives, Hyderabad, April 22–24.

Manimala, M.J. (1992b), "Innovative Entrepreneurship: Testing the Theory of Environmental Determinism" in B.L. Maheshwari (ed.), *Innovations in Management for Development*, New Delhi, Tata McGraw-Hill, pp. 100–118.

Manimala, M.J. (1992c), "Entrepreneurial Heuristics: A Comparison between High PI (Pioneering-Innovative) and Low PI Ventures" *Journal of Business Venturing*, Vol. 7, No. 6, November, pp. 477–504.

Manimala, M.J. (1993), "Growth Venture Policies and their Relationship with Entrepreneur Characteristics", Unpublished MBSc Thesis, Manchester Business School, Manchester.

Manimala, M.J. and Pearson, A.W. (1991), "Hoyle Marine Limited and the T-Disc Oil Skimmer, Case Study on University–Enterprise Technology Transfer", Manchester: MIMTECH-LES.

Manimala, M.J. and Pearson, A.W. (1995), "Growth Venture Policies and Founder Characteristics: Evidence from British High-Growth and Low-Growth Ventures", Paper presented at the EFER 6th Conference, Gent, November, pp. 16–17.

McDonald, S. (1987), "British Science Parks: Reflections on the Politics of High Technology" *R&D Management*, Vol. 17, No. 1, pp. 25–37.

Mitra, J., Cooley, M. and Lakin, C. (1993), "Science Parks and Entrepreneurial Activity: Training at the Cutting Edge", Paper presented at the International Conference on Entrepreneurship and R&D, Hyderabad, January 4–7.

Mitra, J. and Jinkinson, R. (1995), "Science Parks and Research and Development: The Entrepreneurial Experience", Paper presented at the International Conference on Entrepreneurship and R&D, Hyderabad, January 4–7.

Mohan, C. (1992), "A Decade of NSTEDB: Entrepreneurship Development and Employment Generation", *Science-Tech Entrepreneur*, July–September, pp. 5–9.

Monck, C.S.P. (1986), "The Growth of Science Parks: A Progress Report", in C.S.P. Monck (ed.), *Science Parks: Their Contribution to Economic Growth*, UK Science Park Association.

Monck, C.S.P. (1987), "Science Park Tenants and Their Growth Potential and Policy Implications", in H. Sunman (ed.), *Science Parks and the Growth of Technology Based Enterprises*, UK Science Park Association.

Monck, C.S.P., Porter, R.B., Quintas, P.R., Storey, D.J. and Wynarczyk, P. (1988), *Science Parks and the Growth of High Technology Firms*, London: Croom Helm.

Morse, R.S. (1976), "The Role of New Technical Enterprises in the US Economy", Report of the Technical Advisory Board to the Secretary of Commerce, Washington DC.

Nayak, P.R. and Ketteringham, J.M. (1986), *Breakthroughs*, Rawson Associates.

Oakey, R.P. (1991), "High Technology Small Firms: Their Potential for Rapid Industrial Growth", *International Small Business Journal*, Vol. 9, No. 4, pp. 30–42.

Oakey, R.P. (1994), "Placing the Contributions in Context", in R.P. Oakey (ed.), *New Technology-Based Firms in the 1990s*, London: Paul Chapman.

Oakey, R.P. (1995), *High Technology New Firms: Variable Barriers to Growth*, London: Paul Chapman.

Ouchi, W.G. (1980), "Markets, Bureaucracies, and Clans", *Administrative Science Quarterly*, Vol. 25, No. 2, pp. 129–141.

Pavitt, K., Robson, M. and Townsend, J. (1987), "The Size Distribution of Innovating Firms in the UK, 1945–1983", *Journal of Industrial Economics*, Vol. 35, pp. 297–306.

Piramal, G. and Herdeck, M. (1985), *India's Industrialists*, Vols. I and II, Washington DC: Three Continents Press.

Rothwell, R. (1986), "The Role of Small Firms in Technological Innovation", in J. Curran, J. Stanworth and D. Watkins (eds.), *The Survival of the Small Firm*, Vol. 2, Aldershot: Gower.

Rothwell, R. (1994), "The Changing Nature of the Innovation Process: Implications for SMEs", in R.P. Oakey (ed.), *New Technology-Based Firms in the 1990s*, London: Paul Chapman.

Rothwell, R. and Zegveld, W. (1982), *Innovation and the Small and Medium Sized Firm*, London, Frances Pinter.

Segal, Q. (1985), *The Cambridge Phenomenon: The Growth of High Technology Industry in a University Town*, Cambridge: Brand Brothers.

Southern, P.H.S. (1986), "The Experience of English Estates in the Development of United Kingdom Science Parks", Paper presented at the Seminar on Science Parks and Technology Complexes, OECD, Paris.

Storey, D.J. (1982), *Entrepreneurship and the New Firm*, London: Croom Helm.

Storey, D.J. (1985), *Small Firms and Regional Economic Development: Britain, Ireland and the United States*, Cambridge: Cambridge University Press.

Storey, D.J. and Strange, A. (1992), "Where Are They Now? Some Changes in Firms Located on United Kingdom Science Parks in 1986", *New Technology, Work and Employment*, Vol. 7, No. 1, pp. 15–28.

Thompson, J.D. (1967), *Organisations in Action*, New York: McGraw-Hill.

Weick, K.E. (1976), "Educational Organisations as Loosely Coupled Systems", *Administrative Science Quarterly*, Vol. 21, No. 1, pp. 1–19.

Westhead, P. and Storey, D. (1994), *An Assessment of Firms Located on and off Science Parks in the United Kingdom*, London: DTI/HMSO.

Williams, B.R. (1985), "The Role of Universities and Research Institutions in the Development of High Technology Based New Firms", Paper presented at the UK–German Symposium on High Technology Based Firms, Cambridge, 9–10 April.

7

INNOVATIVE NETWORKS IN REGIONAL ECONOMIES: ENHANCING INFRASTRUCTURES FOR TECHNOLOGY CREATION AND TRANSFER

Patries Boekholt[*]

INTRODUCTION: REGIONAL INNOVATION ON THE RISE

With the rise in globalisation, many argue that national and regional economies have shrunk in importance: competition is taking place on a global scale; multinational companies are relocating their activities to those parts of the world that suit their requirements best; capital investments are moving across borders more easily. All these developments appear to diminish the impact of national and regional intervention in the economy. Others argue, however, that the contrary is the case: with capital flowing internationally, economies that have specific factors of competitive advantage can attract new or expanding industrial activity. Indeed companies are more likely to move their business functions, whether this is production, research, distribution or administration, to those locations that fit best with their market needs or where added value is the highest. The process of global sourcing has made firms more aware of the competitive advantages of particular nations or regions. Some analysts go as far as to announce the end of the nation state (Ohmae, 1996). Empirical analyses have shown that globalisation is not as strong as Ohmae (and many others) suggests. Some have refined the generally accepted concept of globalisation. They argue that the idea of the global corporation is a myth. Analysing the world's largest companies shows that they are still very much rooted in their country of origin. Nevertheless, the increased global competition is affect-

[*] This article is based on research undertaken at TNO Centre for Technology and Policy Studies in the Netherlands. Presently the author works in the same field of research for Technopolis, Brighton (UK) and Amsterdam (NL).

ing on internationally operating companies and markets, with
consumer electronics and the automotive industry as the most
obvious examples. Regional economies are influenced by these
changes as much as national economies. Amin and Thrift (1995)
describe two positions in the globalisation versus region debate:

> Thus while some observers perceive globalization in its various
> manifestations as a threat to local diversity and local autonomy,
> others argue that it rather represents a change in the context in
> which local development paths are articulated.

Whichever trend is more dominant, the effect will be that the regional economies are developing a richer mix of global players —
SMEs expanding their cross-border business and SMEs working
on a local scale only.

The growing awareness of this increased international competition is also appearing on the agendas of regional policy makers.
Innovation policy has become a new weapon in the intra-national
and intra-regional competition.

Several developments have led to the emergence of the region
as an active economic entity with its own innovation policy:

- There is a growing understanding of the innovation process as
  an interactive learning process. Following this approach the
  direct environment in which firms — particularly small firms
  — operate, is vital for the development of learning capabilities.
  The institutional environment where firms have easy access to
  innovation support services, informal and formal contacts with
  other firms, availability of skilled labour, are all aspects of the
  firm's learning environment. For these sources of innovation,
  proximity does play a role. It is not surprising that a large proportion of regional innovation actions are aimed at the establishment of links between firms, knowledge suppliers and intermediaries.

- There are now more realistic expectations in the regions with
  regard to the economic potential of attracting (foreign) investment from high-tech and high-growth industries and "building
  high-tech fantasies". At the same time we can see a return to
  an appreciation of the importance of innovation in indigenous
  firms. Regional authorities, especially those in less favoured
  regions, are increasingly aware that offering financial incentives for industrial investment alone is not sufficient for sustainable economic development. Embedding these firms in the

local economy and creating synergy between indigenous firms and the investees is now on many regional politicians' agendas.

- In Europe, the European Commission Structural Funds have shifted their focus from infrastructural and general economic activities to development strategies for regional innovation. Regions have more room to by-pass their national governments and develop their own policies and activities. However, this also has negative effects concerning the crowding out of regional budgets (Steiner, 1995).

- Discussions on subsidiarity in the policy debate has reinforced the argument for designing and implementing policies at the most appropriate level. The regional policy level is increasingly seen as the appropriate level for diffusion-type innovation activities.

NETWORKING AS A VEHICLE FOR INNOVATION

Regional innovation policy is increasingly focused on building network infrastructures for technological support, to enhance start-ups and inter-firm collaboration, and to promote research and development. Cooke (1995) refers to this new approach to regional development as the idea of *networked regional innovation architecture*.

An influential contribution, which emphasised the importance of networking and clusters of related industries, came from Michael Porter (1990) with his book *The Competitive Advantage of Nations*. In his view industries in a particular nation or region have competitive advantage if they are embedded in a wide and deep network. A well-developed, dense network consists not only of inter-firm links within a particular industry, but also with related industries, specialised knowledge centres, education facilities, innovation support agencies and direct links with clients. In an institutional context where co-operative public and private relations can create an environment in which firms find stimuli to upgrade their activities through access to training, finance, business services and sources of knowledge, they are likely to perform better. Many scholars in regional development have expressed their amazement at the public attention that Michael Porter received when he (re)introduced the notion of clusters in 1990. They rightly point out that these concepts were common goods in the regional development literature when describing industrial districts and French *filières*.

Following Porter's line of thinking we can define clusters in a very broad manner: a group of firms, knowledge centres and innovation support organisations with a functional affinity, which co-operate to achieve new market strategies, product or process innovations (Jacobs, 1995). Co-operation can be formal, — that is, with an explicit contract (for example, a supplier contract, a joint venture) — or informal. In the latter case we may think of forms of informal knowledge transfer through relations with "related" industries (that is industries which have no direct horizontal or vertical relationships, but which may share some "economies of scope", such as similar technologies, similar markets).

A crucial element of clusters is inter-firm networks. These can be either horizontal or vertical. Horizontal networks consist of firms within the same sector sharing a technological base, a common market, or purchasing channels. Vertical networks are those of users, suppliers and selected services. Sophisticated buyers need competitive suppliers and vice versa. Governments can stimulate and facilitate the interconnectedness of firms by supporting these co-operation networks. It is however important to have dynamic networks in which firms co-operate in rivalry. Historically, many clusters have declined because of their conservatism. Here the discussion initiated by Patrizio Bianchi and Lee Miller (1992) about progressive and regressive coalitions may be helpful:

> progressive coalitions are capable of filtering various stimuli in order to use what they see as most promising and to discard the rest. . . . A regressive coalition does not have this filtering mechanism, which is more costly both in terms of time and human resources.

Although the relationships in the network should be based on mutual trust, exchange of knowledge and long-term commitment, the outlook of the firm should still be towards the world market (Boekholt, et al., 1993).

When a network of firms is based on a traditional sectoral specialisation in which different elements of the system (for example, specialised suppliers, tool makers, machine builders and services) are present in a relatively restricted geographical area, one speaks of clusters or specialised industrial districts. Thus the concept of clusters can encompass both a spatial component, relating to a regional or local basis *and* a non-spatial component, sectoral or technological in focus. However, firms within a specific cluster do not necessarily need to be linked or networked in a direct co-operative relationship. Without having direct firm-to-firm associations, there can be a dense network based on a common institutional base and infrastructure provision.

THE REGIONAL DIMENSION OF NETWORKS

Examples of very strong clustered industries can often be found in geographically concentrated areas: Silicon Valley, Emilia Romagna, Baden Württemberg (see Porter, 1990; Cooke, 1995; Cooke and Morgan, 1993). Particularly in the last two cases local and regional government policies played a crucial role in supporting and enhancing the network building. Porter stresses the importance of the influence of proximity and geographical concentration on improvement and innovation:

> Rivals located close to each other will tend to be jealous and emotional competitors. Universities located near a group of competitors will be most likely to notice the industry, perceive it to be important and respond accordingly. In turn competitors are more likely to fund and support local university activity. Suppliers located nearby will be best positioned for regular interchange and co-operation with industry research and development efforts. Sophisticated customers located nearby offer the best possibilities for transmitting information, engaging in regular interchange about emerging needs and technologies and demanding extraordinary service and product performance. Geographic concentration of an industry acts as a strong magnet to attract talented people and other factors [of competitive advantage] to it (Porter, 1990: 157).

A series of studies on industrial sectors in the Netherlands inspired by Porter's approach analysed the factors of competitive advantage of these sectors in the Netherlands (Jacobs, Boekholt and Zegveld, 1990). The Dutch studies found that industries with a strong competitive position on the world market were often firmly rooted in a particular region. Determinants of competitive advantage were based on intensive networks with suppliers and customers, a specialised research infrastructure and in some cases collective distribution channels combined with fierce competition on the firm level.

CLUSTERS IN THE NETHERLANDS: THE CASE OF THE FLOWER INDUSTRY

At first sight, the tourist image of the Netherlands as a country of tulips and cheese seems to bear no relation to industrial networks. However, in the Netherlands the tradition of networking, co-operation, and setting up of joint support services originates from exactly these industries with a background in agriculture and horticulture. A striking example of such a cluster is the Dutch cut-flower industry (Jacobs, Boekholt and Zegveld, 1990; Boekholt et al., 1993; Boekholt, 1994).

With its share of approximately 65 per cent of the world export market, the cut-flower industry is the most competitive industry in the Netherlands. The industry has organised itself in a very dense and wide cluster of business activities, from specialised banking to distribution, centres for research, development and demonstration, vocational training facilities and advisory centres. In this sense, this industry could be seen as a miniature system of innovation. Figure 7.1 shows the main elements in this system and how they relate to each other.

Small family-based firms of flower growers

Flower growing takes place in three separate geographically concentrated areas with a closely knit community of families owning small and medium-sized businesses in horticulture. Two areas in particular are well known for its horticulture, the Westland near The Hague and the area around Aalsmeer near Amsterdam. There are strong cultural, social and religious ties within those communities who live and work in a number of villages and towns within a 20 kilometre range. Because of their social ties there are many informal networks. In addition to the many forms of co-operation, rivalry between the growers is still fierce. There is a strong sense of competition to produce the best or an original variety of flowers. A flower grower today has to be highly skilled, not only in the basics of flower growing and trading, but also in computerised climate, watering and feeding control systems, electronic communication with the auctions, and adapting their production process to environmental regulations.

FIGURE 7.1: FLOWER CLUSTER IN THE NETHERLANDS

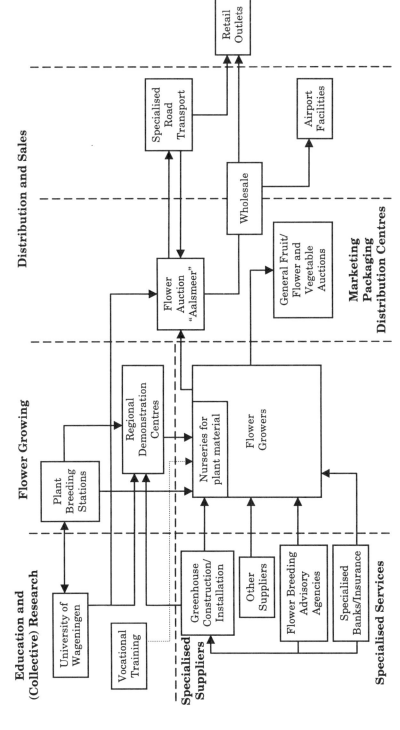

Some growers specialise in producing the nursery stock. These growers play a very crucial role since their plant material is the basis of later quality products. Some concern has been raised in the growers' community because these specialists are exporting their material to foreign competitors.

Specialised and general auctions

The linchpin in this network are the flower auctions. The auctions not only operate as a sophisticated "marketplace", they also organise the distribution between growers and traders through electronic and physical channels, and co-ordinate marketing activities for the whole sector. These co-operative organisations were set up in the 1950s to protect the individual growers from the increasingly powerful supermarket chains and other large clients that were in a position to put pressure on individual clients. Through the sales in the auction, a fee is collected from the growers which is used to finance collective marketing and research activities. The selling techniques used at the auctions make it possible to distinguish between products from particular growers. This encourages competition on the basis of quality, rather than on costs. This has proved a crucial factor in the drive for innovation. In the comparable industry of tomato growing, which uses similar technologies and distribution channels, auction sales are made on the basis of price. This has had such an impact on the quality of the product that some years ago German consumers aired their complaints in the media, urging people to boycott Dutch tomatoes.

The auctions have commissioned research at the Wageningen Agricultural University to improve the quality of the complete product chain, particularly with regard to distribution and transport from auction to retail outlet. By reducing contamination from disease and through quality control measures, the shelf-life of flowers can be increased significantly.

Specialised supplier industry and service sector

The industry depends on a range of specialised suppliers; the most important inputs they provide are greenhouse construction and the installation of climate, water and feeding controls. These suppliers are located in the same villages and towns as the growers and supply custom-made greenhouses for the growers. Constructors and installation companies have to collaborate to deliver a complete product. Greenhouse engineering companies often mediate between growers, constructors and installation companies so that they can design the complete system. Greenhouse construction companies make use of the services of the Netherlands Organisation for Industrial Applied Research (TNO), which has a specialised unit to test and certificate their products. TNO also undertakes contract research for a number of these companies, often in a collaborative project, to test new designs and develop CAD systems. More fundamental research in greenhouse construction is done at the Centre for Agricultural Research (DLO), a publicly funded research centre. Presently these Centres are being restructured as contract research organisations.

Bank branches in the region are also geared to servicing the horticulture sector. They are well aware of the specific investment patterns and needs of the growers who have to make huge capital investments when renewing their greenhouses. Similar service industries are insurance companies who specialise in insuring greenhouses and assessing the risk of damage from storms and hail showers.

Specialised transport and distribution companies and facilities

Traders transport the flowers using specially equipped trucks. These trucks can cover a range of approximately 500 kilometres from the Dutch auctions. They are relatively small so that deliveries can be made directly to city centre shops. To ensure fast transport to Japan, testing facilities to detect plant diseases and insects have been built at Schiphol Airport, where Japanese inspectors can check each batch. Large wholesale companies are having an increasing influence on the trade because of the scale of their purchases.

Basic and applied research and technology transfer activities

The chain of knowledge creation and technology transfer covers all areas from fundamental research (mainly at the Wageningen University of Agriculture), through applied research (in experimental "laboratories") and demonstration in Regional Research Centres. Wageningen engages in bio-technology research into new varieties of plant material and seedlings. The aim of the research is to make plants more resistant to diseases and insects in order to reduce the amount of pesticides needed. The experimental laboratories analyse the optimal growing conditions. The growers are not the only users of the R&D facilities; suppliers such as the specialised greenhouse constructors can also make use of the experimental laboratories to test new constructions or materials. For instance, there are constant experiments in greenhouse construction, using various combinations of light construction methods and larger working surfaces under the glass roofs. The experimental laboratories also test new developments in glass and climate control, feeding methods and so on. The largest one is situated in the Westland, close to the growers and their suppliers. The results of the growth process under different experimental situations is shown to the growers in regional demonstration centres. The flower growers are very active in exchanging knowledge through voluntary study groups which tackle certain topics concerning the growing process.

The role of government

The flower cluster possesses a high degree of self-sufficiency and a strong self-identification. Public intervention was previously focused on creating the research infrastructure, educational facilities and advisory centres. In the last few years many of these facilities have been privatised. The government has, however, provided an indirect but vital supporting role to the Dutch horticulture industry by providing low-cost natural gas to specific branches of industry. Vocational training is provided, but since much of the labour needed in the greenhouses is low-skilled, its impact is not significant.

Knowledge and innovation flows

Although the flower-growing sector could not easily be identified as a high-technology sector, the firms do apply many state-of-the-art technologies, custom-made for their sector. Constant technology transfer throughout the "knowledge chain" is a critical factor for success.

The flows of knowledge and innovation can be found:

- Vertically between the growers and their suppliers and between the growers and the traders mediated through the auctions. For instance, there is collaboration between greenhouse constructors, equipment installers and growers in the design of new greenhouses, which are partly mass produced, partly custom-built. Government regulations on environmental protection are one reason for the need for constant adaptation of greenhouses, installations and breeding methods. Specialised engineering consultancies are increasingly operating as mediators between growers and greenhouse constructors.

- Horizontally between the growers in the exchange of experience and knowledge on breeding methods. Tacit knowledge exchange is the most important vehicle, not only through organised meetings but also through a tight social community in a regionally concentrated area. Religion and family ties play a role which should not be underestimated.

- Between the knowledge centres and the growers through contract research and demonstration facilities.

- Between growers, those in the support infrastructure and vocational training centres.

- Between the auctions and traders on the issue of quality improvements in distribution.

- Government regulation on the environment is a major driving force for innovations in greenhouse construction (waste water management, energy saving) and growing methods (reductions in insecticides and pesticides).

This example shows the multiple flows of knowledge and incentives that keeps the industry at its competitive edge through continuous innovation. It shows the small-scale system of innovation that has been created around a cluster of sectors, not only in the primary industry of cut flowers but also greenhouse construction, vegetable growing, specialised distribution and transport. There are, however, some threats to the competitive position of the sector:

- Increased international competition from countries like Israel, Colombia, and Kenya.

- The environmental damage caused by the horticulture industry is considerable. Pesticides and herbicides are used in large quantities although developments with environmentally friendly methods are spreading. Stricter regulations on waste disposal of these chemicals have at the same time prompted the industry to come up with alternatives, and forced them to make large investments.

- The sector is concentrated in highly urbanised parts of the Netherlands. Given the scarcity of space, serious political discussions are taking place to transfer the complete industry to the more spacious regions in the north-east of the country. Many analysts fear that this will disturb the delicate social structure that has developed over the decades.

CAN CLUSTERS BE CREATED?

The success stories of Silicon Valley, Baden Württemberg and Emilia Romagna have inspired policy makers, authorities engaged in regional development, and technology transfer experts to try to imitate the model in other locations. Various empirical studies have shown how much these success stories rely on networking between firms (Cooke and Morgan, 1995). In Baden Württemberg and Emilia Romagna, institutional networks between companies and a wide set of innovation support infrastructures are put forward as the key to their development.

In the case of Silicon Valley informal networks between innovative entrepreneurs were a key factor.

> The vitality and resilience of Silicon Valley over time and the achievement of its level of excellence were only possible because the Valley itself created social networks among its engineers, managers and entrepreneurs, generating a creative synergy that transformed the drive for business competition into the desire to co-operate for technological innovations (Castells and Hall, 1994: 28).

Universities played a double role as source of information and as providers of highly skilled labour. All these cases, including the Dutch flower cluster, have a history of bottom-up development of indigenous companies triggering the process of network development.

These examples are being followed by regional authorities that have less pronounced specialisation patterns. The question is: can these networks of interlinked firms, knowledge centres, suppliers and services be created? More and more policy makers are setting up initiatives with this objective in mind. Very often these are attempts to create high-tech poles around centres of research. Castells and Hall (1994), who have compared the world's most significant technopoles, have shown how difficult it is to successfully pursue this as planned strategy. It also takes a long time (they estimate 15–25 years) for impacts to become evident. Another common approach is to build clusters around foreign-based multinational companies to counter the problem of these companies operating in a footloose position and failing to build on the strengths (existing or upgraded) of the region in which they have invested. Numerous attempts are being made to create top-down networks. A review of policies designed to support innovative networks in Europe showed an increasing number of public initiatives in this. The review showed a wide scope of activities ranging from initiatives to create completely new networks of collaborative firms to those aimed at renewing existing, often sectorally based, network infrastructures. All the examples of successful clusters show they are not created overnight, it is often a long-term historical process. Even Silicon Valley clusters have gradually expanded to involve related industries, suppliers, knowledge sources, distribution channels and so on. Initiatives, whether public or private, aimed at establishing new clusters from scratch will always be very difficult to implement (Castells and Hall, 1994).

The role of universities in these networks is not always very significant. One of the most urgent topics concerning research–industry links is the problem of bridging the gap between research and the business culture. From the industry perspective research organisations are not able to understand the need for (technological) solutions to specific problems. Working for large companies on big research projects seems less problematic than working with SMEs with highly diverse and short-term R&D needs. Identification of possible clusters of firms with common knowledge issues can offer a strategy for research centres and universities to operate in innovative networks instead of in bilateral partnerships. Universities and research centres can play a vital role in strengthening existing or potential innovative networks, offering access to knowledge and a pool of human resources. This implies a process of mutual understanding and trust-building both from the enterprises and the universities. The match between the available expertise and the demand for knowledge is not self-evident. As Castells and Hall (1994: 230) point out:

> our studies also show that it takes a very special kind of university, and a very specific set of linkages to industrial and commer-

cial development, for a university to be able to play the role it often claims to play in the information-based economy.

BUILDING INNOVATIVE NETWORKS IN THE NETHERLANDS

Recent shifts in Dutch innovation policy shows a clear inspiration from the cluster concept: instead of direct subsidies to either firms or research centres, new public support programmes demand that networks between several firms are formed, together with research centres or universities, to formulate an R&D project. TNO, the largest applied industrial research organisation in the Netherlands, is focusing its strategy for the future around present and potential clusters of firms for which collective actions can be undertaken.

Government interest in inter-firm networks as a policy concept was particularly roused when some of the Dutch "National Champions — medium-sized, internationally operating firms — ran into serious trouble. One of them was DAF, manufacturers of trucks and vans. Due to the collapse of the European market for trucks and vans, DAF had to close down factories and lay off many of its employees. The problems with DAF triggered the discussion on the relevance of "clusters" in the Netherlands. Policy makers stated their concerns that with the closing down of DAF, a whole cluster of suppliers would have to close down as well. This was put forward as a key argument for government support to rescue the company and its cluster.

Currently, public initiatives to stimulate, create and facilitate networks originate at national and regional level. National programmes are implemented centrally and/or involve regionally based Innovation Centres, a network of intermediaries set up by the government in the 1980s. Regional authorities have also increased their activities, often backed up by funding from the European Union.

We can distinguish four types of networking activities in the Netherlands:

1. **Horizontal networks** of firms from the same sector, such as the flower industry. Public action in this area is not directly aimed at networking but more towards supporting sector-based innovation support facilities, such as technology centres. Initiatives come from the firms themselves, as will be discussed below.

2. **Vertical networks** between suppliers and their contractors. A public initiative to support this type of activity is the national Supplier–Contractor Programme. Companies, together with a number of their suppliers, can apply for funding for technological collaboration projects. The objective is to increase the competitiveness of both the contractor and a circle of its suppliers, facilitated through network building. The funding concentrates on one-off projects, so there is no guarantee that the network will persist beyond that funding.

3. **Cross-sector networks** aimed at specific (technological) projects or new product/market combinations. Public initiatives in this field can be found at regional level where Innovation Centres have set up Industrial Partnership Circles and "interweaving" projects. The first initiative starts with series of informal meetings, (seminars, information meetings) between entrepreneurs from all types of businesses. Getting to know each other is a first step in the process of possible networking relations. The Innovation Centres can subsequently support firms in taking a second step: defining collaboration projects between interested parties. A more hands-on approach of creating collaborations can be found in interweaving projects. Here the Innovation Centre's advisors actively look for potential partnerships between firms with different core competencies. The Centres have created a database with core competencies of firms and their interest for collaboration. They are brought together and after a few meetings it is judged whether the network "works" and the participating firms can work out a new product/market combination.

4. **"Star-shaped" networks** around one major original equipment manufacturer (OEM) and its suppliers; An example is the Knowledge Intensive Clustering (KIC) project initiated by the national government. This example will be discussed in more detail below.

Alongside these specific initiatives the Dutch national government is remodelling its traditional R&D instruments in what it calls a "co-operation facility". The new element is that "clustering" is now the integrating concept of business-oriented technology incentive schemes. Most business-oriented R&D subsidy instruments will be replaced to fit this formula. There are two objectives behind this "co-operation facility". Firstly, it should increase co-operation among businesses themselves. This could involve firms within a product chain contributing towards integrated chain management. Secondly, it should increase co-operation between the private sector and research institutes. To qualify for a grant, collaboration projects must represent a new strategic collaboration in the field of R&D between at least one company with a "steering role" and one research institute. In addition, they must develop some form of advanced technology in international terms. The concept of a cluster in this approach is thus at the micro-level of a few collaborating firms.

The model for this co-operation facility or scheme has not yet been elaborated. In a press release in June 1995 the Minister of Economic Affairs announced that the estimated budget would be approximately 40 million ECU.

Knowledge Intensive Clustering (KIC): A Typical Example of Public Network Involvement

In the KIC initiative, a cluster of suppliers with complementary assets is set up around one large or middle-sized manufacturing company. The supported projects must involve joint development of a new product. The objective is to increase the capability of local suppliers for high quality product development, to turn them into strategic partners for the OEM and to involve them in the production of the newly developed products. The network is developed jointly by the OEM and the Innovation Centre who look for the most appropriate local suppliers. The central government, that is, the Ministry of Economic Affairs, has had a large influence in choosing which OEMs were to be involved in the KIC projects. Some experts state that they have opted for a limited number of "national champions" who traditionally have a strong relationship with the Ministry.

An example of such a KIC cluster is the one developed around the photocopier manufacturer Océ. This company is developing new types of colour copiers and printers. Joint development projects with groups of local suppliers are formed for modules of the new products. The early involvement and combination of expertise from different types of supplier is thought to speed up the development process. Océ is very positive about the project and is now contracting out more of its product development than before. However, one of the company's leading executives has stated in the press that the local suppliers still cannot reach the required quality and Océ cannot afford to have more patience with the local suppliers than with global ones. It remains to be seen what the long-term effect of the network will be and if the local suppliers will also be successful in acquiring the production contracts for these new products.

Private Networking Initiatives: A Bottom-up Approach

Networking initiatives do not just come from government: Dutch firms themselves are also actively involved in setting up collaboration through networks. Survival is an important element triggering these activities. One example is a group of shipbuilding companies in the north of the country who have joined forces in order to accept large contracts. The ships are built in modules and each company agrees to build one part of that module. One of the companies then assembles these ships either in their own shipyard or at the location of the customer, which could be in, say, South-East Asia.

One way to support vertical networking is through improving relations between contractors and supplying industries. Again this should not lead to the network as a "safe haven", but as a stepping stone for the supplier to improve its competitiveness on the world market. A recent example of such an approach is the initiative to set up the Twente Sub-Contractors Association (TCA), aimed at enhancing co-operation between subcontractors in the region. The Twente region is faced with serious problems due to the disappearance of the textile industry, one of its major regional industrial activities. The supply industries in the region, often machines and tool firms, were left without their customers and had to redefine their strategies. Those that survived resorted to the general supply market (Praat and van Bemmel, 1994). A large share of the remaining customers in the region, mostly original equipment manufacturers, suffered severe losses in the 1980s. In the process of returning to core business and lean production they demand not only higher quality from their suppliers, but also the capability to manufacture integrated systems instead of components. Only a few of the supplying SMEs were capable of developing from a "jobber" to a main supplier. The TCA initiative, set up as a private company, is designed to bring together the complementary expertise of individual suppliers and thus acquire large sub-contracting projects from the equipment manufacturers. The TMG acts as a "lean" main supplier operating on the Dutch market for complex and multi-functional supply systems Although the firms play an active role in organising these networks within the region, outside catalysts were needed to set up the initiative. The initiative was taken by the Metalworking Trade Association together with TNO, a public-private research organisation. Subsequently the initiative was supported by the Regional Development Agency. So a mix of private–public partnership set off the spark, but it was the economic pressure of having to innovate that made the regional firms enthusiastic to participate. The initiative has only been running for several months so it is not possible yet to reflect on the results. So far, approximately 60 firms have joined the TCA as shareholders.

The crucial difference between this approach and that of the previously described Océ cluster is that here the initiative was taken by the suppliers themselves, who have given their co-operation a formal status by setting up a share-holding company. Given the large number of firms involved and the size of the out-sourcing projects, should this collaboration prove to be successful, the economic impact will be large.

CONCLUSIONS

The Dutch cases of the flower industry cluster and the Twente Sub-Contractors Association initiative, show a large degree of self-sufficiency in which firms play the most active role. We have also put suggested that these clusters need a long time to grow and widen. The almost complete system of innovation in the flower industry took decades to develop. This is also confirmed by documented experiences of other regions with successful industrial clusters. An active role taken by public organisations, including universities, to boost regional economic development by means of creating clusters or networks, will have the best chances of success if it is geared to a bottom-up process in the regional industrial community.

References

Amin, Ash and Thrift, Nigel (1995), *Globalization, Institutions and Regional Development in Europe*, Oxford: Oxford University Press.

Bianchi, P. and Miller, Lee (1992), "Systems of Innovation and the EC Policy Making Approach", Paper for the workshop Systems of Innovation (SPRINT/FAST), Bologna, 5–6 October.

Boekholt, P., Fahrenkrog, G., Jacobs D. and Howells, J. (1993), "Clusters and Networks of Innovative SMEs," background paper for the Policy Forum Workshop, Luxembourg, CEC DG XIII, SPRINT/EIMS, December.

Boekholt, P. (1994), "Methodologies to Identify Regional Networks and Clusters", Presentation for EC RITTS workshop, Luxembourg.

Castells, M. and Hall, P. (1994), *Technopoles of the World: The Makings of the 21st Century Industrial Complexes*, London: Routledge.

Cooke, P. (1995), "Planet Europa: Network Approaches to Regional Innovation and Technology Management", in *Technology Management*, Vol. 2, pp. 18–30.

Cooke, P. and Morgan, K. (1995), "Growth Regions under Duress: Renewal Strategies in Baden Württemberg and Emilia Romagna", in Amin, A. and Thrift, N., *Globalization, Institutions, and Regional Development in Europe*, Oxford: Oxford University Press.

Cooke, P., Boekholt, P., Schall, N. and Schienstock, G. (1996), "Regional Innovations Systems: Concepts, Analysis and Typology", Paper prepared for EU-Restpor Conference on Global Comparison of Regional R&D and Innovation Strategies for Development and Cohesion, Brussels, 19–22 September.

Jacobs, D., Boekholt, P. and Zegveld, W. (1990), *De Economische Kracht van Nederland*, (*The Economic Strength of the Netherlands*), Den Haag: SMO.

Jacobs, D. and Ard-Pieter de Man, J. (1995), *Clusters en Concurrentiekracht (Clusters and Competitiveness)*, Samsom: Alphen aan de Rijn.

Ohmae, Kenichi (1996), *The End of the Nation State, The rise of Regional Economies*, London: Harper Collins.

Porter, M. (1990), *The Competitive Advantage of Nations*, London: Macmillan.

Praat, H. and van Bemmel, Leo (1994), "Towards Value Added Supply Management on a Regional Scale: the 'Twente' Experiment", Paper for the European Network on Industry, Innovation and Territory, Newcastle, October.

Steiner, Michael (1995), *Regionale Innovation, Durch Technologiepolitik zu neuen Strukturen*, Graz: Leykam.

8

INNOVATION, TECHNOLOGICAL TRANSFER AND ENTREPRENEURIAL COMPETITIVENESS

F. Marques Reigado

Summary

Since the pioneering work of Schumpeter, who developed the bimodal concept of innovation, several authors have dwelt over the problems of innovation. Some have introduced, in a more or less explicit way, a social and human component to the meaning of innovation. The concept of an innovative environment has been developed recently by Aydalot (1986), Camagni (1991; 1992) and Cappelin (1993a; 1993b). The links, or symbiosis, between innovative environments, endogenous factors of innovation and technological development have not been properly explored. Thus, in the present context of change, the classical paradigm of economic theory and new propositions related to competitiveness between nations are gaining ground (Porter, 1993). It is necessary to develop the concept of endogenous factors of innovation linked to the local innovative environment.

INTRODUCTION

Innovation, as a realisation of a new idea, is a cyclical process that through history has accompanied the cycles of economic growth. In simple terms, innovation seems to be the result of a process including the diffusion of research, scientific advancement and technological progress, developed in an appropriate environment — the innovative environment. Innovation manifests itself through a set of outputs such as products, improvement of existing products, new ways of packaging, new methods of management and organisation, new ways of penetrating markets, etc.

To take a historical example: the great nautical discoveries would not have been possible without the discovery of the magnetic needle and the astrolabe or without the evolution of the science of navigation, naval construction techniques and the correspondent innovations introduced in the structure of ships and the navigation arts.

The accumulation of technical knowledge, the discovery of new products, the development of trade led by the Dutch East Indies Company and the consequent enrichment of some European countries contributed to two great movements:

- In literature, arts, sciences and ideas and the consequent outpouring of discoveries, inventions and innovations

- The restructuring and modernising of agriculture, the Green Revolution, and the subsequent invention of mechanical looms which were the prelude of the Industrial Revolution.

The aims of this chapter are to develop the concepts of innovation, innovative environments and innovation processes by a systematic and naturally integrated, inter-related approach; to present the innovation process in relation to economic growth and to distinguish between social innovation and entrepreneurial innovation; and finally, to study the evolution of the concept of innovation from a materialistic or economic viewpoint to a more human one.

The chapter is divided into the following sections:

- Introduction.

- A synthesis of evolution and innovation concepts, in particular dematerialisation and the innovative environment

- An exploration of the innovation process, relating endogenous and exogenous factors and introducing the spatial, socio-cultural and temporal variables to this process

- A reflection on innovation and competitiveness

- Conclusions.

EVOLUTION OF INNOVATION AND THE CONCEPT OF AN INNOVATIVE ENVIRONMENT

Schumpeter identifies evolution with changes in the availability of physical factors (land and labour). When the combination of these factors is modified (that is, when there is technical progress), Schumpeter refers to the "development effect". However,

Schumpeter's development concept principally values the economic aspect; other important aspects, such as the access of populations to goods and services, freedom, democracy, justice and independence of social position or geographical location, are subordinated to the economic aspect and do not receive consistent treatment from the author.

Since the pioneering work of Schumpeter (1934), which enhanced the two components of productive forces (i.e. material and immaterial) and drew attention to the important role of research and innovation to economic development, scientific and technological progress have acquired new profiles. The understanding of the Research–Invention–Innovation–Development cycle has occupied a number of researchers, governments, enterprises and universities. By identifying innovation with technological progress based on technical changes, Schumpeter developed a bimodal concept, referring not only to the production of new goods, but also to the use of different methods for the production of such goods.

This concept of innovation included:

- The production of new commodities or improvement of the quality of goods already produced

- The adaptation of a new method of production, based on scientific discoveries already tested in fringe process or a new way of trading traditional commodities

- Penetration into new markets

- The discovery of a new source of raw materials or semi-transformed products

- The introduction of new ways of organisation by any industrial sector.

It remains to be clarified what is understood by "innovation", and only then can the study of the socialisation or humanisation of the innovation process begin.

Innovation can be defined as a "well-succeeded exploitation of new ideas". The introduction into the market of an innovation is invariably aimed at generating competitive advantage, sharing of the market and high growth rates, all of which lead to higher profits. From the economic viewpoint, a distinction must be made between simple innovation and innovation from the base, which not only revolutionises the global economy but also changes society's habits; examples include the discovery of the steam machine, the telephone, radio, television, etc. These innovations do not appear in a continuous way but by leaps causally related to long-term economic cycles. The innovation cycles generate the start of new economic growth cycles, known as "Kondratiev cycles".

A simple innovation manifests itself in the application of new areas of technology or organisational methods, management, marketing etc., already exploited in fringe areas. The understanding of the relationship (innovation process–development) becomes clearer when seen in a global context, integrating in the analysis the spatial, social and temporal variables. The space variable clarifies the local differences of the historical and actual environments where innovation is developed and linked to the innovative environment and its dynamic evolution — the so-called dynamic innovative environment. The temporal variable allows us to examine the effects over time, integrating and articulating the factors linked to innovation and development. Besides being linked to the characterisation of the innovative environment, the social variable distinguishes two innovation concepts: a materialistic/economic or a more socialised one. As already stated, Schumpeter used a narrow concept of innovation and development. However, from the 1980s the social dimension of innovation came under investigation.

The notion of an "innovative environment" emerged in the mid-1980s and was explored in the 1990s by Peyrache, Aydalot and Camagni. Aydalot (1986) was one of the first to contest the materialistic innovation vision, stating that machines were much more than the substance of innovation but were rather its incarnation. Perrin (1991) emphasised the role of communication in the links between economic agents working in different sectors or in different phases of the production process and the importance that these links have in the innovative process. Perrin (1991) devalued the formalisation and programming of innovations and promoted the role of territorial organisation in innovation. Communication and operating in networks were seen as fundamental for innovation. Peyrache (1986) enhanced the role of social structure and drew attention to the socio-economic local environment, stating that the socio-economic dimension gives coherence to the complex network of informal and technical ties that allow the creativity shown by the entrepreneurial structure.

Under such an approach, innovation has an initial impulse to provide a solution to a particular problem in a specific environment. The arrival point will depend upon the sense in which the exploitation of the technical potential content is defined. This approach draws attention to the narrow relationship between technological progress and socio-economic development. However, the production process seems reduced to operations carried out by machines which are the incarnation of the technology selected. Development, or more accurately economic growth, according to this approach, occupies a place along a determined trajectory and derives from induced innovations which are the result of a reaction to the phenomenon of relative scarcity manifested along the process. Location is sometimes the result of interactions between technological and economic variables.

Under the integrated approach, the production process must be seen as an evolutional expression of the environment, considered as a set of technical-productive phases, and it is nothing more than a particular moment in time. In the integrated approach, the essence of production no longer refers to equipment enhancing; rather, its profile is defined by the characteristics of the primary resources. Consequently, technology does not emerge as a specific path to solve the problem but as a human resource able to outline and implement different solutions to different problems. The innovation process can no longer be seen as an adaptation for the development of a given technology, but as a cognitive and learning process resulting in the emergence of completely new and qualified tasks, which even transforms the environment and, in that way, allows the enlargement of the existing hierarchy of problems and solutions.

The integrated approach to the innovation process is closely related to recent developments in the applied sciences. A certain dematerialisation of the production processes related to these developments also highlights the deep changes in worker skills and, above all, the proportions of highly qualified technical staff to unqualified workers[1]. Related to this dematerialisation of the production process and the corresponding integrated approach to the innovative process, the concept of a flexible *atelier* was developed. This is a working unit which is defined by the capacity of transforming non-specific resources into products capable of providing

---

[1] This applies to a new philosophy and social task of the enterprise.

answers to variable specifications[2]. These flexible production systems are no longer just theoretical, but have become reality.

The definition of an innovative environment as a "historical product shaped by local values, culture and customs, by the entrepreneurial spirit of risk and motivation of local populations" is a synthesis of the different definitions provided by several authors — Aydalot, Camagni, Planque and others.

THE INNOVATION PROCESS

It has already been noted that the innovation process develops in space and time and is integrated with invention, scientific and technological discoveries and economic development. The question of the variable space demands careful treatment of the innovative environment while the variable time emphasises the dynamic and non-linear character of the R&D process to entrepreneurial competitiveness and social innovations as well as the temporal feedback effect development has over research and technical progress[3]. Before looking at Figure 8.1, where we will try to emphasise the temporal effects of the symbiosis in the research–innovation–development process, we must draw attention to the relevance of integrating the following aspects in a development model:

- The economic and social development strategies

- The scientific and technological strategies

- Education and training strategies.

Training of staff and adequate investment in science and technology must play an integral part and have first priority in any innovation and development model.

---

[2] This flexibility of the productive process implies the creation of conditions which allow a fast response of the productive process to structural changes.

[3] It is important to note that we consider the innovative environment as a dynamic long-term process, where the time variable influences change in the boundary of space. Together with the social variable, this transforms, by a slow process, some exogenous innovative factors into factors endogenous to the innovative environment.

FIGURE 8.1: DYNAMIC INTERACTION, RESEARCH, INNOVATION AND DEVELOPMENT

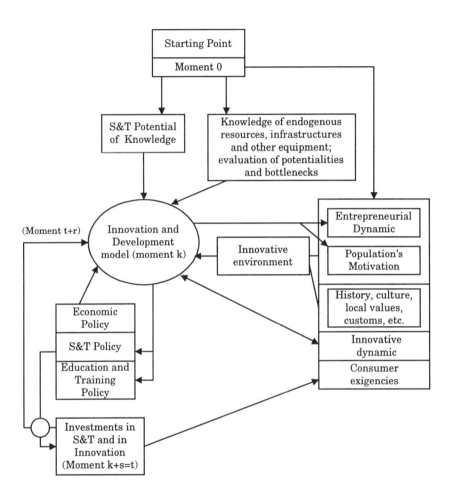

The Chain Process can be synthesised in the following way:

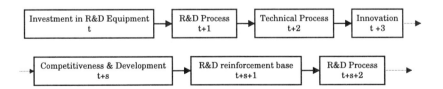

Figure 8.1 synthesises a dynamic process which is based on the current situation and relates to various aspects of national policy — the economic base, the scientific and technological potential, the cultural base, entrepreneurial and demographic motivation; the latter serving as an incentive to motivate innovation. The process as described implies a development model which is characterised by a three-tiered planning system:

- Economic and social planning

- Scientific and technological planning

- Planning for education and training.

In Figure 8.2, the following aspects of the innovative process are distinguished:

- **The innovative environment** which appears divided into a set of elements linked to a long historical process which could only be changed in the very long term; a set of endogenous elements which result from dynamised actions and suffer retroactive effects from the development process. This set of elements, which constitute the innovative environment, we will call endogenous factors of innovation (Reigado, 1995).

- **The exogenous factors of innovation** formed by scientific and technological development, by education and training etc.

The innovator effect is based on and arises from the correct articulation–integration between the exogenous and endogenous factors of innovation, shown in Figure 8.2.

Investments in education, training of human resources, R&D, health and social security, culture and leisure activities are fundamental if the innovation potential factors that characterise the innovative environment are to be transformed into actualised innovation factors. There is no innovation without the spirit of risk. This spirit comes from young people, young entrepreneurs and dynamic managers. As Camagni (1991) points out, managers and young people are attracted not only by material gain, but also and more significantly, by socio-cultural factors.

Throughout history, ways of life and thinking, forms of relationships, cultural traditions and customs have all been connected to the local environment and simultaneously represent both the seeds of particular local methods of innovation and development and barriers to forms of technological development.

FIGURE 8.2: THE INTERACTION OF FACTORS OF INNOVATION

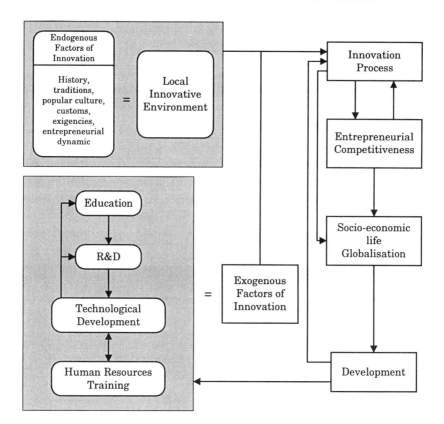

Particularly in a rural area, the socio-cultural environment is the result of a set of dynamic factors:

- The presence and/or passage of several people with diverse cultures and particular ways of life, which somehow marked the *modus vivendi* of populations, in many cases the result of the mixing of several ethnicities.

- The heritage left by those peoples is shown through its architectural, archaeological, cultural and even economic patrimony.

- Concerning the economic and cultural (or artistic) patrimony, the knowledge brought by several peoples, mixed with locally based knowledge and applied to the local geo-economic reality, originated several creative activities, either in the scope of agricultural exploitation or in the transformation of primary products. The transformation of primary products simultaneously assumed an artistic and economic form, having as a result a wealth of creativity and ingenious technology which constitute important starting points for innovation.

- On the other hand, culture, customs and creative activities manifest in many cases forms of knowledge and expressions; demonstration of that knowledge creates benefits which must be used in an innovative sense and directed towards actions to improve the quality of life of the population.

The following set of elements form what we have already called the local endogenous innovative environment: local craft industries, cultural attitudes, ways of relating, daily economic transactions and customs. When this endogenous innovative environment mixes in a harmonic form and is complemented with technological innovation (exogenous factors), we obtain the local innovative process which constitutes the starting point for self-sustained development. This is because it is based on the articulation between knowledge and customs acquired historically and the products of science and technology. The innovative process is formed by the interaction between technological development, consumer demand in terms of quality, customs, history, culture and local knowledge (Reigado, 1995).

INNOVATION, TECHNOLOGICAL TRANSFER AND COMPETITIVENESS

Malecki (1991), organises the studies on innovation into three categories. The first category comprises studies of the impact of innovation on productivity growth. The second category includes research works on the genesis of innovation in the enterprises. In the third category, the author considers studies on innovation diffusion and innovation adoption by firms. This present chapter does not stress the impact of innovation on productivity and economic growth. Rather, particular attention is given to the genesis of innovation, its diffusion and the innovation process. In this section, we consider innovation at enterprise level and its relation to competitiveness. We have already drawn attention to the need for integrating the spatial, temporal, social and technological dimensions in the innovative process; now, we go on to emphasise the enterprise role, not only as an individual unit, but also as integrated in several forms of organisation. But it would not be wise to isolate the enterprise component from the other dimensions or from the different factors of innovation. Relative to the spatial dimension and the set of factors necessary to the realisation of development, it will examine the local background to innovation and its diffusion.

Some authors (Godinho and Caraça (1988), Aydalot (1986), Blakely (1994), Camagni (1991) and Reigado (1995)) emphasise the importance of the following:

- The presence of universities and public entities of research

- Access to important transport and communications networks which, among other functions, allow the absorption of external scientific and technical information

- The presence of human resources duly qualified

- The existence of environmental and cultural factors and of services which create conditions for an attractive lifestyle

- A legal framework favourable to innovation, particularly the existence of a patent registration system

- The availability of risk capital to finance innovations

- Forms and spaces of interaction between the different agents of the innovation system network.

As pointed out by Godinho and Caraça,

> without innovation networks guided according to internal technological development and continuing with the participation of enterprises, as well as public and private institutions of R&D, higher education institutions and the indispensable suppliers of financial products, the absorption and innovation potential of our economy is frankly limited (Godinho and Caraça, 1988: 956).

The factors we have mentioned above alert us to the necessity of: formulating strategies in education and training, and in research and technological development; creating an appropriate environment and adequate fiscal and credit measures; stimulating innovation; developing a good network of transport and communications; and developing methods of stimulating consumers' demand in terms of quality. The role of human resources training and consumer demand is emphasised by Porter (1993) as fundamental to entrepreneurial innovation and competitiveness.

These factors emphasise not only the spatial, temporal and technological dimensions, but also the roles of the innovative environment, the universities and the financial stimulus, among others. The convergence and functioning in networks of the different factors which are at the origin of the innovation process can best be found in an organisation which moves from large-scale production with heavy structures to production which can easily adapt to technological change or to changes in consumer tastes. The idea of a flexible *atelier*, mentioned earlier, is the best example. This structure of flexible production appeared mainly in the 1970s and 1980s in Japan, with isolated appearances elsewhere due to the oil crises of the 1970s. Related to the flexible model of production is the necessity for a permanent innovation system — a desirable system to guarantee self-sustained, spatially balanced development, which still, however, shows significant weakness in its actual functioning. We emphasise that the necessity of this permanent system of innovation is the result of a triple combination of scientific and technological production, the need to reinforce competitiveness at international level and the accelerating obsolescence of products.

Innovation aims to develop at local, regional and national level and development requires strong involvement from the population and institutions and particularly from enterprises, in order to receive competitive gains at international level (Porter, 1993).

An empirical study in the north of Portugal (Silva Costa and Rui Silva, 1995), does not look favourably on the roles of universities and the innovative environment in the innovation process. We believe it is necessary to be careful in drawing such conclusions. The University–Enterprise partnership is, in Portugal, at an embryonic stage, characterised by some timidity and by a lack of mutual trust and reliability. As for the innovative environment, the econometric model applied to determined innovation indicators, does not seem strong enough to include the innovative environment, which by its nature must include a set of latent variables, only quantified by indirect methods and through appropriate indicators. We must point out that the type of innovations detected were generally a result of contagion or imitation; only a few were the result of real technological processes; innovation from the bottom-up was almost absent.

The scheme elaborates synthetically the involvement between, on the one hand, the innovative environment, the R&D process and inventions, and on the other, the production process, all seen as feeding sources for innovation, competitiveness and development.

FIGURE 8.3: RELATIONSHIP BETWEEN INNOVATION, CORRESPONDENT SOURCES, COMPETITIVENESS AND DEVELOPMENT

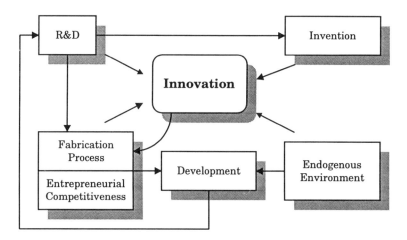

Source: Adapted from Guide sur l'évolution/sélection des projets et des entrepreneurs, edit. EBN, 1992.

Innovation in the enterprise can possess several features and have several sources of stimulus. Features of innovation can be classified according to:

- Innovation of process

- Innovation of product

- Innovation of management and strategy.

Innovation of process is associated with technological changes in production and distribution methods, as opposed to the production of new products. It aims to improve productivity, lower costs, improve product image, increase safety at work, improve market penetration, etc.

Innovation of the production process is linked to the following issues:

- *Production Technologies*: Total innovation in areas such as lowering costs, the introduction of new raw materials or the improvement of products

- The continuous improvement of existing technology

- *Organisation and Production Management:* Introduction of an innovative form of organisation and management of the production process, for example, MRP (Materials Requirement Planning), "Just-in-Time", "Zero Defects"

- Adoption of quality control techniques of the process and the product (TQM)

- Innovation in the "layout" of production

- Use of high quality raw materials or significantly low costs

- "Optimisation" of energy costs

- Improvements in the Rules and Procedures of safety at the enterprise, or in conditions of work in order to increase productivity.

When a new innovation is introduced in the product, the first sales are to innovative buyers followed closely by early adapters, before a new product reaches a regular pattern of diffusion in an expanding market. It is necessary, at this phase of technological and (consequently) product evolution, to take into account the scheme of acceptance of the product in the market and thereafter redefine the marketing strategies. That is, to constantly consider the iterative effect of the enterprise-involving environment in which the market is inserted. The diffusion of the innovative product requires innovation in marketing and its acceptance depends, also, on the characteristics of the consumer to whom the product is offered.

Although essentially related to businesses, innovation must not be reduced to purely business concepts, either when considering the effects it produces, or when examining its supporting base. There are other factors — social, cultural, temporal, etc., not excluding the role of enterprise — articulating and complementing each other mutually. However, in this context, it is important to particularly emphasise innovation's relation to business. We do not claim that only businesses produce innovations, although we readily recognise that the efficiency of technological progress is due in great part to the clearness and range of business aims, which stimulate innovations, which, in turn, stimulates technology and science. These aims would not be immune to social pressures, changes of tastes, quality exigencies of consumers, competition, necessity of conquering new markets, necessity of reducing costs, etc. We remember again, the importance that Peyrache (1986) places on the role performed by sectoral structure — not neglecting, however, the importance of historically acquired know-how. According to Peyrache, the type of innovation diffusion is hard to ascertain due to the complexity of the changes that take place. One of the most celebrated authors of the theory of competitiveness (Porter, 1993) considers innovation as an important competitiveness factor that

> includes not only the technology, but also the methods, including new products, new production methods and new ways of trading, identification of new groups of clients, etc.

According to Porter, innovations that lead to competitive advantage involve an accumulation of little steps and delayed efforts, as well as dramatic discoveries (Porter, 1993: 86). Both innovation and competition have, in fact, dynamic characteristics. They do not stabilise in an equilibrium, but evolve to a perpetual state of change (Schumpeter, 1934). Innovation never ends. Today's advantages are the disadvantages of tomorrow. The contact between enterprises, suppliers and clients is important to innovation. There is a reciprocal influence. As a customer, an enterprise imposes exigencies and tests new methodologies and products. The supplier enterprise introduces new products, new technologies, etc. When possible, co-operative research is desirable and is a way of accelerating innovation.

The innovative process can also be accelerated by competitiveness among co-related enterprises. Rivalry *among* enterprises, manifested as competition, and *inside* enterprises, among departments or centres of profit, is also a factor that contributes to innovation at an entrepreneurial level.

The entrepreneurial spirit and the accumulated knowledge of the population — the acquired know-how — are, according to Maillat (1987), the roots of development. Maillat emphasises a dynamic process of innovation and development linked to the historical dynamic — the past — with all its values, culture, customs etc., carried through to today's cultural dynamic — current and future — and to the entrepreneurial spirit, which, in our view, must be viewed not only as acquired and static, but also as something that began in the past, is based in the present and is moving towards the future. *The entrepreneurial spirit may be in exis-*

tence, but only when it is developed can it become a part of a symbiotic process together with innovation and development.

Let us dwell for a moment on the technological factor, stressing something that was clarified earlier: the innovative process and entrepreneurial competitiveness are a result of the convergence of the innovative environment with technological development. Technology gave to enterprises the possibility of balancing scarce factors with new products and processes (Porter, 1993).

There are two main sources of technological development:

* Scientific and technological research, complemented by the dissemination of its results within each country

* International technology transfer.

The existent literature about technology transfer emphasised — when it did not consider exclusively — the importation of equipment. The imported equipment would carry with it the technology from the countries of origin. The supplier's technical attendance at the moment of installation and experience, would complete the technology transfer.

For the last two decades, other factors, particularly human resources and information, came to be seen as important for technology transfer.

Human resources, mainly technical staff, with the increasing internationalisation of training and specialisation, have a more and more important role to play in technology transfer. The European Commission's Human Resources and Mobility Programmes in 1990, and the Stimulus to Co-operation and Interchange, (SCIENCE 1988) are the best examples of an awareness of the increasing role that human resources have in technology standardisation through its transfer. These programmes, reinforcing the co-operation between and the mobility of researchers in several member states of the European Union made a decisive contribution to increasing technology transfer.

It is, nevertheless, problematic that the levelling effect of technology between countries has been significant. The concentration of mobility and co-operation within the richest countries of the EU could, in the near future, aggravate the tendency for a cleavage between the two Europes. The North Sea–Rhine axis (southern England, northern France, Benelux, Germany, Denmark and northern Italy) have a tendency to benefit from external economies and important synergies, which reinforce themselves with the concentration of R&D projects and mobility and co-operation between researchers. Greater standardisation of technologies will maintain this tendency in these countries, at least in the medium term. The Mediterranean axis will be more and more distanced from the richer, more technologically advanced countries of the European Union.

Modern information and communication processes make the spreading of technologies faster and easier. Television, radio, computers (mainly the Internet and e-mail), are some of the principal means of dissemination and divulgence of scientific discoveries and technological progress. However, we must remember that the spreading of information is still biased in favour of more advanced countries. The less developed countries of the EU have scarce and less powerful means to access and divulge information. The imbalance in the spreading of information, co-operation between researchers and their mobility, in favour of the richer countries of the EU will result in a bias in the technology transfer and consequently the aggravation of inequalities between the two axes.

CONCLUSIONS

Since Schumpeter, the concept of innovation has been deepened by several authors who introduced the concept of the innovative environment and a more socialised dimension of innovation. This has been important in clarifying the process of innovation.

Technological progress, innovation, entrepreneurial dynamics and economic development must be analysed on three fronts: spatial, sectoral and temporal. The growing importance of R&D on economic development justifies the introduction of three subsystems in the system of economic planning: the economic system itself; the scientific and technological system; and the education system.

However, the differences in performance are remarkable in science and technology between and within the major zones at a global level; more important still are the spatial differences of entrepreneurial motivations. The role that the innovative environment takes in the technological progress and in the entrepreneurial dynamic must be stressed. The role of the University in development and, in particular, in the attraction and stimulation of enterprises, has given a special prominence to innovation. Its performance in the near future will depend on how the model of internal management is articulated with regard to the entrepreneurial environment and the concept of development.

References

Aydalot, P. (1986), "Trajectoires Technologiques et 'Milieux Innovateurs'" in Philippe Aydalot, (ed.), *Milieux Innovateurs en Europe*, Paris: GREMI.

Aydalot, P. and Keeble, D. (1988), *High Technology Industry and Innovative Environments: The European Experience,* European Research Group on Innovative Milieux, New York.

Blakely, E. (1994), *Planning Local Economic Development: Theory and Practice*, 2nd Edition, London: Sage.

Camagni, R. (1991), "Local Milieu, Uncertainty and Innovation Networks" in R. Camagni (ed.), *Innovation Networks: Spatial Perspectives*, London: Belhaven Press.

Camagni, R.P. (1992), "The Concept of 'Innovative Milieu' and its Relevance for Public Policies in European Lagging Regions", Paper presented at the Thirteenth Conferenza Italiana di Scienza Regionali, Vol. 7, Ancona.

Cappelin, R. (1991), "International Networks for Cities", in R. Camagni (ed.), *Innovation Networks: Spatial Perspectives*, London: Belhaven Press.

Crevoisier, O. and Maillat, D. (1991), "Milieu, Industrial Organisation and Territorial Production Systems", in R. Camagni (ed.), *Innovation Networks: Spatial Perspectives*, London: Belhaven Press.

Davelaar, E.J. (1989), *Incubation and Innovation: A Spatial Perspective*, Academisch Proefschrift V.U., Interne Huisdrukkerji, The Netherlands.

Davelaar, E. and Mateaccioli, A. (1991), "L'Impact des Réseaux d'Innovation sur les Milieux Locaux: Le Role des Réseaux, des Sociétés de Conseil et des Centres de Recherche en Ile de France", *Revue d'Economie Régionale et Urbaine*, Vol. 3, No. 4.

Freeman, C.H. (1987), "The Case of Technology Determinism" in Ruth Finnegan et al. (eds.), *Information Technology: Social Issues, A Reader*, London: Hodder and Stoughton.

Freeman, C. (1988), "Diffusion: The Spread of New Technology to Firms, Sectors and Nations", in A. Heertje (ed.), *Innovation Technology and Finance*, Oxford: Basil Blackwell.

Ginsberg, A. et al. (1992), "Investigating in New Information Technology: The Role of Competitive Postures and Issue Diagnosis", in *Strategic Management Journal*, Vol. 13.

Godinho, M. and Caraça, J. (1988), "Inovação Tecnológica e difusão no contexto de economias de desenvolvimento interm dio", *Análise Social*, Nos. 103/104.

Godinho, M. Mira (1990), "Interacção Tecnologia: Desenvolvimento em Portugal" *Estudos de Economia*, Vol. XI, No. 1, October–December.

Maillat, D., Crevoisier, O., and Lecoq, B. (1991), "Reseaux d'Innovation et Dynamique Territorial: Un Essai de Typologie", *Revue d'Economie Regionale et Urbaine*, Vol. 3, No. 4.

Maillat, D. (1987), "Les Milieux Innovateurs en Europe", Paper presented at the Colloque International, Les Stratégies Régionales d'Innovation et le Competitivité des Entreprises, Institut de Recherches Économiques et Régionales, Neuchâtel.

Malecki, T. (1991), *Technology and Economic Development: the Dynamics of Local, Regional and National Change*, Burnt Mill, Harlow, Essex: Longman.

Maximiano, A. et al. (1980), *Administraçäo do Processor de Inovação Tecnológico*, São Paulo: Atlas.

Pacqueur, B. (1987), "De l'Espace Fonctionnel à l'Espace Territoire: Essai sur le Développement Local", Thèse de doctorat d'Etat, Grenoble: Université des Sciences de Grenoble.

Pavit, K. (1984), "Sectoral Patterns of Technical Change: Towards a Taxonomy and a Theory", in *Research Policy*.

Perrin, J.C. (1991), "Technological Innovation and Territorial Development: An Approach in Terms of Networks and Milieux", in R. Camagni (ed.), *Innovation Networks: Spatial Perspectives*, London: Belhaven Press.

Peyrache, Veronique (1986), "Mutations Régionales vers les Technologies Nouvelles: Le Cas de la Région de Saint-Étienne" in Philippe Aydalot, (ed.), *Milieux Innovateurs en Europe*, Paris: GREMI.

Porter, Michael (1993), *Avantagem Competitiva das Nações*, Editora Campus.

Reigado, F. Marques (1994), "O Papel das Universidades no Desenvolvimento Regional" in *Congresso Internacional sobre Poder Autárquico*, Câmara de Oeiras e Associação Internacional de Municípos, Oeiras.

Reigado, F. Marques (1995), "Modelo de Desenvolvimento e Necessidades de I & D", Paper presented at Investigação, Inovação e Desenvolvimento Transfronteiriço III, Centro de Estudos de Desenvolvimento Regional (UBI).

Schroeder, D. (1990), "A Dynamic Perspective on Impact of Process Innovation upon Competitive Strategies", in *Strategic Management Journal*, Vol. 11.

Schumpeter, J. (1939), *Business Cycles: A Theoretical, Historical and Statistical Analysis of the Capitalist Process*, New York: McGraw-Hill.

Schumpeter, J. (1934), *A Theory of Economic Development*, Cambridge, MA: Harvard University Press.

Silva Costa, J. and Silva, Rui Mário (1995), "Innovative Behaviour of Small and Mid-Size Enterprises: Territorial Factors vs Enterprises Attribute", Paper presented at the Third Encontro Nacional da Associação Portuguesa de Desenvolvimento Regional, 27–29 April.

Simão, J. Veiga (1994), "Estratégias de I & D para o século XX", Paper presented at Investigação, Inovação e Desenvolvimento Transfronteiriço II, Centro de Estudos de Desenvolvimento Regional (UBI).

9

INNOVATION STRUCTURES: ACTORS, ROLES AND LINKAGES

Eugenio Corti and Corrado lo Storto

Summary

In regions where they are active, Innovation Structures (IS) play an important role in the regional politics of development. To do so they must deliver different innovative services to several local small and medium enterprises, with special emphasis on the technology transfer process of information, including the acquisition and use of technological information and technological diffusion.

In order to have a sufficient number of efficient innovative services, the Innovation Structure has to manage, in an appropriate manner, a network of several actors in the region.

This chapter analyses these aspects in depth, in order to make clear the complexity of the design, organisation, and management of Innovation Structures.

INTRODUCTION

An Innovation Structure (IS) is essentially a complex functional system integrating all available resources by reducing the transfer time of the research outcomes to the applications, removing the barriers to innovation, forming a dense connective tissue among research institutions, industry and services and enabling co-operation between these institutions.[1]

The IS brings together a coherent, whole and powerful territorial innovation system (technology, financial resources, market relations, etc.), a technical culture, some actors, and relations among these. The actors of the IS are the private and public-owned firms, the financial institutions, the local administration agencies, the regional social and professional associations, the local and regional authorities, the universities and research laboratories, education institutions, etc. These actors are very heterogeneous. Therefore, it is a task of the co-ordination agency of the IS to infuse the perception of an atmosphere that gives coherence to the system. Coherence is an outcome of the cognitive dimension of the Structure. The coherence among the actors consists of a common mode of apprehending situations, problems and opportunities. Technical culture comprises the knowledge, know-how, practices, standards and values that are connected with an industrial activity as well as the mechanisms which permit the formation, accumulation and transmission of information and knowledge. The relations include all the manifest and latent exchanges occurring between the actors of the Structure and between the Structure and the external environment. Through formalised and selective linkages with other firms in the Structure or with other external and specialised ISs, local firms may attract the complementary assets they need to carry on their activities. The cohesion of the IS is determined by certain specific forces: a functional interdependence among actors, activities and resources; a structure of co-ordination/power, in terms of a systematically developed capacity to manage the different components of the innovation structure; a structure of knowledge, represented by the experience and knowledge previously acquired by the different actors; a temporary structure, defined in terms of historical development of the IS.

The IS, by promoting and managing the network of linkages among different actors in the territory, contributes to making the local system of small and medium companies more competitive in their markets. In other words, the IS is therefore a means for the regional politics for development (Formica, 1994). As a consequence, the IS has to monitor permanently the different needs of the several local enterprises, and it has to meet those needs through the provision of innovative services. Among those innovative services, the offer of information on the characteristics of the market, of new technologies, of new financial opportunities, and of any other aspects which may be of interest to a firm is very important. But the ISs not only have to provide such information, they have to facilitate the selection and the acquisition of such information, and also the appropriate use of it.

Some information needed by local companies is related to new technologies, derived from the transformation of scientific results, which may solve the particular problems of a single company.

Therefore, the local IS must be organised to support the appropriate transfer of such a technology. That means that the IS has to promote, organise and manage co-operation among the local universities, research centres and local companies.

These local ISs should become "uncertainty-reducing operators", helping firms to overcome their problems with information gathering, screening, transcoding, and selection of appropriate management responses, in a context characterised by wide "failures" of the traditional operators (Camagni, 1991). The mission of an IS is hence to identify, evaluate and select scientific outcomes — the results of the research activity carried out by the actors located in the Structure or elsewhere — transform these outcomes into usable technologies, diffuse information related to them across local firms, begin processes of technology transfer, and help firms in the area to acquire and implement those technologies which could enable them to become more competitive. In this way, they increase the growth of the demand for innovation services. Their role as a co-ordination centre is to develop, amplify and diffuse across local firms the culture of strategic and operative management of technology, thus allowing the system of local firms to overcome the major problem they find in relation to the management of technology, that is, the transfer and acquisition of new technology.

THE MANAGEMENT OF TECHNOLOGY

A firm can manage technological innovation either by managing its technological assets more effectively and efficiently, or by acquiring a novel technology.[2] Both initiatives need other actors apart from the firm to be present: private and public-owned companies, agencies, institutions, etc. This set of actors form what is called the technological system of the firm.

When a firm attempts to know, evaluate, manage and develop its technological assets, it has to deal with three complex problems:

1. The technologies that the firm possesses form a complex system, accumulated over time as a result of the implementation of several technological practices. To describe it, the engineers often introduce simplifications, with the analytic description for the technologies underestimating the power of the technological assets.

2. Technologies contain both explicit and implicit or tacit components. While it is easy to describe and measure the explicit components (machinery, tools, equipment, manual processes, patents etc.), tacit components (culture, skill, capabilities, direct or indirect relationships among the parts, decisional heuristics, informal relations, etc.) can be described only by using approximate verbal judgements. The reduction of firms' technologies to the sole explicit component oversimplifies once again the technological system, and its description reveals limited, or even harmful, information, seriously limiting the potentiality of that technology.

3. Enriching the technological assets of a firm means acquiring new technologies and replacing the obsolete ones. Therefore, the firm must establish a complex relation with some sources of technology (that is, a University, a Research Centre, another firm) and ask for advice from a third actor in the process of technology transfer.

To overcome the problems imposed by the complexity of the technological system, a firm can take advantage of the redundancy of the system. A technological system is decomposable in many different ways, each showing different characteristics. It considers and uses only those capabilities which are functional to the achievement of a specific objective. When a firm utilises a technology, it forces its technical transformation capability within the constraints imposed by the market, finance, and human behaviours. In this way, the firm decomposes the complex technological system limiting the way to carry out its transformation power to that which is more compatible with the defined context.

Usually, the starting point of contextualising the technology is derived from factors over which the firm has a limited manoeuvring capacity. Of course, the market perspective is not the only one the firm can resort to in order to analyse its technological system. For instance, an alternative perspective is to consider the cross-fertilisation capacity offered by the different technologies. A successful firm should develop the capability to apply multiple perspectives to the analysis of a technological system. This is a crucial issue in the strategic management of technology. Indeed, the strategic management of technology for a firm means: (a) to be involved in a continuous analysis of its technological assets; (b) to develop several alternative models, many descriptions, many levels to interpret it; and (c) to continuously simulate new possible descriptions which allow the firm to take into account eventual new constraints and goals. Any attempt to analyse the technological assets represents an exploration of their potentiality. It points out the technical constraints, the functional limits, and any eventual technological gap to be filled with the acquisition of new technologies. Of course, every description of a technological system is partial. A firm can know how to manage effectively its technologies only if it carries out continuous analysis leading to a grasp of the multiple levels of the technological system. Every single description emphasises some specific aspects of the technological system. Only a multiplicity of partial descriptions of the technological system makes it possible to face the issue of its complexity in practice.

Dealing with the problem of the tacitness of a technological system is conversely much more difficult. This problem emerges when, in spite of all the efforts to make the company's technological system explicit, its analytic description remains incomplete and some critical issues are not considered: that is, the cultural aspects, the second-level interactions, the implicit linkages, and the informal relations. The links between explicit and implicit (or tacit) and between formal and informal cannot be ignored. The more one tries to make the system explicit, the greater the tacit aspects; and as the perception that the explicit description of the technology is incomplete, it is more likely that some sort of doubt will arise about the reliability of the description. The incompleteness will introduce uncertainty.

The typical attitude of people involved in the analysis and evaluation of the technological system is to study thoroughly the analytic description, generating — as a consequence — complex models, hard to manage and having the same level of reliability. By limiting the knowledge of the technological system to its explicit component, the reality is forced within the constraints of a simplified model. An alternative solution is to accept the existence of the tacit component, to accept the incompleteness of all the explicit descriptions, and the intrinsic uncertainty. To accept the uncertainty related to a technological system means that we should modify the way we look at technology. Technology should be viewed as a *nucleus* of explicit elements, easily identifiable, certain, surrounded by a *halo* of fuzzy elements, quasi-technologies, unstable linkages, informal relations, unspecified situations, undefined ideas, failed experiments, unsuccessful trails. Thus, technology is an inexact object by definition.

The need to manage uncertainty induces us to understand the dynamics occurring between explicit and tacit components, between nucleus and halo. In the evolution of the technological system, in the life of a company, some of the elements belonging to the nucleus of a certain technology migrate toward the halo, leaving a heritage of experience, skills and capabilities. Conversely, some less important and foreseeable elements, hidden in the halo, that the firm does not necessarily perceive to be a part of its own technological assets, migrate to the nucleus and become explicit elements easily managed by the firm.

The recourse to multiple descriptions of the technological assets or a specific technology, offers a significant assistance to the management of uncertainty. Indeed, for every description, the relation between nucleus and halo is re-built in a different way. What appears sure and unequivocal from a certain perspective is fuzzy, fading and problematic from another perspective. The tacit component becomes identifiable — thus, manageable — only when many levels of analysis of the technical system are available, if paradoxes and juxtapositions are emphasised, but, at the same time, if all the power and insights coming from them are pointed out. The management of uncertainty experiences time elements and assumptions which are contradictory.

From these considerations it clearly emerges why the management of technology is an intrinsically complex process. A firm is forced to modify the halo of every technology when it decides to carry on a process of technological innovation. But few firms, perhaps only the most innovative, have the capability to re-build the technological halos in a short time, with a sufficient quality, without resorting to any professional help. Most firms, and in particular those firms located in late-developing areas, often give up innovating because they do not have any sort of specific capability. In this way they lose any chance of development and growth.

THE DIFFUSION AND ACQUISITION OF TECHNOLOGY

In order for a firm to acquire a novel technology, an external organisation must have the knowledge and willingness to sell it.[3] This information concerns the availability on the market of the technology, a description of its characteristics and possible uses, and the explicit intention to sell it. All this information is limited to the description of the nucleus of the technology.

Usually, organisations whose mission is to develop novel technologies, such as a university department or a public research laboratory, lack the capability or the experience to advertise and promote the sale of technologies. In the same way, even though many firms are fully aware of the existence of the department and the laboratory, they find it difficult to contact these organisations because they do not use the same language of scientists and technicians, or because they do not know whom they have to contact, or what technology to ask for. Likewise, companies seem to show a more marked attitude to promote the sale of their obsolete technologies. However, just because the sale of unstrategic technologies is not a relevant business for a firm, they usually do not pay a great attention to it.

From these considerations it appears evident that a critical issue in the diffusion of information related to novel technologies is the management of the interface between the source of information and the potential users. In the past, Technological Data Banks have been designed and Technological Desks have been introduced, but they encountered a limited form of acceptance by firms. The overall process of acquisition of a technology is much more complex than one can imagine. It includes several steps:

- The creation or strengthening of the sources of technological information willing to transfer useful information[4]

- The promotion and diffusion to potential users of preliminary information relative to specific technologies

- The identification and selection of the source and the desired technology by the firm

- The attainment of information on a specific technology, useful and substantial enough to decide whether to acquire that technology

- The identification of the proprietor organisations which possess that technology and the selection of that organisation willing to sell it under the best technical and economic conditions

- The redesign of the technical and organisational structure, in particular those units which will be involved in the management of the new technology to build the halo

- The purchasing and transfer of the selected technology
- The utilisation of the acquired technology and development of all the necessary technical and organisational supports
- The experiments and the final tests.

From the list of steps indicated above, it emerges that it is important to make clear the mechanism of diffusion of technological information necessary for the acquisition of the technology. In the literature, a linear model of diffusion of technological information has been proposed (Mansfield, 1968; 1977). This model includes a source of information, a social system of individuals or organisations who directly receive the information, and the information itself. If an individual judges the information it receives desirable, they immediately decide to acquire the relevant goods or services. According to the model, each individual's behaviour is independent of other individuals' behaviour, and all the individuals react to the novelty in the same way and at the same time. Subsequent research on the diffusion of hybrid corn in some regions of the United States obviated the fallacy of this simple model (Rogers and Shoemaker, 1971). From the results of an extensive survey, it was demonstrated that the process of diffusion of technical information is not linear, because information does not reach actors of the social system directly from the source in the same instant of time and with the same intensity, but they influence their behaviour by exchanging information, advice and opinions. Furthermore, the diffusion is quicker if the subjects of the social system tend to exchange informal information more frequently. It follows that the probability of obtaining the right information at the right time is higher when the density of the system of the organisations interested in the novelty is higher. Several studies applied the model to the investigation of the diffusion mechanism of different kinds of information, also including technological information, which led to the identification of "adoption curves" in various social systems, such as R&D laboratories, specific industrial sectors, SMEs (Allen, 1979). It is interesting to note that the adoption curve has a shape similar to a gaussian curve for all the social systems investigated, even for the social systems formed by the scientists of a large research centre. On the bases of these studies some managerial implication can be driven. First, in a process of technological information diffusion, it is necessary to displace the adoption curve, so as to accelerate the adoption time for all the subjects. Second, the process of diffusion implies a decision-making process relative to innovation.[5]

Rogers and Shoemaker (1971) proposed a model of the decision-making process relative to the adoption/rejection of innovation in under-developed social systems. Recently, a slightly modified version of this model was proposed in Corti (1997) to understand the behaviour of more advanced organisations. This latter model includes four phases: the collection of information related to the proposed innovation, the evaluation of the utility to adopt or reject such an innovation, the decision-making process as to the adoption/rejection, the confirmation or modification of the previous decision. The rationale behind the model originates from the observation that each member of a social system takes a different length of time to get through the decision-making process. The members of the social system who react in a short time are called "innovators", while those who react very late are called "laggards". In the model, only the firm's phase is usually influenced by formal mass communication. The following three phases can only be affected by informal communication. Some actors have to be involved to make effective the process of acquisition of the diffused information: the source of information; the broker of information; the consulting company providing support for the acquisition; the end-user. A major problem is how to co-ordinate the activities of these actors. In areas where the density of innovative companies is high, the co-ordination occurs more or less spontaneously, but this is not so in the areas where there is a considerable lack of development. In these latter areas the IS can represent a mechanism for co-ordination of the actors involved in the innovative activity.

THE MANAGEMENT OF THE TECHNOLOGICAL TRANSFER PROCESS

The relation explicit/tacit is particularly critical in technology transfer. Indeed, the techno-economic transaction established between the source of a technology and the firm wanting to acquire it is concerned with the explicit part of the technology (e.g. patent, a prototype, a blue print, a manual, etc.). However, it is obvious that the economic value of that technology depends — indirectly — on the tacit, or rather, the "presumed" tacit component. The transfer of this tacit component is the true problem in the transfer of technology. Indeed, as we stated before, the tacit component of a technology cannot be precisely defined, unless it is done through a very generic and universal assessment of the processes involved. Thus, the clauses of a contract of technology transfer cannot include it. For this reason, many projects of technology transfer were unsuccessful simply because the tacit component was not transferred, or the buyer of the new technology was not able to develop a suitable halo around the nucleus of the acquired technology.

A technology, contextualised in the place where it has been generated, has a nucleus and a halo that are more or less ample and harmonic. The nature of the halo is strictly tied to the past experiences that led to the materialising of the technology — that is, all the past experiences that transformed one or more scientific outcomes in that usable technology, and all the competencies used to generate it. When this technology is purchased and hence moved to the buying company, it is the nucleus to be transferred and set up in the new place, according to the contractual clauses. Soon after the purchase, the novel technology has the same nucleus it had before the transfer, but a halo which is almost non-existent. The contract of technology transfer should necessarily include some initiatives aimed at developing the proper halo for the buying firm in an acceptable time. The nature of the halo depends on the process of integration of the novel technology in the new environment, and hence its use, and contextualisation. Thus the new halo will show different characteristics as compared to the halo before the transfer, and it will be more or less useful depending on the effort made by the firm to absorb the novel technology. Indeed, in a different environmental condition (in the same or in another firm) the same nucleus can give rise to a different halo. In other words, the same nucleus can be associated with many halos, depending on the contextualisation process. Thus it happens that some halos can lead to a successful transfer of the technology, while others cannot.

The previous result explains the following, well-known situation: during the diffusion of information relative to a certain technology across a multitude of different firms, not all the firms acquire that technology in the same time, and not all the firms among those receiving the technology are able to implement and use the same technology with the same degree of success.

From this discussion it follows that it is correct to say "diffusion of technological information", while it is not appropriate

FIGURE 9.1: VIRTUOUS CYCLE OF A TECHNOLOGY TRANSFER
PROCESS STARTING FROM MARKET DEMAND

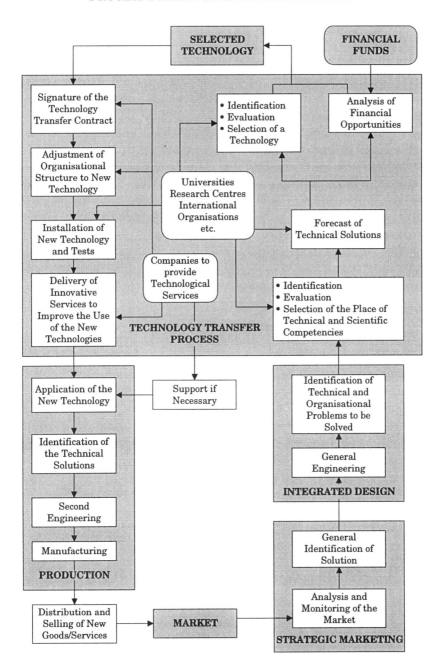

to say "diffusion of technology". It is also correct to say "transfer of technology" and not "transfer of technological innovation". The latter expression finds a justification in that, while a technology (or better, its nucleus) is an object that can be sold or bought and, therefore, transferred, the technological innovation is the result of an appropriate use of that technology, which necessarily must include the halo. This halo, as we discussed earlier, is never transferable, but only buildable by the firm which has already acquired the nucleus of the technology.

Let us consider the case of a firm which possesses a certain technology it has already experimented with and applied to manufacture some of its products. This firm possesses the nucleus around which a halo has been developed. Over time, as a consequence of the particular use of the technology and its relations with other technologies, competencies and activities — broadly speaking, with its context — this halo will change. When the technology is moved to the new context, the halo is still almost non-existent and the firm should learn how to use the technology in the new context to develop an adequate halo. The learning process occurring during the use of a technology mastered by the firm, which is to be applied for the first time to a new product, requires the generation of a new halo. Unfortunately, very often this process needs too much time. Therefore, the firm is compelled to intervene to accelerate the growth of the halo and make it harmonic with the nucleus and the context. Frequently, firms do not have the resources or the capability to make this intervention and, consequently, have to ask for advice from consulting companies providing services in the field of technology management (see Figure 9.1).

For the sake of clarity, the relevant conditions leading to a successful process of technology transfer are summarised below. The potential receiver of the novel technology must:

- Be able to identify the need to acquire a new technology to solve one or several problems that the firm is facing

- Be able to identify the sources of technological information and the organisations which own the technology

- Develop a strong and positive interest and a motivation towards the purchasing of that technology

- Know how to select the organisation willing to transfer the technology at the best technical and economic conditions

- Possess enough financial and professional resources to acquire the technology

- Know how to get further financial and professional resources if it lacks them

- Be able to carry out the negotiation to buy the technology and draw up the contract

- Be able to overcome all the barriers to innovation that will follow the introduction of the novel technology

- Have actual and realistic possibilities to use the technology at a profit

- Have a sufficient quantity of qualified professional resources to manage the utilisation in time of the technology at a profit and rapidly increase the halo

- Be able to redesign the organisation of the functional departments of the firm which are involved in the use of the new technology

- Be willing to revise the distribution of power and privileges in the departments where the new technology will be implemented.

The owner organisation must:

- Have the willingness to transfer that technology at realistic economic conditions and with different contracts

- Be able to assist the buyer with all the technical issues arising during the period in which the transfer of technology occurs

- Become convinced that in the negotiation for a technology transfer there are neither losers nor winners, but only two organisations that must both remain satisfied.

These conditions emphasise the well-known findings that a successful technology transfer is usually a market-oriented process (Nicolò, 1995).

THE PROCESS OF TECHNOLOGICAL INNOVATION AND THE INNOVATION STRUCTURES

The early studies on technological innovation tended to reduce innovation to a single focal point — the entrepreneur or the firm — thus not considering the influence of the spatial context on the creation of the new technology (Gordon, 1991; Perrin, 1991). Innovation was supposed to be essentially random and indifferent to the specifics of the place of occurrence, while geographical regions were treated essentially as a sort of collection of entrepreneurs, their importance being assessed only with respect to the presence or absence of some appropriate psychological or cultural predisposition for the emergence of individual innovative capabilities. Sometimes, space was also considered an exogenous variable like technology itself, and the production of new technology dependent on the geographical availability of cost-efficient combinations of specific production factors.

The advent of new computer-based technologies has given force to the reverse idea that autonomous regional initiatives can create new industrial formations. Analysis based on location characteristics, shifting the focus onto area variables (some specific attributes of a certain area that can favour the emergence of a high technology industry), explains the prerequisites for the re-emergence of classical entrepreneurialism in terms of interacting spatial factors of production and capability creation (Hakansson, 1987; Stohr, 1986; Freeman, 1991). Technological innovation has become more and more frequently a product of social interaction, a process happening both at the intra-regional level in the form of a collective learning process, and through inter-regional linkages facilitating the firm's access to different local innovation capabilities, fed by such social phenomena as intergenerational transfer of know-how, imitation of successful managerial practices and technological innovations, inter-personal face-to-face contacts, formal or informal co-operation between firms, tacit circulation of commercial, financial and technical information. Territorial factors and organisations act not only as a complement to firms and market forces, but also play a major role in the innovation process (Camagni, 1991). In order to innovate, a firm must procure resources and information from outside. To analyse the innovation process, one must therefore investigate the mechanism governing the whole of the firm–environment system. In this context, innovation is no longer produced by one isolated firm, but rather it is the result of an organisation built on a set of interdependencies between local and non-local elements (Aydalot, 1985; Scott, 1986; Crevosier and Maillat, 1991; Maillat and Perrin, 1990).

The innovation process occurs indeed as a technical exchange among different actors, such as individuals, firms, and institutions. As a consequence, it is useful to see innovation as the product of an interaction between two or among several actors, a *network of innovators*, rather than the product of a single actor. New knowledge in terms of ideas to develop new products or processes, or information useful to solving technical problems, frequently arises from the interface between different areas of technological knowledge (von Hippel, 1977; Hakansson, 1987). In those situations in which exchanges among various actors occur, different forms of knowledge combine to give rise to innovative situations. Technical solutions identified by an actor to solve technical problems in a certain context can be usefully adopted by another actor belonging to the network in order to solve similar problems in a context which is slightly or totally different. A network configuration can foster the process of technological innovation for two reasons. On the one hand, to be part of a network increases the probability and the potential improvement of the quality of the interaction among the actors. On the other hand, one must not forget that products are frequently based on the combination of various, often numerous, technologies which need competencies from different technological domains. To establish steady collaborative relations among the units which participate in the process of innovation can favour the creation of an interface and a bridge between specialised actors who possess specific competencies. The actors within the network often have to adapt, modify and redefine technological knowledge in order to contextualise it to the different situations. In the network perspective, the innovation process is strongly characterised by learning, adaptation and socialisation among units. All these elements require resources which every actor does not always possess. The interaction process within the network enables the actors to utilise — by sharing — critical resources possessed by some of the units. That is true both in the case of immaterial and material, financial and professional resources necessary to the implementation of an innovative process.

However, information essentially remains the critical resource throughout the process. Elaborated by the units of the network it becomes new technology, material or immaterial, available for new applications. Thus, the process of technological innovation becomes — in the network perspective — a process in which information relative to a certain technology is transferred from the place in which it has been developed to the place in which it will be utilised (Fisher, 1980). Actually, even though a certain amount of information and knowledge is embodied in a physical object when the technology is used, technological innovation is essentially an activity of search, selection, treatment, and utilisation of technical and managerial information aimed at the solution of specific technical, managerial and organisational problems. These problems represent an answer to determined or latent needs of the market.

The distinction between the processes in which new technology is generated and the following transfer of technology is not clear (Sahal, 1981). Because of the nature of technology itself, as we previously discussed, the transfer of technology does not occur as easily as the purchase of a product or a blueprint. The unit which receives the technology has to devote resources to assimilate, adapt, and improve the original technology, to re-generate a halo around the nucleus that makes it possible to use the technology. Modifications and further improvement of the technology constitute an integral part of the transfer. Technology is developed in a specific context and can hardly be introduced into a new environment without any change (Allen, 1990).

Each actor in the network contributes to the process of innovation by enriching the value of information, processing it in order to make it possible to use it. The availability of information, and the capability of the actors who participate in the process of innovation and the co-ordination of the processes to search, select and process information, are as a consequence critical (Kanter, 1983; Tushman, 1979a; 1979b). Therefore, organisations have to acquire some units able to monitor the external environment and the development of the technology. Allen (1970) found that some difficulties related to the transfer of information across the boundaries of organisations emerged due to the lack of professional roles of "boundary-spanners" or "technological gatekeepers". Several studies have emphasised how technology can only be transferred through direct contact between individuals and that the transfer of technology often requires the transfer of skilled people to overcome cultural barriers.

An attempt to understand how an innovation structure becomes a catalyst and "producer" of innovation may be made by considering the scheme illustrated in Figure 9.1. It illustrates the *virtuous cycle* of the process of technology transfer when a new product or service is developed. The model emphasises the roles that some institutions can play in the technology transfer. In particular, university departments, public-owned research laboratories, international technical organisations or some other analogous organisations can be identified as sources of technology. They play the roles indicated in Figure 9.1. Without any effective analysis of financial opportunities, either public or private, the processes of technology transfer cannot be performed. Therefore, the sources of finance are critical subjects to include in these processes. A third typology of actors which play an important role is formed by agencies and companies which provide technological services (the technical, organisational, contractual and fiscal support) to the firm which wants to purchase the technology.

These three types of actors, which are shown in Figure 9.1 by rounded oblongs, usually do not co-ordinate spontaneously. Thus, the lack of co-ordination and integration among the various actors can determine a dangerous lack of efficiency for the process of technology transfer. Market and technological opportunities, and the availability of financial resources, can, alone or together, stimulate the emergence of new ideas able to generate technological innovation. The activation of internal and external resources and the use of competencies internal to the organisation or coming from the external environment make it possible to refine the initial idea by solving practical problems. The innovation process thus occurs — involving several units spread throughout the territory — as a set of chained cycles of research, selection, transfer, processing and synthesis of information and knowledge from the market and the sources of the technology, which combining with competencies and resources belonging to the organisation, create new useful knowledge.

Spatial proximity not only reduces physical distance but also makes the exchange of information easier, facilitates the adoption of similar cultural psychological attitudes and enhances the frequency of interpersonal contacts and co-operation. All these elements are crucial. They determine the local response capability to a changing external environment and its innovativeness (Camagni, 1991). However, they are far from being sufficient. Even though geographical elements are relevant, the solution is not of a spatial, but rather of an organisational nature. Indeed, several studies emphasise how some specific activities, which are able to co-ordinate and integrate the actors and the resources which take part in technological innovation, have a positive effect upon the process, because they increase the amount and quality of the information diffused, enhance the success rate of the technology transfer processes and improve the firm's innovation capability (Hakansson, 1987; Allen, 1977; Twiss, 1980; Camagni, 1991).

The level of development of the geographical area strongly affects the emergence of difficulties in the diffusion and transfer of technology. The diffused innovation capability, typical of the areas where the density of firms which continuously introduce new products is high, and the presence of imitation and simulation behaviours of the firms, largely increases the probability of diffusion of technical information across the system of firms. Vice versa, the barriers to innovation are often insurmountable in those areas where the density of innovative firms is low.

The social and economic characteristics of the area where the IS is located heavily influence its growth and development. Thus an IS located in a late-developing area differs from an IS in a developed area.

The late-developing areas are characterised by a lack of connective tissue linking together the places where the technical and scientific knowledge are created, the sources of technology, and the places where this technology can be utilised. The connective tissue between the sources of technical and scientific knowledge is formed by a great number of factors which operate in the area:

- Manufacturing and craft firms having different size and innovation capability

- Firms providing innovative services; often these firms are absent from the under-developed areas

- Economic and financial institutions, which in the slow-developing areas (late-developing areas), tend to collect local savings and transfer them elsewhere rather than investing to foster local entrepreneurship

- Commercial and sales/distribution agencies, particularly those which operate in international markets, and which are usually not present in slow-developing areas

- Local administration offices, which should foster innovation processes are, on the contrary, perceived by local firms as centres of political influence in the slow-developing areas.

In a late-developing area the linkages between these different factors are absent or weak. As a consequence, the connective tissue is fragmented, co-operation and association between firms scarcely pursued by local entrepreneurs, innovation services are missing, sales markets are bounded to the local area, the few innovation attempts do not have any sort of positive effect upon other firms, often local public administration hampers innovation processes.

An IS in a late-developing area should organise, promote and implement suitable interventions aimed at developing the connective tissue between the sources of the technical and scientific knowledge and the users of the scientific outcomes in the area.

The major goal of an IS in a slow-developing area is to start a wide process of innovation continued over time, able to gradually involve all the economic actors of that area.

Summing up, an IS must design, organise and manage:

- The promotion and supply of services enabling firms to identify new market opportunities, at national and international level

- The supply of technological information services, market and competitor intelligence, financial opportunities information

- The supply of services to start specific technology transfer projects, creating new professional roles and re-qualifying people when needed

- The initiatives aimed at diffusing and fostering the sensitisation of the culture of technology management across local firms

- The monitoring of the technological assets of firms in order to enhance their competitive capabilities

- The supply of consultancy services in the field of business organisation and management, and the training of entrepreneurs, managers and professionals of the local small firms

- Initiatives aimed at identifying, assessing, and selecting opportunities for new entrepreneurship, assisting the creation, growth and development of new firms

- The individuation of the public and private sources of financing, to absorb the cost of innovation projects

- A management system supporting firms in their decision-making activity with regard to innovation activity.

CONCLUSION

In conclusion, we summarise the major concepts discussed in the previous paragraphs relative to the role of the IS:

1. The ISs operate with the objectives of contributing to local social and economic development. Consequently, an IS acting in a region where the density of the innovative organisations is high, and the sources of new technologies are numerous, should have a quite different role and behaviour compared to an analogous structure which operates in a region experiencing considerable delays in development. In the first case, the IS will be mainly involved in promoting new research projects and new high-tech processes, taking advantage of the fact that the relationships between universities, research centres and local companies are, in general, strong. In the second case, the IS will act to stimulate the local organisations to acquire and use, at a profit, conventional and well-known technologies.

2. In order to achieve the objective of the previous point, any IS must be related to many different local actors: universities, research centres, financial organisations (i.e. banks, venture capitalists, etc.), local government, small and medium companies, innovative services companies, etc. Sometimes these relationships consist in participating as partners to the managing company of the IS. For instance, the company which runs the Science and Technology Park at Calabria in southern Italy, has at present about 70 partners of the types listed above. Each partner can take part in specific innovative projects promoted by the IS, thus playing an active and important role according to its professional and entrepreneurial capability, alongside many other actors. The local university and research centres play the educational role, the banks and local venture capitalists play the financial role, the consultancy and service companies the role of the Innovative Service Office, the local companies the entrepreneurial role, etc.

3. As the mission of the IS is to contribute to the development of the local socio-economic system, such a structure should organise and co-ordinate appropriate projects aimed at promoting and developing the local entrepreneurial culture. Briefly, the IS will support the companies in learning how to take advantage of acquiring new technologies from the local universities and research institutions, strengthening the co-operation between these actors and creating, as a consequence of this co-operation, new companies primarily though a process of industrial and academic spin-offs. To achieve results like this is quite difficult, and the IS has to organise qualified professionals, with the task of stimulating, maintaining and following up on hundreds of contacts with managers and academicians in order to select any interesting potential entrepreneurial opportunities.

4. The diffusion of technologies implies that at least two actors must have a part in the process, one as the source of technical and organisational knowledge, and the other as the potential final user. Frequently, a third actor, such as a company providing innovative services, supports the final user in identifying and selecting the appropriate source and getting the appropriate information. The local IS can promote and co-ordinate the activities of the above three actors.

5. The transfer of technologies is — as discussed previously — a complex process which usually requires, as in the diffusion of technologies, at least three actors having an active role: the technology source, the final user of the selected technology and a consultancy company which supports the final user in defining the technical and economic clauses of the contract to acquire the new technology. Often a fourth actor, such as another consultancy company, could help the user of the technology learn how to implement the acquired technology in a more effective way. In this case, too, the local IS can promote and co-ordinate the activities of the above four actors.

6. Finally, the role of the managing company of the IS is to promote initiatives, select opportunities, co-ordinate local actors, integrate local resources, and to programme large-scale innovative regional projects. For this reason the IS is sometimes called an Innovation Regional System.

Notes

[1] In several industrialised countries the typical *Innovation Structure* may be called either Technopolis, or Science and Technology Parks, or Technopark, or Business Innovation Centre, or Development Agencies, etc. In the last few years definitions and classifications for such structures (we remind the reader that, a few years ago, the European Community gave some precise definitions about those different structures, but now those definitions have been called into question because it was clear that a distinction should be based not on their name but on their missions and functions).

[2] For the sake of clarity, we recall the following definitions (Corti, 1997): *technology* means a homogeneous set of technical and organisational knowledge, the use of which allows its owners to perform expected goals. Moreover, *technological change* means only a possible technical modification of a given technology; *technological innovation* means a suitable technological change which helps the operator to achieve a specific expected goal. Therefore, not all technological changes lead to a successful result.

[3] "Information constitutes the first and general input into the innovation process. It is mainly produced in a diffuse way, quickly exchanged at not excessively high costs, and nearly always rapidly rendered 'obsolete' by production of new information. Since, moreover, it can almost never be fully appropriated (except in the short-term), it gives rise to numerous spill-overs that contribute to cross-fertilisation of different territorial systems. Knowledge implies some specific qualities in the receiver of the information, and adequate receptive structures. The information is not in fact always used by the receiver, or in other words the receiver is not always able to internalise it in a structured, organised way into his own information system. This nearly always means that knowledge takes place selectively. Competence adds a further element, that of 'know how': it is connected with the individual's and the collective's learning process and is therefore stimulated by performance of the productive stage that most exploit the process of learning by doing. Creativity, in the last place, emerges from the synergic meeting of information, knowledge and competence, combined in a specific context. It is almost non-exchangeable and is not necessarily localised in the central area." (Bramanti and Senn, 1991, p. 97)

⁴At times the source of technological information is a broker organisation; more frequently it is the organisation which owns the technology.

⁵ The literature on innovation is extremely wide. The term "innovation" has been used with different meanings. We suggest the reader refer to the following authors: Bhushan and Easwaran (1995), Boyden (1976), Brown (1981), Camagni (1991), Corti (1997), Drucker (1985), Foster (1986), Freeman (1982), Marquis (1969), Roberts (1986), Rothwell (1972), Sahal (1981) and Tomlin (1985).

References

Allen, T.J. (1970), "Communication Networks in R&D Laboratories", *R&D Management*, Vol. 1, pp. 14–21.

Allen, T.J. (1977), *Managing the Flow of Technology: Technology Transfer and the Dissemination of Technological Information within the R&D Organization*, Cambridge, MA: The MIT Press.

Allen, T.J. (1990), "People and Technology Transfer", Working Paper, No. 3201-90-BPS (Business Policy and Strategies), Cambridge, MA: MIT.

Aydalot, P. (1985), *Economie Régionale et Urbaine*, Paris: Economica.

Bhushan, Y.K. and Easwaran, S. (1995), "Innovation: the Concept, the Process, the People", Paper presented at the Conference on University–Enterprise Partnerships in Action, University of North London, June 22–23, London.

Boyden, J. (1976), "A Study of the Innovation Process", Sloan School of Management, Cambridge, MA: MIT.

Bramanti, A. and Senn, L. (1991), "Innovation, Firms and Milieux: A Dynamic and Cyclic Approach" in Camagni, R. (ed.), *Innovation Networks: Spatial Perspectives*, London: Belhaven Press, pp. 89–104.

Brown, L.A. (1981), *Innovation Diffusion: A New Perspective*, London: Methuen.

Camagni, R. (ed.) (1991), *Innovation Networks: Spatial Perspectives*, London: Belhaven Press.

Corti, E. (1984), "Il Trasferimento delle Innovazioni Tecnologiche in Agree Geografiche in via di Sviluppo", *Problemi di Transizione*, No. 15, July.

Corti, E. (1994), "Technology Diffusion and Transfer in the Eastern Countries", NATO Advanced Research Workshop on Science and Innovation as Strategic Tools for Industrial and Economic Growth, Moscow, Russia, October 24–26.

Corti, E. (1997), *La Gestione dell'Innovazione e dei Progetti*, Naples: CUEN Ed.

Corti, E. and Piperno, O.W. (1996), "The Science and Technology Park of Calabria", Paper presented at the Conference on Small and Medium-Sized Enterprises in a Learning Society, June 20–21, London.

Crevosier, O. and Maillat, D. (1991), "Milieu, Industrial Organisation and Territorial Production Systems: Towards a New Theory of Spatial Development", in R. Camagni (ed.), *Innovation Networks: Spatial Perspectives*, London: Belhaven Press, pp. 13–34.

Drucker, P.F. (1985), *Innovation and Entrepreneurship: Practice and Principles*, New York: Harper & Row Publishers.

Fisher, W.A. (1980), "Scientific and Technical Information and the Performance of R&D Groups", *TIMS Studies in the Management Sciences*, Vol. 15, pp. 67–89.

Formica, P. (1994), "Co-operative Competition between SMEs and Major Industrial Companies: A New Way to Secure Technology Transfer and Cooperation for a Competitive Advantage", Paper presented at the Conference VISION-EUREKA — Small and Medium-Sized Enterprises: Technology Transfer and Co-operation for Competitive Advantage, Oslo Technology Park, Lillehammer.

Foster, R.N. (1986), *Innovation: the Attacker's Advantage*, London: Macmillan.

Freeman, C. (1982), *The Economics of Industrial Innovation*, London: Frances Pinter Publishers.

Freeman, C. (1991), "Networks of Innovators: A Synthesis of Research Issues", *Research Policy*, No. 20.

Gordon, R. (1991) "Innovation, Industrial Networks and High-Technology Regions", in Camagni, R. (ed.), *Innovation Net-*

works: Spatial Perspectives, London: Belhaven Press, pp. 174–195.

Hakansson, H. (1987), *Industrial Technological Development: A Network Approach*, London: Routledge.

Hill, C.T. (1979), "Technological Innovation: Agent of Growth and Change", in C.T. Hill and J.M. Utterback (eds.) *Technological Innovation for a Dynamic Economy*, New York: Pergamon Press, pp. 1–39.

Kanter Moss, R. (1983), *The Change Masters*, New York: Simon and Schuster.

Lo Storto, C. (1996), "Technology Nature, Communication Pattern and Performance in Technology Transfer Projects", Paper presented at the Annual Meeting of the Academy of Management, Cincinnati, August 9–14.

Maillat, D. and Perrin, J.C. (eds.) (1990), *Actes du Colloque GREMI*, Paris: Economica.

Mansfield, E. (1968), *Industrial Research and Technological Innovation: An Econometric Analysis*, New York: Norton.

Mansfield, E. (1977), *The Production and Application of New Industrial Technology*, New York: Norton.

Marquis, D.G. (1969), "The Anatomy of Successful Innovation", *Innovation*, Vol. 7.

Nicolò, N. (1995), "Markets and Systems-driven Knowledge and Technology Transfer for Economic Development", Paper presented at the Conference on University–Enterprise Partnerships in Action, University of North London, June 22–23, London.

Perrin, J.C. (1991), "Technological Innovation and Territorial Development: An Approach in Terms of Networks and Milieux, in Camagni, R. (ed.) (1991), *Innovation Networks: Spatial Perspectives*, London: Belhaven Press, pp. 35–54.

Petroni, G. (1994), "Le Agenzie Locali per l'Innovazione Tecnologica", Rapporti CNR: Progetto Finalizzato al "Funzionamento della Pubblica Amministrazione", Roma.

Raffa, M. and Zollo, G. (1992), "Il Rapporto tra Innovazione Tecnologica e Oranizzazione nelle Piccole Imprese Innovative", *Piccola Impresa / Small Business*, No. 2.

Rapp, F. (1981), *Analytical Philosophy of Technology*, Dordrecht: D. Reidel Publishing Company.

Reigado, F.M. (1995), "Innovative Environment, Technology Transfer and Entrepreneurship Development", Paper presented at the Conference on University–Enterprise Partnerships in Action, University of North London, June 22–23, London.

Roberts, E.B. (1986), "Generating Effective Corporate Innovations", *Business Development Review*, Spring.

Roberts, E.B. et al. (1981), "Commercial Innovations from University Faculty", *Research Policy*, Vol. 10, pp. 108–126.

Rogers, E.M. and Shoemaker, F.F. (1971), *Communications of Innovations*, New York: The Free Press.

Rosenberg, N. (1976), *Perspectives on Technology*, Cambridge: Cambridge University Press.

Rosenberg, N. (1982), *Inside the Black Box: Technology and Economics*, Cambridge, MA: Cambridge University Press.

Rothwell, R. (1972), "Factors for Success in Industrial Innovations, Project Sappho, A Comparative Study of Success and Failure in Industrial Innovation", SPRU.

Rothwell, R. and Zegveld, W. (1982), *Innovation and Small and Medium-Sized Firms*, London: Frances Pinter Publishers.

Sahal, D. (1981), *Patterns of Technological Innovation*, Reading, MA: Addison-Wesley.

Scott, W.R. (1987), "High Technology and Territorial Development: the Rise of the Orange County Complex, 1955–1984", *Urban Geography*, Vol. 71, pp.3–45.

Stohr, W. (1986), "Territorial Innovation Complexes", in P. Aydalot (ed.), *Milieux Innovateurs en Europe*, Paris: GREMI, pp. 29–55.

Sunman, H. (ed.) (1989), "The Role of Science Parks in Promotion of Innovation and Transfer of Technology", Proceeding of the UKSPA's Annual Conference.

Tomlin, B. (1985), "Technical Ventures as a Technological Innovation Strategy", Sperry Management Summer School, St. Paul de Vence, August.

Tushman, M.L. (1979a), "Managing Communication Networks in R&D Laboratories", *Sloan Management Review*, Winter, pp. 37–39.

Tushman, M.L. (1979b), "Work Characteristics and Sub-unit Communication Structure: A Contingency Analysis", *Administrative Science Quarterly*, Vol. 24, pp. 92–98.

Twiss, B.C. (1980), *Managing Technological Innovation*, London: Longman.

Von Hippel, E. (1977), "The Dominant Role of the Users in the Semiconductor and Electronic Subassembly Process Innovation", *IEEE Transaction on Engineering Management*, EM 24 pp. 60–71.

Von Hippel, E. (1988), *The Source of Innovation*, Oxford: Oxford University Press.

Winter, S.G. (1987), "Knowledge and Competence as Strategic Assets", in D.J. Teece (ed.), *The Competitive Challenge: Strategies for Industrial Innovation and Renewal*, Cambridge, MA: Ballinger, pp. 159–184.

10

TECHNOLOGY-BASED ENTREPRENEURSHIP: ACADEMIC SPIN-OFFS IN LESS DEVELOPED AREAS

Emilio Bellini and Giuseppe Zollo

Summary

This chapter explores the hypothesis that encouraging *academic spin-offs* should be an effective policy for the economic development and diffusion of technological innovation in less developed areas. It is based on field research carried out by the authors. The weakness of relationships between university and small firms is due to several cultural, organisational and managerial barriers. As suggested by the analysis of some technology-based firms and by a close inspection of the cultural aspects of academic research groups, academic spin-offs seem to be a very effective way to overcome those barriers. The chapter discusses the role that science and technology parks can play in developing policies and actions to encourage the increasing involvement of universities in generating new business ventures.

INTRODUCTION

It is widely recognised that academic research may represent an important resource to overcome some structural weaknesses of less developed areas (LDAs) such as:

1. The high rate of mortality of small firms during their first years of life, due to their inability to renew their technological competencies

2. The structural problem of job creation for graduate and undergraduate youth

3. The difficulties of local economies in grasping the opportunities raised by technological breakthroughs.

The utilisation of researchers' competencies to generate academic spin-offs (ASOs) is regarded as an important way to connect universities to the local economy and to maximise the endogenous resources of LDAs.

Contrary to what a naïve theoretical approach seems to suggest, the presence in the same area of both large technological universities and a large number of small firms is not a sufficient condition for the development of effective relationships between university and small and medium-sized enterprises (SMEs). The Campania Region in Southern Italy is such a case.

In Campania there are seven universities, which account for more than 120,000 students and 3,000 teachers and researchers. The presence of technical knowledge is testified by four Faculties of Engineering, which account for about 20,000 students, 500 teachers and researchers and about 150 doctorate students. These figures, together with the presence of laboratories in many departments and with the international reputation of the local scientists, show that scientific and technical capabilities in Campania are deeply rooted in the academic tradition. Nevertheless, compared with the well-established academic environment, the economic involvement of the university shows a lasting weakness.

The university's involvement in industrial and commercial activities can take different forms. A taxonomy for university–industry interorganisational relationships identifies six different types (Bonaccorsi and Piccaluga, 1994):

1. *Personal Informal Relationships*, such as individual consultancy, informal exchange forums and workshops

2. *Personal Formal Relationships*, such as scholarships and exchange of personnel

3. *Third Parties*, such as liaison offices and applied research institute

4. *Formal Targeted Agreements*, such as training of employees and co-operative research projects

5. *Formal Non-Targeted Agreements*, such as research grants

6. *Creation of Focused Structures*, such as research consortia and innovation centres.

Campania's university involvement in industrial and commercial activities is concerned with the first two types of relationships, and the presence in co-operative research projects, training activities and research consortia between universities and large companies. The university is generally absent as an active institutional subject in promoting the direct exploitation of the results of research developed in the university's laboratories. Nowadays the prevalent commercial exploitation of scientific and technological knowledge is realised by university scientists (teachers or researchers) as a private commitment. The common path of academic spin-offs follows the model suggested by Richter (1986): in the incubation stage the university scientists develop considerable consulting practices for private companies, and at the same time they manage research teams that have the character of "quasi-firm". It is sufficient that the perception of a profitable market occasion should convince the scientists to move from ordinary consulting activities into entrepreneurial activities.

The first issue with which this chapter is concerned regards the significance of academic spin-offs in sustaining the economic development of the Southern Italy region. The second issue regards the strengths and weaknesses of spontaneous spin-offs. The final issue concerns how and to what extent political guidance of academic spin-offs is possible, and what institutional actors should do to promote it.

This chapter is organised as follows:

- The first section develops several issues concerning economic development sustained by SME networks

- The second section presents some cases of ASOs in Campania and discusses the role of technical entrepreneurs during the firm's growth path

- The third section analyses the ASOs issues from the point of view of university researchers on the basis of field research on 80 research groups in the University of Salerno

- The fourth section discusses the barriers and the motivations of academic researchers to develop ASOs

- The final section draws some guidelines for developing ASOs in LDAs.

SYSTEMS AND NETWORKS OF SMALL FIRMS

The System Perspective

The economic development of north-east Italian areas and the success of Italian industrial districts during the first half of the 1990s raise the issue of an economic development based on systems formed by small firms. Scientific investigation and political debate are focusing on the identification of success factors of small firms and on the possibility of exporting the development model of an industrial district to less developed areas of the country.

The analyses carried out on SMEs and industrial districts, starting from the middle of the 1970s (Bagnasco, 1977) and developing though the 1980s (Bagnasco, 1988; Becattini, 1979, 1987, 1989; Brusco, 1986) have clearly shown how industrial growth based on small firms is strongly linked to the local context, because of the strong interdependencies that firms have consolidated over time (Gandolfi, 1990). These analyses implicitly or explicitly concluded that the systems factors sustaining the success of industrial districts were not reproducible because they were the result of long and complex evolutionary processes, involving economic, social and cultural aspects. No industrial policy had the possibility to plan and develop complex actions to get effective long-term results (Cotugno et al., 1982; Gros-Pietro, 1995).

The fundamental argument which justifies these conclusions is that the small firm is an "incomplete" economic actor, because the small firm is always a part of a system from which it derives most of its human, cultural, financial, economic and social resources. The industrial districts are able to develop and renew their resources because of the "entrepreneurial ambience" (Becattini, 1979) that creates proper environmental conditions. That ambience is a system's resource, the result of an historical development based on entrepreneurial traditions, managerial practices, shared values, specialised production, specialist workers, financial institutions, business services, personal relationships and reciprocal trust.

Unlike the large firm, the small firm cannot implement organisational structures and practices and develop an internal cultural environment, which defines the main competitive features of its own resources. It does not have the necessary resources to finance its own long-term development (Huppert, 1981; Marc, 1982; Nagel, 1981), it has simple decision-making processes based entirely on the expertise of the entrepreneurial group (Raffa and Zollo, 1988), and it needs external support for strategic activities such as training, marketing and technological research. Under such conditions small firms try to reduce fixed costs and maximise the use of human resources (Lassini, 1990) and the use of the resources available in the environment (Brown and Schwab, 1984; Oakey, 1984; OECD, 1982, Rothwell and Zegveld, 1982; Rothwell, 1984), especially technological and professional resources (Bianco and Luciano, 1982; Del Monte et al., 1982). It is more appropriate to think of a small firm as an entity which "revives" every day by acquiring its resources from an outside environment and "dies" every evening when its resources go back to the environment.

The performance of the small firm depends mainly on what happens to its resources when they are part of the environment, out of the control of the firm. This fact explains why a single small firm can possess limited abilities and insufficient know-how and, at the same time, can show positive performances: it is sufficient that the small firm belongs to an appropriate system (Lorenzoni, 1979; Norman, 1977).

The implications of this system's view on industrial politics are discouraging. If the system plays the key role in the small firm's success, regional economic development based on small firms becomes impossible. Of course, industrial policy can sustain the development of small firms through appropriate interventions in sustaining entrepreneurship, export, financing, employment training, innovation, but *the system view claims that industrial policies are unable to produce by themselves a self-sustaining industrial development.*

The Network Perspective

Nevertheless, during the 1980s this conclusion began to be challenged by several analysts who, on the basis of a closer inspection of the reality of industrial districts, proposed the category of "network" as an intermediate organisational form between the current categories of "firm" and "system". By using the network category, successful industrial systems can be analysed from a new point of view, which opens interesting perspectives for the definition of development policies of SMEs in less developed areas. This new point of view sees the system just as one of many possible forms of relationships between different companies and institutions, probably the most advanced one. The network category is based on the recognition that co-operation is a possible way of governing economic transactions, intermediate between the classic alternatives of "hierarchy" and "market". Within the conceptual framework of the "co-operation" and "network" model, new organisational types appear, among which are the "quasi-markets" (Barney and Ouchi, 1985), the "quasi-firms" (Eccles, 1981), the "macro-firms" (Dioguardi, 1983), the "satellite companies" (Lorenzoni, 1985) and "business networks" (Dioguardi, 1986; Lorenzoni, 1987).

Traditional forms of relationships between companies (production cluster, consortia, third party manufacturing, joint ventures and industrial districts) should be considered as more or less evolved forms of networks. Albino et al. (1992) developed a classification of possible relationships, pointing out seven criteria for identifying the networks: the symmetry of relationships, nature of links, degree of formalisation of relationships, geographic range, nature of the actors, horizontal or vertical relationships, and spontaneous or planned relationships. The widening of perspectives that this taxonomy introduces has the advantage of providing a general framework to recognise various types of networks ranging from the most simple relationship between two economic actors to the most complex type of network corresponding to the industrial system. The relevant consequence of this approach is that it makes it possible to establish more or less complex networks, from which eventually an industrial system could develop. In other words, the network viewpoints tell us that it is possible to build part of the entrepreneurial ambience by designing appropriate relationships between local firms and other institutions. The network should play the role of an artificial entrepreneurial ambience, that overcomes the specific constraints of local environment.

The Technological Ambience

One of the most important parts of the entrepreneurial environment or ambience is the technological one, because technology and innovation are fundamental resources to sustain competitive advantage in turbulent and global markets. Stadenmaier (1985) defines three dimensions of the "technological ambience" sustaining emerging technologies: "technological support network", "technical tradition" and "systems". The "technological support network" includes the many technical capacities of a given society, capacities embodied in hardware or in the skills and knowledge of its people. The "technical tradition" is a cognitive reality, that is, the conventional rationale, practice, procedure, method and instrumentation accepted by a relevant community of technological practitioners. The "systems" are the intercommunicating units and activities interrelated within a unifying principle of integration (theoretical model), that makes them elements of a single functional artefact. This artefact is a working paradigm, forming both technological problems and solutions.

It is necessary to emphasise that a technological ambience, as part of the larger entrepreneurial ambience, is an historical artefact, made by a community and by a tradition. The technological ambience sets up the possibilities for a firm to be innovative because it defines the personal and immaterial resources fuelling technological innovations: skills, practices, references. The firm should operate within an appropriate technological ambience in order to be innovative. Usually the large firm is able to build up an artificial technological ambience within the organisation in order to compensate for the deficiencies of the outside environment. For small firms the issue of innovation is more complex, because the technological ambience is something belonging to the environment, out of control of the single small firm. The small firm can only choose the amount and the typology of investment necessary to use and upgrade a given technological ambience. For this reason networking is a critical activity. Through networking two small firms can realise the most effective balance between complementary and shared resources. Usually complementary resources are those directly involved in primary activities supporting the firm's competitive advantage, while shared resources could be considered as "black boxes" that the firms incorporate in their current activities in order to raise their general efficiency and effectiveness. When a technological ambience is well developed the amount and quality of the available "black boxes" is very high and includes: technical expertise, suppliers, financial services, and so on. When small firms are part of a network, the "black boxes" circulate within the network, as information, services and products that firms exchange with each other. From this point of view it is normal that small firms which possess a small amount of distinctive competencies can display good performances because they are able to incorporate within their activities a large number of "black boxes".

An unsolvable problem arises when Small Innovative Firms (SIFs) operate within an environment where the local technological ambience is very poor. In those situations the SIFs are pushed to make higher investments in order to connect with non-local technological sources, and in the long run they are forced to lessen their innovative capabilities.

Nevertheless, a very interesting situation arises in LDAs (e.g. Campania and Calabria in Southern Italy) where the "technological ambience" is poor, but there exist actors, such as university, research centres, large companies, which could become potential sources of technological resources. In those cases it is possible to build up an artificial technological ambience through networking. In the next two sections we explore the possibility of universities participating in the development of such a network, on the basis of two field research activities.

CHARACTERISTICS OF ACADEMIC SPIN-OFFS

There is general agreement on the usefulness of the involvement of universities in economic activities, even if the positive effects lag by several years (Berman, 1990). As suggested by Piero Formica and Jay Mitra (1996: 156–159), the university–industry network creates a supportive environment for three types of spin-offs:

- Enterprises set up by teaching or research staff of university and other research centres, which wish to exploit commercially the results of research conducted in academic environments

- Enterprises founded by graduates to exploit commercially the results of research in which they have been involved at their institution

- Enterprises run by people from outside the university (such as employed professional mangers in the private sector moving from their job to business ownership), who decide to exploit commercially the results of the university's or their own research.

According to this point of view the university–industry network could represent an effective environment for the creation of enterprises in Southern Italy. It is important to emphasise that even before the recent economic recession the creation of new enterprises in Southern Italy was the lowest in Italy (Fumagalli et al., 1988). However, other economists (Del Monte and Giannola, 1989) believe that, while the birth of new firms in Southern Italy is feasible, the real problem is the high mortality rate due to difficulties faced by new firms in establishing their business and sustaining their growth.

The above different points of view imply that, for the creation and/or development of different industrial policies, it should firstly be necessary to establish a policy for the formation of new enterprises. Secondly, an effective industrial policy should support the growth of existing enterprises.

In the first case the main ingredients are the availability of professional services, the skills and culture of the potential entrepreneur and the financial support at the start-up stage. In the second case an industrial policy should remove the growth barriers, that is, availability of financial resources, organisational and entrepreneurial weakness, availability of specialist suppliers and of professional services.

As regards university involvement in the implementation of such policy: in the first case, academic spin-offs are regarded as an important key for economic development, while in the second case, consultancy activities, training of employees, and joint research and development projects are regarded as more important.

The aim of this study is not to choose one or another point of view, or to establish whether it would be more effective to favour the birth of new entrepreneurs or the growth of established firms. Nevertheless, this debate is important, because we can derive a significant conclusion from it: at the start-up stage of a new enterprise the central issue is the entrepreneur, while at the maturity stage the central issue is the organisation, that is, the established relationships between the firm and internal and external resources. In reality these issues are strictly linked, because the organisational weaknesses in the maturity stage is often the result of the weaknesses of the entrepreneurial culture in the initial stage. In our opinion, political guidance of academic spin-offs should support, together with adequate services and financial support, the formation of an adequate entrepreneurial and managerial culture that will display positive effects in the maturity stage.

According to this point of view, the following key questions arise:

• What is the role played by the culture, education and skills of the academic entrepreneur in sustaining the competitive advantage of small firms?

- How do entrepreneurs adjust their know-how in the course of the firm's life?

- What are the inter-relations between initial know-how and a firm's development?

- What are the limits of spontaneous academic spin-offs?

- Is it possible to have political guidance in order to move from spontaneous actions to the generation of planned ones?

To attempt to answer those questions, several academic spin-offs (ASOs) in Campania were analysed in order to understand their weaknesses and strengths and to derive ideas and directions on what support should be more appropriate to sustain the economic role of universities.

Start-ups are common in emerging industries, such as personal computers, software, industrial control, biotechnology and so on. These sectors are characterised by the presence of many competing and often "redundant" companies, created under the double opportunities of availability of resources and growing market demand. A wide range of strategic and organisational choices are available for these firms, because traditions, habits, culture, standard process technology and reference examples are almost completely absent (Kao, 1991). In such conditions the entrepreneurs must deal with a high degree of uncertainty both internally and externally. The original culture, vision and skills of the entrepreneur are the unique factors which can turn the original ambiguity, uncertainty and disorder into a successful organisation (Filion, 1991).

An increasing number of studies refer to the personal characteristics of the entrepreneur as the key to the success of the firm in the early stages of its life (Miller et al., 1988; Lefebvre and Lefebvre, 1992). Roberts and Hauptman (1986) demonstrated that founders' characteristics were associated with the technological level of the firm's product. Moreover, Roberts (1991) presents a schematic model which assumes that new companies are dependent at their formation on the technological base learned by the entrepreneur from the incubating source, that is, former companies, university laboratories, engineering departments. Personal abilities and commitments and individual attitudes are seen to be the critical factor of successful entrepreneurial technology transfer.

This does not imply that the firm's performances should be attributed to entrepreneurial characteristics only. During the passage from organisational infancy to adulthood the firm undergoes crises of centralisation and direction (Greiner, 1972), due to the necessity of reducing the central role of the entrepreneur. The literature shows that a growing firm must have a minimum size, hold internal skills and maintain a network of stable linkages with external economic agents in order to support its innovation capability successfully.

In summing up current knowledge on the subject, it can be observed that the technical founder-entrepreneur plays a crucial role during the first stage of the firm's life, while during the growth stage, a more complex set of resources is necessary to sustain the firm's activities. According to Roberts (1991), only a few research studies focus on detailed aspects of the technical base of new firms during both stages. In order to explore those aspects a sample of small software firms founded by academic entrepreneurs with strong scientific and technical backgrounds have been studied (Raffa et al., 1994).

Small software firms were chosen for two reasons:

1. The software industry displayed a high growth rate in the last decade, and several new firms were founded by technical entrepreneurs, mainly coming from universities' laboratories and technical departments of large companies. In Campania, during the 1980s, about one-third of software companies could be considered academic spin-offs.

2. In the last three years, because of the economic recession and the general crisis in the information industry, the software sector went through a difficult period and the original technical culture of the academic entrepreneurs displayed weaknesses which prevented them from overcoming economic uncertainties.

During the years 1983–84, 132 software firms were studied, representing 84 per cent of the software firms in Southern Italy. The core of the software industry in Southern Italy was made up of small firms: 58.27 per cent of the sample have less than 10 employees, and 21.26 per cent have between 11 and 20 employees, whole only 4.72 per cent have more than 100 employees. The medium-sized firm range is very narrow in this sector (15.75 per cent).

The research revealed that 34.4 per cent of the firms entered the sector with technical know-how. This know-how is basically held by technicians who have left large firms operating in the information and electronics sector, or who have a university background. New entrants with technical know-how played a particularly important role when the market growth rate was particularly high.

For a lot of those firms detailed case studies were developed, and several firms were analysed at different stages of their life. In the years 1993–94 a new field survey was carried out around the small firms from the sample studied in the years 1983–84. The new survey was aimed at analysing organisational changes, development paths, product strategies and firms' performances, allowing for some considerations to be made as to the relation between initial know-how and the firm's development. A large number of indicators emerged from the research, but the present work summarises only the results related to six small firms, which were founded by academic entrepreneurs in Campania, and which are considered as a typical example of how the original culture of the entrepreneur affected the growth path of the firms.

The six firms surveyed followed various paths of growth, leading them to explore the opportunities provided by the market. Besides the original activities, some new activities were added, which sometimes even replaced the original ones. These choices tended to exploit and expand the existing know-how and, in some cases, the initial entrepreneurial skills were dropped and new skills were created.

The life of the small innovative firms was marked by changes that could give rise to different outcomes, such as growth, survival or death. In any case the small innovative firms had to cope with external changes (competitors, market and technology) and internal changes (professional skills, organisation and management). The high growth rate of the software industry in the 1980s should have driven small firms to focus their attention on growth issues to follow market expansion and to have access to new market segments. On the contrary, the technical background of the entrepreneurs allured them to focus on product development, enabling them to drive the firm into a market niche. In every surveyed firm the academic entrepreneurs were simultaneously responsible for management and software development. The firms maintain this organisational configuration for a very long time, with the entrepreneurial group, or even the single entrepreneur, performing all activities of the firm without any clear distinction between responsibilities and functions.

Moreover, entrepreneurs, under different forms, are directly involved in project development. This organisation is typical of the early stages in the life of firms founded by technical entrepreneurs. The firms usually focus on a single or few products and meet some difficulties in sustaining the innovation capability over time. As technical skills are mainly embodied in the entrepreneurial group, when the entrepreneur becomes more and more involved in management issues, the firms face many difficulties in renewing their technological background and, after a few years, they lose their strong technical advantage. Consequently, they experience the highest technological performances at the beginning of their life, then gradually settle down at lower innovation levels (new releases, program updating) and end up managing only the current market.

The cases illustrated in Table 10.1 display some typical growth paths of academic spin-off. These cases show that the technical culture usually drives the firms in a niche market, from which they have difficulty escaping. The prevalent destiny of those firms is to survive in the niche market. They are able to escape the niche boundaries only after completing and updating their initial know-how:

- By establishing new relationships with large firms, which transfer new managerial and market competencies to the small firm (Case 6)

- Integration of new competencies by external collaborations (Cases 2, 4 and 5)

- New relationships with the external environment that allowed the firm to strengthen its competitive capabilities (Cases 3, 4, 5 and 6).

In conclusion, the software case studies in Campania show that spontaneous ASOs occur in industries characterised by technological discontinuity, when the market growth rate is high. The technical culture of the entrepreneur drives the enterprises into niche markets. After a few years, when the original business ideas had been fully exploited, a lot of firms left the sector. Usually, the chances of firms surviving and growing are linked to the acquisition of new managerial competencies. For these reasons, spontaneous academic spin-offs play only a limited role in sustaining regional economic development.

TABLE 10.1: INITIAL ENTREPRENEURIAL CULTURE AND PATTERNS OF GROWTH

Cases	Initial Entrepreneurial Culture	Initial Market	Critical Event	Main Results
1	Entrepreneurs with academic experience	A software product for local market	The firm is forced to use new hardware technology	The firm survives around a single product
2	University professor	Accounting products for local market	Shifting to UNIX system; Introduction of marketing and production competencies	Size grows during the early 1980s; the firm maintains its current activities
3	Two electronic engineers with academic experience	Local market	Diversification towards professional services linked to software production	The firm survives in a local niche market
4	Three technicians and an engineer with academic experience	Hardware and software systems	Separation of software activities from hardware sales activities	The firm survives around its original competencies
5	Entrepreneurs with academic experiences	Software and services for local market	Diversification towards professional services linked to software production	Reduction of software development activities
6	Two university professors and some graduates	Custom software for local market	Participating share by a large firm	The firm became a production unit for a large firm

CULTURAL BARRIERS OF ACADEMIC SPIN-OFFS

An empirical study of the potential role of the University of Salerno in Campania in the innovation process and in potential ASOs has been carried out by the *Science and Technology Park of Salerno and Internal Areas* in the period 1995/96. The study was developed through interviews with researchers and data was gathered from official documents and other written material of the University Research Groups. The study's analysis unit was the "Research Group" (RG), because the university administrative classification (Faculties, Departments, Institutes) was not suitable for the purpose of analysis. The RG has been defined as "the group of teachers, researchers, doctorands, students and fellows involved steadily in research and scientific production activities".

The University of Salerno accounted for 130 RGs organised in 10 faculties (2 Faculties of Engineering, 2 Faculties of Economics, Faculties of Science, Pharmaceutics, Law, Political Science and Literature). A total of 80 research groups, equal to 100 per cent of RGs operating in the Faculties of Engineering, Science, Pharmaceuticals and Economics, were interviewed. The research carried out for other Faculties have been considered inappropriate for ASOs and the technology transfer process. The surveyed variables were the following: organisation, scientific expertise, scientific partnerships, scientific production, degree of transferability of knowledge to SMEs, knowledge transfer methods, perceived benefits. The data gathered during the interviews were developed with the aim of underlining the tendency towards relationships with SMEs and developing ASOs. The information collected was classified into two groups of variables:

1. Structural variables (composition of RGs, outputs of RG activities, etc.)

2. Perceptual variables (expected benefits, transferability of academic knowledge, vision of economic opportunities, etc.).

The average number of components for each group was 6.3 researchers. In general, research groups were relatively small and therefore flexible, consequently the co-ordination and communication developed without particular problems. Scientific partnerships with other academic structures were well-developed. The data showed a greater intensity of relationships with American scientific partners than national or European ones. In some cases, permanent relationships were at a worldwide level, and in six cases the local research group was the leader of international research programmes. Table 10.2 shows data on perceived benefits from relationship with SMEs. It is important to emphasise that the most important perceived benefits did not involve the University as an institution but the research group ("Research Funding") and the students ("Student Placement" and "Class Programs"). An orientation of research programmes toward industrial applications was not considered to be very important and perceptions of benefits derived from commercial exploitation of research results were absent. The data is consistent with the outputs of activities carried out by RGs (Table 10.3). Every RG is deeply involved in academic competitiveness by publishing papers and participating at conferences. Some of them offer their expertise as consultants, mainly to large firms. Table 10.4 illustrates the perceived efficiency of transfer methods of results by RGs. It is important to underline that RGs believe that it is more efficient to transfer personal knowledge, rather than the results of their activities, which suggests that the research programmes are not aimed at the solution of specific industrial technological problems. The gap between outputs of research and technological needs is considered too high to develop efficient relationships on the basis of joint activities (research, industrial applications, commercialisation). This fact implies that to build effective relationships between university and industry, it will be necessary that an entrepreneurial culture enters the university and shapes the research programmes from their beginnings. Further data reinforces this conclusion. Table 10.5 illustrates the RGs' knowledge about the potential industrial exploitation of their results. Several indicators are shown concerning the vision of business aspects connected with the RGs' activities. The lack of knowledge of the business world is impressive. In many cases there is only a general idea of firms, markets and competition in some way connected with the activities of RGs. For many RGs it is very difficult to understand that their results could be analysed not only from a technical point of view, but also from an economic point of view. In a very few cases, the RGs have some relationship with potential customers (Table 10.6).

TABLE 10.2: PERCEIVED BENEFITS FROM RELATIONSHIPS WITH SMES (%)

	Major Benefits	Minor Benefits	No Benefits	Total
Research funding	60	30	10	100
More applications-oriented research	24	57	19	100
Partnership in EC Research Programmes	36	24	40	100
Curricula improvement	3	12	85	100
Orientation of academic courses	63	21	16	100
Student placement	66	24	10	100
Exploiting of innovative ideas	21	12	67	100
Other (e.g. graduation thesis, sponsorship)	35	65	0	100

TABLE 10.3: ESTIMATED OUTPUTS OF RESEARCH GROUPS (%)

	High	Medium	Low	Total
Scientific publications (Papers, Conferences)	100	0	0	100
Textbooks	20	17	63	100
Texts for practitioners	15	18	67	100
Feasibility studies	18	47	35	100
Applied Projects	28	29	43	100
Test on-site with industries	12	48	40	100
Prototypes	18	42	40	100
Patents	9	39	52	100
Consultancy	36	45	19	100

In conclusion, the field survey strongly confirms that the university is a closed system, and that autonomy from the economic environment is reinforced by the objectives pursued by RGs, the of economic implications of their activities. This analysis confirms the results illustrated in the previous paragraph: in this situation the ASOs are difficult to develop, and in most cases they are the results of strong pressure from the market.

TABLE 10.4: PERCEIVED EFFICIENCY OF DIFFERENT METHODS OF
KNOWLEDGE TRANSFER (%)

	Very efficient	Fairly efficient	Not very efficient	Total
Training of SMEs personnel	55	35	10	100
Technological check-up	40	51	9	100
Studies of new processes	37	25	38	100
Studies of new products	31	40	29	100
Joint R&D GDR-SMEs	9	27	64	100
Prototypes	12	24	64	100
Patents	6	12	82	100
Joint commercialising of R&D results	3	9	88	100

TABLE 10.5: INDICATORS OF BUSINESS VISION OF RESEARCH
GROUPS (%)

	High	Medium	Low	Total
Ability to identify firms and sectors	33	26	41	100
Knowledge of competitive forces and the market	3	32	65	100
Knowledge of main market segments	15	18	67	100
Knowledge of main marketing levers	18	47	35	100
Knowledge of main competitors	28	29	43	100

TABLE 10.6: INDICATORS OF BUSINESS RELATIONS OF RESEARCH
GROUPS (%)

	High	Medium	Low	Total
Relationship with firms	35	36	29	100
Relationship with potential customer	9	39	52	100
Relationship with key economic players (banks, chamber of commerce, firms, associations)	36	45	19	100

MOTIVATIONS AND BARRIERS OF ACADEMIC SPIN-OFFS

It is time now to generalise the results of our field research. In less developed areas, universities do not usually promote the direct exploitation of research results developed in their laboratories. One of the most accepted explanations is that this situation is due to:

- The time lag existing between economic exploitation of the university research and the emergence of positive effects in the economic environment (Berman, 1990)

- The gap between the technological problems raised in laboratories and technological problems the firms currently face.

Consequently universities become auto-referential systems, which have strong relationships with other universities and are separated from the local industrial environment.

On the other hand, the entrepreneurs of small innovative firms located in less developed areas show a low propensity to integrate their competencies with external ones. This behaviour is due to two fundamental reasons:

- The entrepreneur as a product of the laboratories of large companies replicates a self-sufficient behaviour learned in their incubating source (Roberts, 1991)

- During the passage from organisational infancy to adulthood, the entrepreneur shifts their attention from technological aspects to marketing issues (Meyer and Roberts, 1986; Raffa and Zollo, 1994).

The consequence is that both the relevant actors (researchers and entrepreneurs) are not interested in investing time and effort in technological co-operation, because they evaluate that such investment does not guarantee benefits related to their own mission.

Table 10.7 sums up the motivations of the University's Research Groups to co-operate with industry. The Research Groups' motivations are due mainly to financial motivation, because of the progressive reduction of public funding for research (Varaldo and Piccaluga, 1994; Mian, 1994; Martinez and Pastor, 1995). The other motivations play a secondary role, and the deliberate decision to transfer the results to industry is quite absent. It is important to emphasise that the public policies sustaining research projects, particularly EC programmes, are trying to strengthen university–industry relationships to answer the "European paradox", characterised by the high scientific performance of European research and the poor performance of science-based industries. The educational and services motivations, poorly developed in the past, are becoming more important as the trend toward a greater autonomy of universities progresses. Indeed, autonomy fosters competition and the quality of educational programmes among universities. Consequently, effective relationships with local and social environments will become more important.

TABLE 10.7: MOTIVATION OF UNIVERSITY TO CO-OPERATE WITH INDUSTRY

Mission "Research"	• Research funding
	• Developing field research
	• Participating with pre-competitive research programmes
	• Direct exploitation of innovative results
Mission "Education"	• Better teaching orientation
	• Student placement
Mission "Public Service" (support to local economy)	• Increasing the role of university in local area
	• Strengthening relationship with local key-players
	• Attracting private investment of large sums

Nowadays there is more attention paid to transfer activities from university to industry. Unlike the prevalent culture of the recent past, linkages between the academic and economic fields are encouraged and rewarded as manifestations of the social value of research activities. The cultural and institutional environment is changing, both in the academic and industrial fields. For example, the universities of Campania and of other LDAs are directly involved in the activities of the new scientific and technology parks. They fit into the definition of the organisational structure to promote projects aiming to transfer technologies from university laboratories to local firms and are involved in management and consulting through several professors and researchers. For the first time the universities are involved as institutions, not only through the private commitment of their scientists. Furthermore, recently the curriculum of engineering studies has been reconsidered and modified in some parts in order to integrate traditional competencies with a new sensibility for organisational issues. A new engineering degree in Management Engineering was introduced in 1991 at the Faculty of Engineering at Naples, in the belief that the engineer should regard the firm as a complete system and learn how to link technology with people and products with markets in order to achieve successful results.

The experience of Odisseo is equally relevant. Odisseo is a research centre of the Department of Computer Science and Systems of the University of Naples. It was established as a result of research activities in the areas of industrial economics and business organisation carried out in the Faculty of Engineering at Naples since the second half of the 1970s and concerns itself with the relationships between technology and organisation, technological innovation processes and innovative sectors. Odisseo is constituted by a permanent group of professors and researchers working at the Department of Computer Science and Systems and of a variable number of collaborators (graduates, students) from the Faculty of Engineering. The aim of Odisseo is to link the technological culture of engineers with managerial and economic issues. In its decennial activities Odisseo developed field research, workshops, seminars, training activities and joint research projects with private companies and public institutions. Odisseo actively participated in the planning of the Scientific and Technology Park of Salerno.

From the point of view of the industrial culture, a new approach was realised by Law 44 of 1986, aimed at supporting the start-up of enterprises founded by young people in Southern Italy. Up to 15 March 1996, 4,063 new projects were presented for approval. There were 1,056 projects approved (employing 20,662 people for an investment of L3.079 billion (approx. £1.2 million)). The universities participate in evaluation committees, in supporting the proponents by consulting services, in training and tutoring activities. The activities set up by this law could represent an important reference point for further initiatives.

The general impression is that the universities, even in LDAs, are slowly moving from a "Mercantile Model" to a "Lever Model" (Varaldo and Piccaluga, 1994) through innovation and the continuous adjustment of the training processes, the focus on effective research programmes, a proactive attention towards the economic value of research results. The ASOs are part of this process, because they in many aspects anticipate the "Entrepreneurial University" model suggested by Piero Formica (1994), which defines academic institutions as "ideas firms", open to both scientific and business environments.

Several barriers stand in the way of co-operation between university and industry in LDAs (Table 10.8). The results of field research confirms the conclusions of several authors (Varaldo and Piccaluga, 1994; Harmon et al., 1995; Martinez Sanchez and Tejedor Pastor, 1995; Fontes and Coombs, 1995) who distinguish three categories of barriers: cultural, organisational and managerial. These barriers play different roles. The first group is particularly relevant to LDAs, while the second one is relevant to countries where the university's autonomy is very low, and the third one is related to general problems in university–industry relationships.

TABLE 10.8: BARRIERS AGAINST UNIVERSITY–INDUSTRY RELATIONSHIPS

Cultural Barriers	• Compatibility of different Missions
	• Lack of "shared culture"
	• Auto-referential behaviour of the university system
Organisational Barriers	• Incompatibility of deadlines
	• Fragmentation of university disciplines
	• University bureaucracy
	• Legal aspects
Managerial Barriers	• Structure and procedures for joint activities
	• Financial difficulties
	• Inadequate skills to manage agreements
	• Secrecy and security of R&D results

The most important barriers concern the cultural aspects. Most of the problems arise because researchers and entrepreneurs use different methods and categories in framing their evaluations (language, explicative arguments, perceptions, expectations). In such conditions it is very difficult to co-ordinate a collective action. The auto-referential behaviour is clearly shown by the fact that the RGs consider the scientific community as an almost exclusive "client" of their activity.

Furthermore, from the organisational point of view, while the industry focuses on "time to market", the RGs focus on "time to novelty" with the consequence that research programmes' deadlines become incompatible with firms' innovation projects. Finally, the fragmentation of disciplines, university bureaucracy and contractualism dramatically influence the development of effective relationships and appear to be inadequate for long-term agreements.

Within these constraints, it is very easy to understand that consulting and spontaneous ASOs could be considered by RGs as one of the most efficient methods of interaction between the academic and business worlds. Indeed, the ASOs both maximise motivations and neutralise the most important organisational and managerial barriers.

CONCLUSIONS

The above initiatives clearly show that in recent years a small network of formal and informal relationships between university and industry has been created and several spontaneous ASOs developed. The decisive question now, as pointed out by Schimank (1988: 330)

> is how and to what extent political guidance of the technology transfer between universities and firms is possible. What can political actors do to promote the realisation and the effectiveness of transfer interactions between university researchers and firms?

Policies directed at encouraging and fostering stronger networks and ASOs should support the personal commitment of the scientist-entrepreneur by offering several services promoting an increasing involvement of universities in their economic environment. As suggested by Piero Formica and Jay Mitra (1996), the Science and Technology Park could play a central role in promoting and driving proper actions for developing university–industry relationships and ASOs. Particularly, policies and actions for developing ASOs could be grouped in five categories, according to the common pattern of establishing a new business (Capaldo, 1996):

1. Defining the business idea

2. Defining the entrepreneurial group

3. Defining the business plan

4. Funding

5. Starting up (see Table 10.9).

Usually scientific and technology parks are suitable for realising these actions by playing the role of networking companies, because they consist of several different actors interested in joining their competencies, such as universities, research centres, local authorities and public local financing agencies, and large private firms. In order to act as a networking agency, scientific and technology parks should learn to manage immaterial assets, such as knowledge, values, competence, relational skills, technological know-how and political relationships with local actors. All these elements should be utilised and combined in specific projects from which each participant could gain competitive advantage so that, in the long run, they generate added value. In the end the effectiveness of a policy for developing ASOs is linked to the creation of a new university culture regarding the utilisation of science and technology as a resource for social and economic development.

TABLE 10.9: POLICIES AND ACTIONS FOR DEVELOPING ACADEMIC
SPIN-OFFS IN LESS DEVELOPED AREAS

Steps	*Policies*	*Actions*
Defining the business idea	• Permanent monitoring of new business ideas deriving from results of academic research and firm's technologists • Permanent monitoring of market opportunities	• Data bank of "business ideas" • Brainstorming with academics, students and firm's technicians to develop creativity • Monitoring of market opportunities
Defining the entrepreneurial group	• Promotion of multi-skill entrepreneurial groups • Training graduates and scientists in entrepreneurship • Mentoring new entrepreneurs	• Data bank of potential new entrepreneurs • Workshops for permanent diffusion of entrepreneurship culture • Meetings with entrepreneurs • Consulting
Defining the business plan	• Joint definition of technological, marketing and financial aspects	• Project management • Supporting networking activity • Consulting • Providing information
Funding	• Maximisation of public funding for new business • Activation of innovative financial tools (venture capital, seed capital)	• Agreements between universities and financial and local institutions • Creation of focused structures: e.g. consortia between universities and investors (venture capitalist, merchant banks)

References

Albino, V., Costantino, N. and Garavelli, A.C., (1992), "I Sistemi di Imprese: Criteri per una Tassonomia Organiszzativa", *Atti del Convegno AilG "Le nuove configurazioni dell'impresa e ddei mercati"*, Bari, 16 October.

Bagnasco, A. (1988), *La Costruzione Sociale del Mercato*, Bologna: Il Mulino.

Bagnasco, A. (1977), *Tre Italie: Le Problematich dello Sviluppo Italiano*, Bologna: Il Mulino.

Barney, J.B. and Ouchi, W.G. (1985), "Costi delle Informazioni e Strutture Economiche di Governo delle Transazioni", in Nacamulli, R.C.D. and Rugiadini, A., *Organizzazione e Mercato*, Bologna: Il Mulino.

Becattini, G. (1979), "Dal Settore Industriale al Distretto Industriale", *Rivista di Economia e Politica Industriale*, No. 1.

Becattini, G. (ed.) (1987), *Mercato e Forze Locali: Il Distretto Industriale*, Bologna: Il Mulino.

Becattini, G. (1989), "Riflessioni sul Distretto Industriale Marchalliano come Concetto Socio-Economico", *Stato e Mercato*, No. 25.

Berman, E.M. (1990), "The Economic Impact of Industry-Funding University R&D", *Research Policy*, Vol. 19, No. 4, pp. 349–355.

Bianco, M.L. and Luciano, A. (1982), *La Sindrome di Archimede*, Bologna: Il Mulino.

Bonaccorsi, A. and Piccaluga, A. (1994), "A Theoretical Framework for the Evaluation of University–Industry Relationship", *R&D Management*, Vol. 24, No. 3.

Brown, W.B. and Schwab, R.C. (1984), "Boundary-Spanning Activities in Electronics Firms", in *IEEE Transactions on Engineering Management*, Vol. EM-31, No. 3.

Brusco, B. (1986), "Small Firms and Industrial Districts: The Experience of Italy", in Keeble, D. and Wewer, E. (eds.), *New Firms and Regional Development in Europe*, London: Croom Helm.

Capaldo, G. (1996), "Le Creazione di Impresa nelle Aree in Ritardo di Sviluppo: Risultati di una Indagine Empirica" in Capldo, G., Raffa, M. and Persico, P. (eds.), *Economia e Gestione delle Piccole Imprese del Mezzogiorno*, Naples: CUEN.

Cotugno, P., Del Monte, A., Di Luccio, L. and Zollo, G. (1982), *Mezzogiorno e Terza Italia: Il Modello Casertano,* Rome: ESI.

Del Monte, A., Ciambelli, C., Raffa, M. and Zollo G. (1982), *Decentramento Internazionale e Decentramento Producttivo,* Turin: Loesscher.

Del Monte, A. and Giannola, A. (1989), "I Problemi dello Sviluppo Industriale del Mezzogiorno e i Riflessi di Queti nella Determinazione del Quadro di Politica Industriale", in Battaglia, A. and Valcamonici, R. (eds.), *Nella competizione globale: Una Politica Industriale verso il 2000,* Bari: Laterza.

Dioguardi, G.F. (1983), "Macrofirms: Construction Firms for the Computer Age", *Journal of Contructon Engineering and Management,* March.

Dioguardi, G.F. (1986), *L'impresa nell 'Era del Computer,* Milan: Il Sole 24 Ore.

Eccles, R.G. (1981), "The Quasi-Firm in the Construction Industry", *Journal of Economic Behaviour and Oranisation,* No. 2.

Filion, L.J. (1991), *Vision et Relations: Clefs du Succès de l'Entrepreneur,* Montrèal: Les éditions de l'entrepreneur.

Fontes, M. and Coombs, Rod (1995), "New Technology-Based Firms and Technology Acquistion in Portugal: Firms' Adaptive Responses to a Less Favourable Environment", *Technovation,* Vol. 15, No. 8, pp. 497–510.

Formica, P. (1994), *Mutanti Aziendali,* Naples: Edizioni CUEN.

Formica, P. and Mitra, J. (1996), "Co-operation and Competition", *Industry and Higher Education,* June, pp. 151–159.

Fumagalli, A., Rovida, F. and Vivarelli M. (1988), *La Formazione di Nuove Imprese: Aspetti Teorici e Analisi Sistematica,* Centro Studi sull'Imprenditorialità Furio Cicogna, Università Commerciale Luigi Bocconi.

Gandolfi, V. (1990), "Realizionalità e Cooperazione nelle Aree-sistema", *Economia e Politica Industriale,* No. 65, pp. 95–117.

Greiner, L.E. (1972), "Evolution and Revolution as Organisational Growth", in *Harvard Business Review,* July–August.

Gros-Pietro, G.M. (1995), *Nord-Est dei Miracoli,* Milan: Il Sole 24 Ore, p. 6.

Harmon, B., Ardishvili, A., Cardozo, R., Elder, T., Leuthold, J., Parshall, J., Raghian, M. and Smith D. (1995), "Mapping the University Technology Transfer Process", Paper presented at the Babson Conference.

Huppert, R. (1981), "Stratégies de Développement des PMI Fran-caises", in *Revue d'Économie Industrielle,* No. 17 (Italian translation in *Problemi di Gestione,* No. 3/4, 1982).

Kao, J. (1991), *The Entrepreneurial Organisation,* London: Pren-tice Hall.

Lassini, L. (1990), "Forma e Determinanti della R&S nelle Piccole Imprese", *Economia e Politica Industriale,* No. 66.

Lefebvre, E. and Lefebvre, L.A. (1992), "Firm Innovativeness and CEO Characteristics in Small Manufacturing Firms", in *Jour-nal of Engineering and Technology Management,* No. 9, pp. 243–277.

Lorenzoni, G. (1979), *Una Politica Innovativa nelle Piccole Medie Imprese,* Milan: Etas Libri.

Lorenzoni, G. (1985), "Dalla Singola Impresa Agli Aggregati di Imprese: La Costellazione", in Balloni, V., (ed.), *Esperienze di ristrutturazione industriale,* Bologna: Il Mulino.

Lorenzoni, G. (1987), "Costellazione di Imprese e Processi di Svi-luppo", *Sviluppo e Organizzazione,* No. 102.

Marc, F. (1982), "De la Difficulté d'Innover dans le PMI", in *Revue Française de Gestion,* June/July/August.

Martinez Sanchez, Angel and Tejedor Pastor, Ana Clara (1995), "University-Industry Relationships in Peripheral Regions: The Case of Aragon in Spain", *Technovation* Vol. 15, No. 10, pp. 613–625.

Meyer, M.H. and Roberts, E.B. (1986), "New Product Strategy in Small Technology-Based Firms: A Pilot Study", in *Management Science,* Vol. 32, No. 7.

Mian Safraz, A. (1994), "US University-Sponsored Technology In-cubators: An Overview of Management, Policies and Perform-ance", in *Technovation* Vol. 14, No. 8, pp. 515–528.

Miller, D., Droge, C. and Toulose, J.M. (1988), "Strategic Process and Content as Mediators between Organisational Context and Structure", *Academy of Management Journal,* Vol. 31, No. 3, pp. 544–569.

Nagel, A. (1981), "Strategy Formulation for the Smaller Firm: A Practical Approach", *Long Range Planning,* Vol. 14, August (Italian translation in *Problemi di Gestione,* No. 11–12, 1982)

Norman, R. (1977), *Management for Growth,* New York: John Wiley and Sons.

Oakey, R. (1984), *High Technology Small Firms*, London: Frances Pinter Publishers.

OECD (1982), *Innovation in Small and Medium Firms*, Paris: OECD.

Raffa, M. and Zollo, G. (1988), *Software Tecnologia e Mercato*, Bologna: Il Mulino.

Raffa, M., Zollo, G. and Caponi R. (1994), "Entrepreneurial Education and Growth Paths of Small Firms", *Internationalising Entrepreneurship Education and Training*, Stirling, 4–7 July.

Raffa, M. and Zollo, G. (1994), "The Role of Professionals in Small Italian Software Firms", *Systems Software*, No. 26, pp. 19–30.

Raffa, M. and Zollo, G. (1995), "Il Ruolo del Parco Scientifico e Tecnologico nel Sostegno delle Piccole Imprese Locali", *Caserta Economia e Lavoro*, No. 2, pp. 33–40.

Richter, M. (1986), "University Scientists as Entrepreneurs", *Society*, July/August: pp. 73–88.

Roberts, E.B. (1991), "The Technological Base of the New Enterprise", *Research Policy*, No. 29, pp. 283–298.

Roberts, E.B. and Hauptman, O. (1986), "The Process of Technology Transfer to New Biomedical and Pharmaceutical Firms", *Research Policy*, No. 15, pp. 107–119.

Rothwell, R. (1984), "The Role of Small Firms in the Emergence of New Technologies", in *Omega*, Vol. 12, No. 1.

Rothwell, R. and Zegveld, W. (1982), *Innovation and the Small and Medium-Sized Firm*, London: Frances Pinter.

Scimank, U. (1988), "The Contribution of University Research to the Technological Innovation of the German Economy: Societal Auto-Dynamic and Political Guidance", *Research Policy*, Vol. 17, No. 6, pp. 329–340.

Stadenmaier, J.M. (1985), *Technology's Storytellers: Reweaving the Human Fabric*, Cambridge, MA: The MIT Press.

Varaldo, R. and Piccaluga, A. (1994), "Un Ponte tra Industria e Università per Rilanciare la Ricerca", in *L'Impresa*, No. 8, pp. 4–14.

11

EVALUATING REGIONAL INNOVATION POTENTIAL: ASSESSMENT OF TRENDS AND IMPLICATIONS FOR POLICY[*]

Claire Nauwelaers

Summary

This contribution is based on an EIMS project involving a "horizontal" inventory and critical analysis of existing studies on the measurement and evaluation of regional innovative potential.

After the presentation of a conceptual scheme aimed at reflecting on the functions of a "Regional System of Innovation", the main trends in methodological approaches to the evaluation of regional innovative potential in the European Union are discussed, pointing to the necessity of moving progressively towards a methodology which takes into account interactions, both locally and externally, between the various components and actors of the innovation process. There is no single best-practice methodology in this respect: the use of an "eclectic" assortment of methodological approaches is investigated and the recommendation made to develop databases on innovation at the regional level.

Implications for regional innovation policies and the role of universities in economic development are proposed in the concluding section of the chapter.

---

[*] This contribution is based on a study by the author and A. Reid (both in the RIDER programme at the Catholic University of Louvain, Belgium, at the time of the study) for the European Commission, and published in the EIMS collection, no. 21, under the title "Innovative Regions".

INTRODUCTION

The purpose of this contribution is, first, to reflect on and widen the range of methodologies available to regional planners in charge of performing evaluations of the innovative potential of their regions; and second, to derive some policy implications from this and to briefly discuss the role of universities in the development of innovative regions. Such an objective corresponds to a general recognition of the importance of a better understanding of the functioning of the innovative process at regional level, as a key dimension of the competitiveness of regions. The study on which it is based is part of the third action line of the former SPRINT programme managed by the European Commission (DG XIII-D), and included in the INNOVATION programme within the European Innovation Monitoring System (EIMS) which provides the European programme with a "horizontal" dimension, allowing policy research results to be turned into tools for those with responsibility for implementing practical programmes.

This project involved a horizontal inventory and critical analysis of existing studies on the measurement and evaluation of regional technological innovation services and infrastructure, innovative networks and other aspects of the regional innovative potential. Each of the four research teams[1] originally involved in the project undertook this horizontal review for a distinct geographic zone, covering both the EU (the 12 member states at that time) and the other members of the triad. This study does not attempt to provide a single or definitive account of best practice in regional innovation evaluation methodology. On the contrary, the aim is to extract from a survey of existing studies, which have measured and assessed regional innovation systems, the most coherent and widely applicable approaches currently being used throughout the EU, Japan and North America. It should be underlined that the horizontal review did not have a remit to deal with the question of the innovative potential of firms, since its main objective was to evaluate the role of innovation support organisations (ISOs) in the contribution to the innovative performance of the regions.

TRENDS IN EVALUATION METHODOLOGIES FOR REGIONAL SYSTEMS OF INNOVATION

Conceptual Framework

Before reviewing the main trends in methodological approaches for the evaluation of regional innovative capacities, it is essential to provide a conceptual representation of innovation dynamics at the regional level. The importance of this exercise is that it serves as a framework within which the results of the horizontal review can be interpreted in terms of methodological and related policy trends, rather than merely listing the various determinants and indicators of regional innovation capacities and infrastructure.

A considerable body of literature has developed in the last ten years on the concept of national systems of innovation (NSI). In part this is due to the gradual realisation that in terms of technological innovation, "the accent has shifted from the single act philosophy of technological innovation to the social process underlying economically oriented technical novelty".[2] In parallel, studies carried out at the regional or local level by a number of research teams underline the importance of organisational capacities and networks of innovation in promoting regional economic and technological development.

In the last decade or so, a fundamental break has occurred from the previously dominant model of the linear research-to-market model. In this model, innovations in product or processes were held to originate in research laboratories before being developed and finally placed on the market. The influence of other institutions or factors such as market demand or education systems were acknowledged without particular attention being paid to the interactions between the various actors and the flow of knowledge between them.

Increasingly, however, the deficiencies of this linear model and, in particular, its lack of attention to the role of final demand and interactions between the numerous actors in the wider process of innovation led to the development of what has been referred to as interactive or "chain-link" models of innovation.

The recognition of the fact that the transfer of knowledge from the science-producing sector into commercial innovations in the productive sector is all but an automatic process, has led authorities at regional level to create a wide range of innovation support organisations (ISOs) with the aim of favouring a better diffusion of scientific and technological advances into the industrial fabric of the region. The role of these ISOs in assisting innovation in the regions of the European Union is one of the core issues of this study.

A simplified and schematic model of an interactive regional system of innovation (RSI) is presented in Figure 11.1. The concept of an RSI is consistent with the interactive model of innovation in that it is characterised by continuous interactions and feedback between the different stages of the innovation process. Moreover, the notion of an RSI also draws on the "innovative environment" approach by stressing the importance of both collaborative networks and the "openness" of the local environment to internal and external factors influencing the innovation process.

Depending on the fundamental concept of the innovation process (linear or interactive) adopted, these relations may be described rather differently.

In the linear vision of the RSI (broken lines and arrows in Figure 11.1), a sequential flow occurs from pure and applied research activities, and possibly internal R&D activities of firms, through design, production and finally commercialisation. Science and technology are, in short, exogenous to the system.

In the interactive vision of the RSI (bold arrows and feedback loops in Figure 11.1), the sequential scheme is substantially modified by a number of interactions and feedbacks in the process.

Within firms and industries, feedback loops between each of the phases lead to an increasingly integrated process, resulting in circular dependency between market forces and technological development effort. The supply-side of the system becomes more and more influenced by the demand-side. The intermediate organisations, created from the recognition that the relationship between science-producers and final science-users should be supplemented by interface mechanisms, become central players in an interactive RSI. Another, perhaps still more important, type of relation in the interactive vision of the RSI, is networking between firms, between ISOs, and between research organisations.

A move from the classical linear view to the modern interactive vision of the innovation process at the regional level leads to a radical shift in the design of indicators. It is argued here that indicators of the performance of a regional innovation system are basically of two types, corresponding to the two visions of the RSI.

FIGURE 11.1: REGIONAL SYSTEM OF INNOVATION: LINEAR AND
INTERACTIVE VIEWS

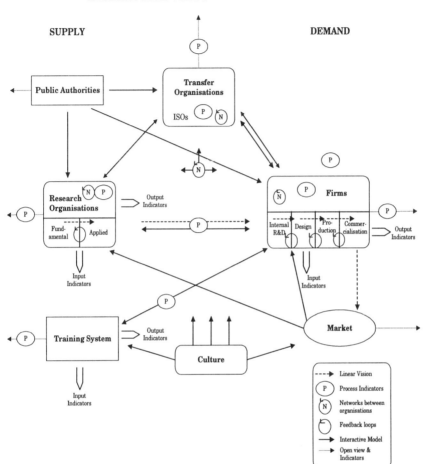

Under the traditional linear view of technological innovation, "bean counting" or the quantification of the endowments of the system (the inputs) and the results in terms of research and development (the output) predominate. Moreover, the input/output indicators tend to be quantitative and static by nature, offering the advantage of being easy to replicate and based on existing and relatively cheap statistical sources.

With the advent of the interactive vision, a new emphasis should be placed on process indicators which capture networking activities and relationships in the system. This second form of indicator is more qualitative and dynamic. However, process indi-

cators have the disadvantage of being relatively difficult to dupli-
cate over time within one region, while their territorial specificity
makes them difficult to transfer from one region to another. As
they measure the systemic aspects of the performance of an RSI,
they depend heavily on questionnaire and interview techniques
which are also less easy to compare on an inter-regional level.

**Trends in Methodological Approaches for the Evaluation
of Regional Innovative Capacities**

The main trends in methodological approaches to the evaluation
of regional innovative potential in the European Union, identified
in the study, are the following:

- Studies aimed at problem solving rather than knowledge
  building

- The linear vision of innovation continues to dominate regional
  innovation capability evaluations

- Process indicators are neither particularly robust nor reproducible

- An interactive approach implies a focus on qualitative data

- There is an inappropriate focus on high-technology sectors

- A failure to take into account the degree of openness of the regional system of innovation is highly common

- The content of evaluation studies depends on the orientation of
  related policy measures

- Regional data on innovation potential remains limited and of
  poor quality.

A first conclusion of the horizontal review is that policy makers
have the tendency to adopt problem-solving as opposed to knowledge building approaches. In many respects this is to be expected
since many studies attempt to search for or justify a "single powerful approach" (science park or some other specific ISO) rather
than producing a coherent set of generic findings. However, a sufficient theoretical framework for an all-inclusive and predictive
analysis of regional systems of innovations is rarely constructed
or applied. Such a framework requires explicit treatment of the
key causal determinants of a model of regional innovation capacities, yet many implicit assumptions are used in methodologi-

cal design and subsequent analysis of RSIs. As a result, regional technology development programmes, to date, have not been constructed on the basis of an explicit diagnosis of regional innovation capabilities.

Second, methodologies and indicators continue to be heavily influenced by a linear vision of the role of innovation in regional development. Such studies are based on an inventory and description of main components of the regional system of innovation. Descriptive indicators can be useful devices for tracking change over time and comparing different regions. However, due to the general failure, noted above, to adopt an adequate theoretical model as a foundation for evaluation methodologies, the development of indicators of technology-based regional development is sometimes an empty exercise. In particular, such indicators are unable to identify and measure the complex relations between the different elements and within the system as a whole. A static one-off description of the endowments of the RSI is provided, as opposed to a dynamic evaluation of the interactions between the various components. Moreover, the linear vision of the innovation process tends to produce an over-emphasis on the supply side of the RSI and consequently on input indicators.

Third, a clear gap can be identified between, on the one hand, the prevailing concept of an interactive RSI, as revealed by a review of key determinants of regional innovative performance; and, on the other hand, the indicators used to assess its performance. Indicators suitable for measuring the systemic aspect of the performance of the RSI are not matched by existing databases and therefore are mainly qualitative with a low level of duplicability and robustness. In short, appropriate developments in indicator-building are hampered by the non-existence of suitable data.

Fourth, a related trend detected with respect to less advanced regions was an attempt to compensate for a lack of qualitative data by employing an increasingly large number of quantitative indicators. Such an approach, focusing on quantity rather than quality, is not only methodologically suspect but in general inoperative due to the high costs, both in terms of financial and human resources, for the regional authority.

Fifth, as far as data collection techniques are concerned, a correlation was found between an emphasis on "system" aspects and the use of more qualitative data, generated by *ad hoc* data collection devices: mail or telephone enquiries, interviews, expert meetings, and analysis of documents (reports of activities, etc.).

The collection of such qualitative, and hence subjective, data which tries to capture new dimensions of the innovation system (networking, clusters, contractual behaviour and performance, etc.) tends by nature to be a costly process, both financially and in terms of human resources. As a result, regions which have begun to adopt such approaches tend to focus their efforts on particular segments of the RSI through case studies. Clearly this reduces somewhat the acquisition of a systemic vision of the innovation process in a region.

Sixth, as a result of the above-noted constraints which focus efforts on particular aspects of the RSI, many of the studies identified explicitly excluded the primary or tertiary sectors from the scope of analysis. Paradoxically, the importance of these two sectors for, respectively, less-favoured and advanced regions should not be underestimated as a potential source of innovation. In the same vein, an overemphasis on leading-edge technologies or research-oriented firms may not only be inappropriate for certain regions but may very well ignore potential product or process innovations in traditional or "low-tech" sectors.

Seventh, few of the identified studies took into account the degree of openness of the RSI. The failure of studies taking adequate account of the open character of the regional innovation system seems to arise from a lack of awareness of the importance of external relations for the RSI, rather than from conceptual difficulties in integrating this dimension. In the case of the numerous studies relying on *ad hoc* new data collection methods, there should be few difficulties in adding this dimensions to the data collection methods employed (surveys, questionnaires, interviews, forums, etc.).

Eighth, regional governments with relatively high levels of competence for research and innovation policy are identifiable in a number of member states of the European Union. However, the ability or freedom of action to support economic development through innovation-related activities is not the sole inducement to the creation of regional innovation surveys. More specifically, a number of surveys are conceived and written under the auspices of higher levels of government, both national and European. National authorities may be stimulated to promote such analyses due to a need to have a better understanding of the allocation of research and innovation capacities throughout their respective jurisdictions. Such information may form the basis for a policy of decentralisation of R&D capacities from metropolitan or "capital" areas to less-favoured regions. In consequence, regions undertake this type of exercise not only to assess their strengths and weaknesses in this sector, but also as a lobbying action in order to secure the widest possible share of public funds devoted to R&D and innovation towards their region. Some questions may thus be raised with respect to their objectivity.

Finally, in general, information gathered in the form of concise and classified databases remains not only limited but is essentially only a number-counting exercise. Moreover, such information is often of dubious accuracy. It goes almost without saying that inter-regional comparisons, either within a particular member state or transnationally, should be made with a great deal of caution.

Classical versus Innovative Evaluation Methodologies

In sum, the various methodological approaches identified may be viewed as different steps on a continuous path starting from what could be called the "classical choice", and striving to reach an "innovative choice" for evaluating regional innovative potential. An overall assessment of the selected studies leads to a simplified categorisation of the two contrasting methodological choices for regional innovation studies, and hence, for the basis for constructing regional policies to foster innovation.

TABLE 11.1: TRADITIONAL VERSUS INNOVATIVE METHODOLOGIES
        FOR EVALUATING REGIONAL INNOVATIVE
        PERFORMANCE

Classical Choice	*Innovative Choice*
Inventory and characterisation of local innovation actors	Evaluation of the capacity of the RSI to favour learning processes and synergies
Focuses on:	Focuses on:
• Description • Components of the RSI • Technology creation • Homogeneity between regions • Quantitative indicators • Input/output indicators	• Evaluation • Interfaces in the RSI • Technology diffusion • Regional diversity and specificity • Qualitative indicators • Process indicators

NEW METHODOLOGIES AND INDICATORS FOR
MEASURING INNOVATIVE PERFORMANCE

On the basis of the main trends outlined above, a clear need can be identified for an evolution of regional innovation evaluation methodologies and indicators towards an approach which corresponds to the interactive vision of the innovation process. Regions which to date have not, or have only partially, undertaken the more descriptive approaches to evaluating their innovative potential clearly still need to build up a suitable set of data permitting them to make, for instance, a comparative inter-regional analysis. Regions which have already established a relatively advanced level of data collection should be able to refine their established evaluation techniques through an identification of outdated or superfluous indicators. In addition, the latter should be considering means of evaluating the interrelations between the components of the RSI.

FIGURE 11.2: MAIN DIMENSIONS OF THE RSI AND ASSOCIATED
                  METHODOLOGIES

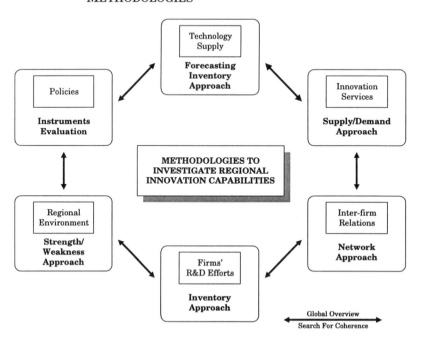

Source: ISI-Karlsruhe, final report.

Currently, the evaluator of regional innovation capabilities is faced with a multiplicity of approaches, each one possessing particular strengths and weaknesses. Moreover, all the approaches only partially deal with the question in hand. The best way to exploit the information gathered through this EU-wide study is therefore to recommend an eclectic, multidimensional approach to the question.[3]

To this end, six different types of methodologies can be proposed, according to the part of the RSI focused on an evaluation. Figure 11.2 is a graphical representation of the six main dimensions of a regional system of innovation, along with the corresponding methodological approaches to investigate them.

Technology Supply (Forecasting Inventory Approach)

The aim is to assess the technology supply potential of the region, to identify the deficits in the supply/demand relation of this potential and to define the position of the region in the context of inter-regional/international competition. Technology supply has at least two dimensions: first, which technologies are of regional importance (according to branch structure, technological competence and regional technological demand); and second, how and by whom are these technologies being utilised and how can access to these technologies be improved. In a more prospective view, two more dimensions have to be included in a regional technology supply analysis. Firstly, the question of regional "best practice" in technology utilisation, that is, which are the "appropriate" technologies allowing the attainment of regional economic strategies. Secondly, which are the relevant emerging technologies which should be exploited to improve regional competitiveness and secure the economic base of the region in the future. Three types of determinants are important in this respect:

- The potential regional influence of higher education institutions

- The receptivity of the regional economy

- The regional importance of the transfer.

The potential regional influence of higher education institutes is determined by the quantity and quality of research and teaching. The determinants of the receptivity of the regional economy are the degree of correspondence between the offer of the higher education institutes and the industrial branches and firm size structure. Other important factors are the financial possibilities for acquiring know-how, the industrial R&D capacity, the promotion of NTBFs (new technology-based firms) and the regional environment. The regional significance of technology transfer from institutes of higher education can only be interpreted by examining the regionalisation of third-party funding (the localisation of contract-givers). However, this information is often difficult to obtain. Another dimension to take into account is the supra-regional orientation of the institutes, which can be interpreted as a sign of excellence. Written questionnaires, interviews, discussions with experts and evaluation of statistics, reports and plans, quantitative data and other information on the above indicators are to be collected, and are then to be qualitatively evaluated with respect to the regional importance of new technologies (science offer in relation to branch structure and regional demand), and the exploitation of new technologies in the region and their importance for regional economic performance and competitiveness. The instruments and methodologies of technology foresight (e.g. expert panels, delphi studies) should also work on a regional scale, although most of these studies refer to the national level.

Innovation Services: Supply/Demand Approach

The aim is to identify deficits in innovation services supply according to the regional demand. The achievement of objectives of ISOs may be measured through the matching of the declared aims of the organisation and the degree of coherence and complementarity between ISOs active in a region, as well as the degree to which expectations of the clients of ISOs have been fulfilled. To this end empirical information should be gathered from written questionnaires, interviews and evaluation of documents relating to suppliers and users of innovation services (R&D institutions, transfer and advisory offices, technology and incubator centres). Quantitative data and qualitative assessments should be collected on:

- The aims of the innovation services

- The organisation and resources of the institutions

- The scope and quality of the offer

- The intensity of use and the user structure

- The evaluation of services by users and their expectations

- The impacts of the ISOs and their services on enterprises and on the regional economy.

Whereas the innovation services and the use made of them can be relatively easily recorded, ascertaining the real impact of the ISOs and their services involves a considerable expenditure of resources (e.g. isolation and measuring impacts). There is often a lack of sufficiently detailed data recorded over long periods, in addition to already operational aims, which could be used for comparison. Moreover, the evaluation of innovation services by users remains, by necessity, somewhat subjective: in the analysis, standardised evaluation criteria would have to be developed, which is generally not the case in the documents surveyed.

Inter-Firm Relations: Network Approach

The aim is to evaluate the firms' propensity to network as a variable of the innovation ability, to determine the regional dimension of those networks, and to characterise them in terms of strengths/weaknesses for the region. The characterisation of firms' innovation-related networks has to be based at first on the identification and localisation of the partners and innovation-related sources. Two dimensions appear to be of fundamental importance in the definition of networks: the type of partner involved (firm, institution, consultants, etc.) and their localisation (within the region, outside the region, in neighbouring regions). A third dimension is the content of the information exchanged or the extent of innovation-related co-operation. Finally, the nature of the links (informal relation, formal co-operation) merits an investigation. The analysis should not be limited to firms and should take other possible actors in networks into consideration.

The localisation/identification of innovation-related networks can be realised through a matrix-based data-collection process, with the two main dimensions being :

1. *Type of partners*: listing of possible contacts, as wide as possible (firms of the same group, of the same industry, of other industries, suppliers, equipment suppliers, other suppliers, consultants, private research institutes, professional associations, etc.)

2. *Localisation*: definition of geographical area — "region", "neighbouring region", but also a distinction between national and foreign-located information.

In addition, the nature of the relation should be recorded. The use of matrixes in surveys allows a binary encoding of the answers, offering interesting data-crossing possibilities.

Information should also be gathered on companies' use of external innovation and information resources (higher education institutions, engineering firms, transfer and consulting firms, other companies in the sector, customers and suppliers), using written questionnaires and interviews with firms and innovation services, evaluation of statistical sources and discussions with experts, chambers of commerce and associations. This mainly involves the collection of quantitative data, but also qualitative assessments relating to the indicators mentioned above.

Firms' R&D Efforts and Innovative Behaviour: Inventory Approach

This dimension is recorded here for memory, in order to indicate its importance for a complete description or evaluation of the RSI. However, since this dimension has not been included in the "horizontal review", methodologies and indicators are not discussed here.

Regional Environment: Strengths & Weaknesses Approach

The aim is to identify, in a general fashion, regional weaknesses and opportunities or advantages. The approach is essentially based on concepts of regional development, and makes use of statistical data and planning documents of the regional, urban and European authorities containing basic information on a number of areas of importance to regional development. This information should be complemented by discussions with experts from policy, industry and planning offices in the region on the qualitative evaluation of data and on future development perspectives.

Policies: Instruments Evaluation

- The aim is to assess the regional impact of policy measures and programmes, including an identification of unfulfilled needs, and to analyse the coherence between policies formulated and applied by different levels of government (regional, national and European). It leads to the identification of possible means of improving policy measures and programmes. The methodology used is based on surveys on regional policies and instruments that should cover the following elements:

- Principal aims of regional policy, (e.g. inward investment, technology transfer, support of small and medium-sized enterprises, urban regeneration, support of traditional industries)

- Relative importance of the actors involved, (e.g. central government, regional government, local authorities, institutions of higher education, chambers of commerce, economic organisations, public–private partnerships, business-led initiatives)

- Instruments used (e.g. technology policy grants, sectoral grants, EU grants, regional marketing, consultancy, technology transfer, technology centres)

- Organisation and transparency of the policies, networking aspects

Relations between the central state and the region (degree of regional political authority).

Empirical data should be collected from interviews with policy-makers, experts and entrepreneurs in the region under investigation.

CONCLUSION AND POLICY PERSPECTIVES

On the methodological side, three major findings arise from this comparative review of methods used for assessing regional systems of innovation (RSI). Those conclusions, when translated to the policy area, have important implications on the way regional innovation policies should be conceived, and on the role of universities in regional development.

The first conclusion of the study relates to the question of the appropriate approach to analysing RSI given the acknowledged conceptual shift from a linear to an interactive vision of the innovation process. It was suggested that while those two distinct approaches can be identified from a conceptual point of view, the majority of European regions continue to focus on the more "traditional" descriptive component oriented form of evaluation. Consequently, despite the theoretical jump to an interactive vision, practical evaluation methodologies are likely to change only incrementally towards the more innovative approach suggested in this study.

A second main message centres around the lack of a single best-practice methodology: this would suggest that regional planners interested in gaining a better understanding of the innovation process need to use an "eclectic" assortment of tools in order to evaluate the various dimensions of the RSI.

Finally, the numerous studies and reports analysed as part of the European-wide review highlighted the dearth of robust, reproducible and comparable statistical sources on innovation at the regional level. In many respects, this reflects the relatively poor level of indicators used in studies of the RSI both in Europe but also in the US and to a lesser extent in Japan. Hence, a principal recommendation of this overall review is that greater resources should be allocated to building up a more comprehensive and comparable set of data on RSI, by both European and regional authorities. A particular effort should be directed towards the improvement of process indicators and a more selective series of indicators better able to capture the systemic aspects of the innovation process at regional level.

In the neo-classical approach, technology is considered as exogenous to production, free access is secured to knowledge sources, and technology is viewed as generic, codified, accessible and context independent; one is faced with a market failure in the form of private under-investment in R&D (because of indivisibility, non-appropriability and risks related to R&D activities). Therefore, in a linear vision, the role of public policies is mostly to sustain the science-producing sector, secure free access to knowledge and protect inventions.

In contrast, within the modern innovation approach, technology is endogenous to the production process, access to knowledge resources is not free, technology is specific, often with a tacit and embodied character, and context dependent; and the knowledge base of industrial firms is built through interactions with institutions, and exchanges and co-operations with the research and industrial sectors. The policy issues in this context are not so much geared to the knowledge-producing sector, but relate to the identification and support of nodal points in the systems, to the favouring of exchanges, synergies and co-operations in the system, and to the development of human capital and training.

In this systemic approach, the role of universities can be seen, first, as providers of a skilled and educated workforce able to develop links between the education and research system and industry and, second, as diffusers of knowledge into the industrial sector with the help of interface structures such as liaison cells, technopoles, transfer organisations, etc. Depending on the regional context, universities may also form a breeding ground for new technology-based firms as spin-offs of HEIs or act as knowledge sources for larger firms which may be present in the regional environment.

Notes

[1] The four teams were: INFYDE (Spain), CIRCA (Ireland), ISI-Karlsruhe (D), and RIDER (B).

[2] *Technology and the Economy: The Key Relationships*, OECD, Paris, 1992

[3] The rest of this section is extracted from the final report of ISI-Karlsruhe for the horizontal review.